READING SHAKESPEARE'S SONNETS

by the same author

poetry

NIL NIL

GOD'S GIFT TO WOMEN

THE EYES

LANDING LIGHT

ORPHEUS

RAIN

aphorism

THE BOOK OF SHADOWS

THE BLIND EYE

editor

101 SONNETS

ROBERT BURNS: SELECTED POEMS

LAST WORDS (with Jo Shapcott)

DON'T ASK ME WHAT I MEAN (with Clare Brown)

NEW BRITISH POETRY (with Charles Simic)

Reading

SHAKESPEARE'S SONNETS

A NEW COMMENTARY BY

Don Paterson

faber and faber

First published in 2010
by Faber and Faber Ltd
Bloomsbury House
74–77 Great Russell Street
London WC1B 3DA

Typeset by Faber and Faber Ltd
Printed in England by T. J. International Ltd, Padstow, Cornwall

A CIP record for this book
is available from the British Library

The facsimile on page XXIII
is the title page of the 1609 Quarto
(courtesy of the Bodleian Library,
University of Oxford)

ISBN 978-0-571-24502-4

2 4 6 8 10 9 7 5 3 1

To Nora

Contents

Introduction

Since their first publication in 1609, Shakespeare's Sonnets have appeared in countless editions, and have been translated into every major living language, as well as many minor, dead, synthetic and intergalactic ones, too. Basque, Latin, Esperanto and Klingon have all have played host to these verses, written 400 years ago by a bald Englishman who didn't even consider poetry his main literary medium. The Sonnets have been awarded the ultimate accolade human culture can bestow: proverbialism. 'A Shakespeare sonnet' is almost as much a synonym for 'love-poem' as 'Mona Lisa' is 'beautiful woman'. As soon as something becomes proverbial, however, everyone feels like they already know it. In recent times, this has relieved us of the trouble of reading the Sonnets properly.

About a year ago, I decided that I'd stop pretending to myself and to my students that I knew these poems better than I did. I'd made a couple of fairly thorough passes in my twenties, and knew a respectable number of the Sonnets well, and had a few by heart. However, a hideously exposed bluff at a party, much too painful to recall here, prompted me to re-examine my avowed familiarity. I have the charmless habit of imputing my own larger ignorances to everyone else – otherwise they'd be too much for any one man to bear – but this time, I had the strong suspicion that I might not be completely alone. A straw-poll of my non-academic acquaintances quickly confirmed as much. Shakespeare's Sonnets are not quite poetry's *A Brief History of Time* – i.e. a book everyone owns, and no one has finished – but they're close. We all know Mark Twain's definition of the classic, 'something that everybody wants to have read and nobody wants to read'. We might add, less memorably, that a classic is a book you can safely avoid reading, because no one else will admit they haven't read it either. Don't get me wrong: everyone said they *loved* the Sonnets. They just tended to love the same ten poems. (My control, incidentally, was Tennyson's *In Memoriam.* Everyone who said they loved *that* knew it backwards and inside out.) Was this because there are only ten good poems? Were those ten *really* the best ten? What about the other hundred and forty-four? Even more worryingly, more than one apparently well-read individual remarked 'They're addressed to a *man*, I believe', as if the information had only recently come to light through ingenious advances in 21st-century cryptography. So I started to make a list of questions: do the Sonnets really contain what we *believe* them to contain? Do we still talk about love in the same way, and are these poems still useful to us? Do they still move us, speak to us, enlighten us? Is their reputation deserved, or have they simply hitched a ride on the plays? What are these poems to us *now*?

I formed a vague plan to read one or two sonnets a day, keep a record of my thoughts, feelings, gut reactions and reflections as I reread them, and make notes on their arguments and form, on their poetic technique and compositional method. I revised these notes as little as possible, and hope that this book has retained the feel of the 'reading diary' that it was. Essentially, I tried to read the poems in a way which was sympathetic to them, and suited the questions I'd posed. Compared with every other available commentary this book was written, quite intentionally, in a tearing hurry, and no doubt it shows. A book with different aims would have been written in a far more cautious and considered fashion, and there are plenty of excellent commentaries which are, written by people for whom caution and consideration come far more naturally. I'll talk about why I went about it in this way in a moment, but first, a word about the Sonnets themselves.

~

I'll give no more than the very briefest introduction to the Sonnets here. All the business of their authorship, composition, dramatis personae, publishing history and controversies will be touched on in the course of the commentary itself. I've also included two short essays as appendices; one on the form of the sonnet, and one on the Sonnets' metre. (If you're after an informative, scholarly and reliable single essay on the Sonnets, I can heartily recommend those with which Colin Burrows, Katherine Duncan Jones and John Kerrigan introduce their own editions.)

The Sonnets are a collection of one hundred and fifty four poems, first published in 1609 as '*SHAKE-SPEARES SONNETS. Never before imprinted.*' A bit of a fib, that, as early versions of Sonnets 138 and 144 had previously appeared in a something called *The Passionate Pilgrim*, a dog's dinner of an unauthorised miscellany, published by William Jaggard in 1599, claiming to be by Shakespeare but containing the work of several other authors too. In the 1609 volume we also find *A Lover's Complaint*, a long poem written in rhyme royal, a seven-line stanza introduced by Chaucer into English: a rather lovely, weird poem it is too. This first printing of the Sonnets is generally referred to as the Quarto edition (the Q, hereafter), and was published by Thomas Thorpe, which we know from his having entered it in the Stationer's Register, the nearest thing the Elizabethans had to copyright law.

Controversy still rages over whether the Q was authorised by WS or printed without his permission, and nothing can be definitively proven either way. However, I fall very strongly into the 'there's absolutely no damn way Shakespeare didn't authorise it' camp, as the Q has been ordered in a meticulously careful, sensitive and playful way that can only indicate the author's hand. (Reasoning: publishers care, editors care – but none of them care *that* much.) The Sonnets seem to have been composed between 1582 and their date of publication, 1609, i.e. between Shakespeare's eighteenth and forty-fifth birthdays. This, I admit, is a staggeringly useless piece of information. However the 1582 date refers to an isolated piece of juvenilia, Sonnet 145, while the so-called 'dating sonnets' seem to imply that the larger part of the project was likely over some time before 1609. Most commentators still argue that the poems were written in a six or seven-year span in the mid-1590s. True, Frances Meres refers to them in 1598 – *The witty soul of Ovid lives in mellifluous & honey-tongued Shakespeare, witness his Venus and Adonis, his Lucrece, his sugar'd sonnets among his private friends, &c.* – but I'm wholly suspicious of the claim that they were *all* composed in this period.

What we do know is that the Sonnets were part of an extraordinary fashion for sonnet-cycles in the 1590s. These were wildly competitive affairs. The bar had been set high by Philip Sidney with the 108 sonnets of *Astrophil and Stella*, which had been in private circulation from the early 1580s. A poet would be judged on more than the length of his sequence, of course, but size counted for something, and padding was epidemic. Shakespeare's own sequence falls into three principal sections. It begins with the so-called 'procreation sonnets', a rather dull run of seventeen poems where WS urges an unnamed young man to marry and reproduce, so his loveliness will survive; these sound somewhere between a warm-up exercise, a commission, an apprentice-piece and an elaborate exercise in seduction, and I'll explore all four possibilities. (I apologise in advance for my lack of enthusiasm for these poems; it seems a bit much to begin a book in such a negative way, and still expect you to keep reading on – but the alternative would have been lying about their quality.)

Things look up dramatically at Sonnet 18, however. WS seems to have fallen in love with the young man, and the next 108 sonnets are given over to an account of their love-affair's progress – although the jury's out as to whether it's always the same guy being addressed. I have no settled opinion on the matter, but the poems do seem to have a clear dramatic narrative. (The question 'was Shakespeare gay?' is so stupid as to be barely worth answering, but for the record: of *course* he was. Arguably he was a bisexual, of sorts; though for all the wives, mistresses and children I'm not entirely convinced by his heterosexual side. Mostly, his heart just wasn't in it; when it was, his expressions of heterosexual love are full of self-disgust. The young man is often referred to by commentators as 'the Fair Youth' – one of those sly euphemisms that aestheticises WS's relationship, and keeps everything just the right side of sodomy. I prefer 'the Young Man'. Even more sinister is the convention of reducing WS to the status of cast-member, referring to the author of the Sonnets not as Shakespeare but 'the poet' – in the desperate hope that these screamingly autobiographical poems might be construed as a fiction or a dramatic monologue.) Sonnets 126–52 have as their subject an unnamed mistress, traditionally known as the Dark Lady, and are for the most part a bitter essay in misogyny, lust, post-coital suicide and self-hatred. The last two sonnets improvise on a Greek epigram.

The Sonnets are next-to-impossible to read in one sitting. If you tried to, you wouldn't be reading them well: they're too various, and no normal human could make the crazy, poem-to-poem gear-changes in mood that WS demands without losing their mind. They are alternately beautiful, maddening, brutally repetitive, enigmatic, sweet, prophetic, pathetic, bathetic, triumphant, trite, wildly original, contorted, screamed, mumbled, plain-speaking, bewildering, offensive, disarming and utterly heartbreaking.

~

This is a book which makes a distinction between two kinds of reading, and then attempts to steer a path between them. Literary criticism, in either its academic or journalistic flavours, is ideally geared up for 'secondary reading' – by which I mean all the kinds of reading that require us to generate some kind of secondary text: the paraphrasing and unpacking of a poem's multiple senses, the careful analysis of its deep structure, the thick description of the poem as a historical, social and cultural symptom; the poem's relationship to and development of the literary tradition, and so on.

By contrast, a primary reading isn't necessarily required to articulate its findings. Sometimes it does, sometimes it doesn't. It engages with the poem directly, as a piece of trustworthy human discourse. That doesn't sound too revolutionary, does it? But the truth, alas, is that many readers don't feel like that about poetry any more, and readers often start *in* with a secondary reading on the assumption that 'that's how you read poetry' – before they have made any attempt to read the poem for the simple pleasure of doing so. How this situation has arisen is complex, but let's just say there have been faults on both sides, and many readers now simply assume that the poem is something that has to be translated before it can be meaningful, and that 'meaning' is something the poet has deliberately withheld. It doesn't, and they didn't. (It's all summed up alarmingly well in Billy Collins's *Introduction to Poetry*: '*all they want to do / is tie the poem to a chair with rope / and torture a confession out of it. / They begin beating it with a hose / to find out what it really means.*') But that isn't the kind of the first reading most poems hoped they were going to get. They had much more direct designs on you.

So what does our direct reading of the poem give us? Three things, I think: what the poem is saying; what the poem is saying about us; and what the poem is saying about the author. We can usually get all this through the simple act of rereading – rereading being what is most distinct about the act of reading poetry, and the reason poetry books are so thin. However, Shakespeare's Sonnets have increased in difficulty in proportion to our distance from them, and their concerns, conceits, language and idiom have become more and more unfamiliar with every passing decade. Nonetheless, if we're to claim them as great poems *now*, we have to show them as poems still capable of inviting and rewarding the kind of primary reading I've described, and this is what this book sets out to do.

An honest answer to 'What are these poems to us now' required me to have a good long think about that 'now' and that 'us'. The first thing I did was to rephrase the question as 'What are these poems to *me* now', since I can't speak for you. My 'now' had to be an honest one. So rather than lock myself in the library, I wrote this book while I was teaching, editing, writing, marking or giving lectures, writing other books, poems, and bits of journalism. I wrote it when I was wide awake, bored, half-asleep, full of the cold, drunk, or hungover; I wrote it feeling happy, frustrated, serene, elated, smart, befuddled and stupid. I wrote in on the train, in bed, in the bath and in my lunch-break, at 7 a.m., midday, and 2 a.m.; I wrote it while reading another book, stuck on a level in *Call of Duty*, while I watched the kids, old episodes of *Larry Sanders* or the view out the window. I wrote it pretty much the way folk usually read poems – fitting them round their work-routine and domestic obligations, into their leisure and dead time.

Poetry is an interactive pursuit. It's a cultural sign in a form of words, and it says 'it'll be worth your while to read in to this'. You can tell you have to read in to it, because the poem often doesn't make complete sense on a first reading. The reason for that is quite simple: the poet was trying to put into words something that hadn't been before, and the result will be something partly unfamiliar. (Difficulty is built into the system, which is why I think poets should strive to make their poetry as clear as they can: because it's just *never* going to be that clear.) You have to read a poem in the way you read an interesting stranger. Some features, expressions and traits are familiar enough to be universally understood, but others will require far more careful interpretation; this is where the fun starts, because this is where *you* enter into the picture. Poetry *demands* of us a personal response. The problem with a poem like the Sonnets is that most of the available criticism is necessarily impersonal in nature – otherwise it wouldn't count as scholarship. But in a non-scholarly context, to try or pretend that you've made a wholly disinterested and impersonal response is to betray the poem, and articulate the opinions of a non-existent, consensual *they*. *They* don't exist. There's just you.

Reading a Shakespeare sonnet is an act of authorship. Some of the time this will involve violently disagreeing with the reading of *this* reader. It should: Shakespeare is great because we all see ourselves in him. While half of this book takes the form of textual analysis, a lot of it is just an 'articulated primary reading' where thoughts I'd normally keep to myself got written down. I'd usually keep them to myself, because I know folk will just disagree, and I hate being wrong as much as you do. But poems are unstable signs, and deliberately ambiguous because of the space the poet has left for the reader to place themselves in the heart of the poem. (As Antonio Porchia once said, 'I know what I have given you; I do not know what you have received'.) I won't apologise for reading Shakespeare in my own way. I *will* apologise, of course, for the stupidity, prejudice, ignorance, bias, bad temper, bad taste, crudeness, excess, childishness, impatience and error that my reading has brought to the poems, but (a) you'll bring your own, and (b) this isn't physics. It's love, for better or worse.

While it will be immediately apparent that this is not a scholarly work, I've made use of most of the available scholarship. Anyone is of course welcome to read the Sonnets without a commentary – I mean, be my guest – but the reality is that unless you're a Renaissance scholar, have the OED by heart or are channelling Ben Jonson, you're likely to miss about 30–40 per cent of the poem. Reading-conventions have changed at lot in the last 400 years, at least half of Shakespeare's allusions are unfamiliar, and many senses, puns and proverbial usages have been completely lost. As a result, WS's word-game – complex enough at the best of times – can be simply bewildering. Far simpler to go in with a native guide. While the Sonnets' interpretations are largely my own, much of the scholarship is gratefully borrowed. The only expertise I have to contribute is some knowledge of the practical and theoretical side of poetic composition, which I'll bring in where it's appropriate. (This is the only area where academic critics tend to be wide of the mark – as you would be, when you write about something of which you've had little first-hand experience. It's one thing to say that the ball missed the fairway, but quite another to say what went awry with the swing.)

When making this reading, I bought, borrowed and downloaded just about every damn commentary available (thank you, St Andrews research allowance and the Internet Archive) and used most of them here and there, but ended up drawing most heavily on half a dozen or so, especially those edited by Stephen Booth, John Kerrigan, Katherine Duncan Jones, Helen Vendler and Colin Burrow. (I also consulted several websites, though my favourite has to be G. R. Ledger's gloriously ramshackle resource – a treasure-trove of scholarly criticism, unusual secondary material, and wild surmise.) I've also made heavy use of Blackwell's recent and excellent *Companion to Shakespeare's Sonnets* (ed. Michael Schoenfeldt).

After their first appearance, these critics will go by their initials. As the humans who have provided the smartest recent interpretations of WS's poetry, they inevitably form a part of the dramatis personae of this reading, and I was in conversation with them throughout. I would recommend them all, though for different reasons. As a handy, well-designed, navigable, scholarly, passionate and readable commentary, Katherine Duncan Jones's Arden edition is still unsurpassed. Kerrigan's book is full of laser-sharp and unexpected insights you won't find anywhere else, and Burrow's is a wonderfully even-tempered and unexcitable account, which compliments KDJ's nicely. Booth's is an exhaustive and exhausting exegesis, a sublimely intelligent and discriminating digest of all earlier criticism, and for the last thirty-odd years has been the standard work to which any book on the Sonnets is obliged to refer. It is a book of immense scholarly sensitivity, but also one of horrible vivisection, and an attention to the text that sometimes borders on clinical paranoia. Either way, I will never be parted from it. If you want one critic to have annotated the complete works of man, it would be Stephen Booth.

Vendler's book *The Art of Shakespeare's Sonnets* is a special case, and needs some separate consideration. It is not a work of *scholarly* criticism in the usual sense, or perhaps in any sense. Her book is a supreme example of the kind of book there should be more of: you want to rise to your feet and applaud such intelligent, freewheeling and shamelessly experimental engagement with the text. Vendler reminds us of the *point* of criticism – to keep the work alive, to ignite or reignite our enthusiasm for the book, and to engage it in lively, violent debate. *The Art of*

Shakespeare's Sonnets served as the primary inspiration to come up with something that was at least as annoying, even if it's only a tenth as smart.

To those annoyances: while I've been the grateful beneficiary of Vendler's guidance for many years now, my misgivings over her critical method have steadily grown, and this is where I finally lost patience. There is a hidden threshold in the poem, a point past which you go on insightfully identifying things *that are not there*, and *The Art of Shakespeare's Sonnets* saw Vendler cross it. She is too quick to impute her own formidable intelligence to the poet, and quicker to read the poem as the kind of word-puzzle she herself enjoys solving. But there *are* no 'key words' or 'couplet ties' in WS's sonnets, 'defective' or otherwise (these are, respectively, the deliberately repeated words, one per quatrain, which unlock the theme of each poem, and the word in the couplet which echoes some other key term in the other twelve lines of the sonnet), and some of the subterfuges whereby Vendler has uncovered these – such as 'orthographic hiding' – strike me as plain kabbalistic. WS's frequently demonic concentration of theme and his attraction to rhetorical parallelism will *naturally* produce repeated words. His intense patterning of sound will also throw up many connections which look like carefully contrived correspondences, but they're really no more than echoic effects. Once in a while, yes, I think he indulges the Elizabethan passion for code and cipher. But the kind of structural complexity Vendler claims for his poetry would simply have acted directly against its pleasurable composition.

Despite their final inevitable, symmetrical, and even crystalline appearance, poems are generally far more chaotic affairs than Vendler's analysis could possibly admit, and that chaos is necessary to provide the wild connections whereby a brilliancy or serendipity might be pursued. Vendler has a remarkable gift for uncovering the structural and argumentative shape of Shakespeare's poetry, but misrepresents the extent to which these structures were developed in the dynamic process of composition itself. Structure (and by this I mean the structure of argument and rhetorical shape – not, say, the simple rules of the sonnet) is most often an emergent phenomenon. Structures are negotiated. Poems are written by poets who don't quite know what they mean yet, and the poem is their way of discovering it. My contention is simply that Vendler's hypostatising of those vestigial, ghostly, unconsciously developed and half-articulated structures overstates their importance at the expense of far more important things the poem is doing and saying.

Nonetheless, *nonetheless* . . . one happily pays the price of Vendler's near-occultism as one tolerates Yeats's theosophical fantasies, as the necessary line along which she has developed her insight. I'm having my copy of *The Art of Shakespeare's Sonnets* rubberised so I can catch it again after I've thrown it at the wall.

~

I'd like to offer my thanks to the folk at Literature & Latte for *Scrivener*, the best drafting software in this galaxy, at least; my colleagues at St Andrews for their encouragement and advice, especially Neil Rhodes; and Matthew Hollis at Faber, who sowed the seed, cracked the whip and turned the screws. Finally I would like to thank my partner Nora Chassler, who did her best to excise the larger stupidities; those that remain are her fault alone.

SHAKE-SPEARES

SONNETS.

Neuer before Imprinted.

AT LONDON
By *G. Eld* for *T. T.* and are
to be solde by *William Aspley.*
1609.

SHAKESPEARE'S SONNETS

TO.THE.ONLIE.BEGETTER.OF.
THESE.INSVING.SONNETS.
Mr.W.H.ALL.HAPPINESSE.
AND.THAT.ETERNITIE.
PROMISED.
BY.
OVR.EVER-LIVING.POET.
WISHETH.
THE.WELL-WISHING.
ADVENTVRER.IN.
SETTING.
FORTH.

T. T.

The strange, lapidary dedication to the Sonnets has inspired a thousand crackpot theories. It is now, in Colin Burrows's words, a 'dank pit in which speculation wallows and founders'. In other words, a fun place to start.

Diving headlong into the pit, it strikes me that this must surely allude to John 3:16: *For God so loved the world, that He gave His only begotten Son, that whosoever believeth in Him should not perish, but have everlasting life*. 'Son', in all the bibles WS would have been familiar with, would have been spelled 'Sonne'. So here we have Mr WH as the only begetter, i.e. God of the 'Christ' of the sonne-ts; though he's also promised everlasting life (*eter-nitie*) by an immortal (*ever-living*); but the trinity doesn't map neatly to the WS, the YM and sonnets or anything like it, and it suggests just free play, rather than anything more neatly crypto-graphic. Eternity for the beloved through the immortality of his verses is just what WS will promise, over and over again. 'Ever-living poet', though, could just be an elaborate epithet for God, the eternal maker (*poet*: maker, from its etymology; 'maker' as in the one you go to meet).

I think the first part of this dedication is mighty clever for 'TT' – Thomas Thorpe, the publisher, who's naturally credited as the author of this little enigma; I think we're within our rights to see WS's hand here. For what little it's worth, my own hunch is that WS might have contributed the first half, and TT the second. The two are typographically separated, and the second part is a very awkward grammatical continuation of the first. Had WS written the whole thing, I'll bet he would have extended the trinity conceit into the second half. (On the other hand, if we count Ws as two Vs, the letters add up to an alarmingly deliberate-looking 144: a numerological figure of great significance – 12 x 12, 12th Fibonacci number, all sorts of stuff. Might it also direct us to the sonnet of that number? Sonnet 144 explicitly discusses the whole sorry love-triangle that lies behind the entire sequence. Improbable, isn't it.)

Most of the crazy speculation naturally revolves round the identity of the dedicatee Mr WH, the prime candidates by some distance being William Herbert, or Henry Wriothesley, via the minimum encryption of inverting his initials for discretion's sake. I think it's entirely possible that it's *both* men, since you asked, and that WS probably had a thing for them both. There's actually no need to see the YM sonnets as having a consistent addressee: the fact that we'd prefer them to have one is neither here nor there. As to the identity of the well-wishing adventurer – it could be anyone. It could be the poet, the book itself, or the publisher underwriting the risky undertaking of publishing the Sonnets – or Mr WH, who might have sponsored the enterprise. (I suppose I should mention that one tireless sleuth, by forming an 18 x 8 grid from the letters of the dedication, has found 'Henry Wriothesley' buried word-search style; but his surname is spilt into three bits, which downgrades the discovery from 'cool' to 'huh'.)

The paranoid reader – i.e. me; it's 2 a.m. – might also hear 'fourth' in 'forth', and 'planting' in 'setting', and read it as another injunction to the dedicatee to breed, and produce a 4th Earl: both Herbert and Wriothesley were 3rds. Let me be the first to say that I consider this theory to be garbage, although I've just found some precedent for this use of 'set' in Sonnet 16. 'Set forth' commonly just mean 'publish'.

1

From fairest creatures we desire increase,
That thereby beauty's rose might never die,
But as the riper should by time decease
His tender heir might bear his memory:
But thou, contracted to thine own bright eyes,
Feed'st thy light's flame with self-substantial fuel,
Making a famine where abundance lies,
Thyself thy foe, to thy sweet self too cruel:
Thou that art now the world's fresh ornament
And only herald to the gaudy spring,
Within thine own bud buriest thy content,
And, tender churl, mak'st waste in niggarding:
  Pity the world, or else this glutton be,
  To eat the world's due, by the grave and thee.

Multiplication. That's the name of the game. The alternative is to diminish the world's store of beauty by subtraction, and this gorgeous creature is about to do just that, through his refusal to breed. Now tense up, or set your alarm clock, or something – because we now have 17 poems which say exactly the same thing. Things look up dramatically at sonnet 18, but for now, we'll have to be patient.

The argument here runs something like: 'We want the lovely things to breed and perpetuate themselves, so that they don't disappear from the earth. You're a lovely thing yourself – but alas,

you're also a preening narcissist, and instead of spreading the
1 love, you hoard yourself. Oh – you're jack-the-lad right now, you're the one-and-only, you're gilded youth incarnate, you are; but you've sunk your happiness into your own youth [*Within thine own bud buriest thy content*]. If you don't have some sympathy for the world, you'll be remembered as the guy who consumed himself in self-love, and whom the *grave* ate, without the world seeing any return on its investment in you.'

If you know what's coming, you might well detect an unconsciously expressed hope that maybe this fair creature just doesn't *want* to breed with a woman; maybe he's just not a woman's guy. Otherwise why is WS so concerned? We get *seventeen* poems of this stuff: the laddie doth protest too much, methinks. Poems never, ever, engage with their subjects disinterestedly; and these are *love* poems – which are almost always written out of self-interest, even if their author imagines otherwise. However, there's an alternative theory, and it's probably the better one. Remember that the Young Man hasn't been declared as the beloved yet. WS may not even have *met* him, and as we'll see, these early poems may well have been produced to commission.

I feel I may be alone in thinking that this opening sonnet was composed later in the sequence of procreation sonnets, though. Why? Firstly, it's markedly superior to most of the others placed nearer the start of the sequence, and I sense he wrote it after hitting his stride; secondly, there's no doubt in my mind that WS oversaw the ordering of the poems, and you just don't start with a bad one. He'd have wanted to appear, at least, to hit the ground running.

Here is not the place to expound on my theories of sound and sense (I'll do all that later) but suffice to say that they're much the same thing for poets, inseparable aspects of the same sign. The most immediate corollary of that statement is that if you unify the music of a line, you'll also unify its sense. Look at *Feed'st thy light's flame with self-substantial fuel*, and the way WS consolidated his meaning by making the line complicit in its own song, here composed of lots of *l*s and *f*s and nasals. The line itself feeds its own flame: say it aloud, and hear how it's almost *licking* itself in self-admiration.

l.3 *But as the riper should by time decease* is tricky. I think the intention is something like 'But while the older (roses, things generally) are obliged to die in time'.

l.4 appears to contain a very convoluted but clever pun: *mulier* (Latin for woman, wife) was erroneously supposed by the Elizabethans to have been derived from *mollis aer* ('tender or soft air'; though the 'soft' part was probably correct). So *tender heir* can both the son that bears his father's memory, and the wife that carries the child. WS riffs on this in *Cymbeline*, V. v:

SOOTHSAYER *(to Cymbeline):*
The piece of tender air, thy virtuous daughter,
Which we call mollis aer*; and* mollis aer
We term it mulier*: which* mulier *I divine*
Is this most constant wife, who, even now,
Answering the letter of the oracle,
Unknown to you, unsought, were clipp'd about
With this most tender air.

l.5 *contracted* is a lovely pun. Both 'reduced to' and 'legally bound to'.

2

When forty winters shall besiege thy brow
And dig deep trenches in thy beauty's field,
Thy youth's proud livery, so gazed on now,
Will be a totter'd weed of small worth held:
Then being asked, where all thy beauty lies,
Where all the treasure of thy lusty days,
To say, within thine own deep sunken eyes,
Were an all-eating shame, and thriftless praise.
How much more praise deserv'd thy beauty's use
If thou couldst answer 'This fair child of mine
Shall sum my count, and make my old excuse',
Proving his beauty by succession thine:
   This were to be new made when thou art old,
   And see thy blood warm when thou feel'st it cold.

'When you're old and look like a train-wreck, and you're asked where your beauty went, and you answer – *within mine own deep sunken eyes* – well: that's an all-consuming shame. But how much better to say *look – look at this lovely kid of mine; here's where it went.* That'll warm you up.' A great poem resists such easy summary. This isn't a great poem. While there are little flourishes, puns and double senses to be appreciated here, I don't think that paraphrase does the poem such a terrible disservice; it proves these little effects so much window-dressing. It is, however, a stonkingly heterosexual poem for all appearances, and gained a great deal of popularity shortly after Shakespeare's death, for that reason alone. Which is pretty funny.

Although 'forty' just means 'a lot' (as in 'forty days in the wilderness') it also tells us how forty-somethings were expected to look in Elizabethan times, i.e. like me, not Johnny Depp. The conceit is still going strong, though, but watch how WS becomes steadily exhausted with it, and how his exhaustion exposes its insincerity.

(By the way: whenever I say anything like 'this is boring', or 'this sucks the chrome off a trailer-hitch', please be assured that I'm *always* adding, under my breath, 'for Shakespeare'. But you'd get tired of me saying that. I'll say it once, though: I'd still take the least of WS's poems over just about anyone else's best. It's something to do with his preternaturally acute ear, and the effortless arrogation of authority to his own voice, an authority that lends even his misfires a weird rhetorical force. You can't *not* pay attention to this guy, even when he makes no sense. Does he ever stop to ask himself, for example, 'who the hell am *I* to be offering this kid advice?' Not for a second. This is *way* beyond normal human arrogance; it's the kind of unalloyed, unthinking self-conviction we often find in religious mania and psychosis, and occasionally – as here – poetic genius.)

l.4 *totter'd weed*: tattered garment, though we can also just about read it within the metaphor of *beauty's field* as a plain old *weed*.

l.11 naturally, *make my old excuse* doesn't refer to 'I'm washing my codpiece tonight', but something like 'excuse or pardon my age', I think, with *old* being wrestled into a noun here.

ll.13–14 A long run of monosyllables was as ugly a thing 400

years ago as it is now. It renders the lines as nastily staccato as
2 a sewing machine, and with little shape they can draw from the
interior rhythm of the words themselves.

3

Look in thy glass and tell the face thou viewest
Now is the time that face should form another,
Whose fresh repair if now thou not renewest,
Thou dost beguile the world, unbless some mother.
For where is she so fair whose uneared womb
Disdains the tillage of thy husbandry?
Or who is he so fond will be the tomb
Of his self-love, to stop posterity?
Thou art thy mother's glass and she in thee
Calls back the lovely April of her prime;
So thou through windows of thine age shalt see,
Despite of wrinkles, this thy golden time.
  But if thou live remember'd not to be,
  Die single, and thine image dies with thee.

A better poem, this one, and an elegant and straightforward affair. 'Look at yourself (in the mirror, where you probably are right *now*, you vain twerp): if you don't breed now, you'll deny the world your beauty.' *For where is she so fair whose uneared womb / Disdains the tillage of thy husbandry?* is a lovely example of a decorous Shakespearian periphrasis. Let's just say there are cruder ways of putting it. The poem goes on: 'You're your mother's double, and you recall *the lovely April of her prime*.' WS compares the YM to a woman *a lot*, and rejoices in his feminine features. 'So like her, you'll also see, through your hazy, aged

eyesight, your own youth again in *your* children.' *Windows* were
3 rubbish in 1590, and not the handy off-the-peg metaphors for
'clear vision' they are now.

What I *don't* quite get is WS's easy assumption that self-love and reproduction are mutually exclusive. George Foreman, for example, has eight sons, all of whom are called George Foreman. I think the false logic might point to some other and possibly-as-yet-unconscious preoccupation on WS's part. Oh, I can understand the 'you're too beautiful to deny the world replicas of yourself, and that makes you *really* selfish' as a one-off conceit, thrown out in the passing; but seventeen poems? Nah. It's too weak an idea, i.e. it's too revealing of another agenda. What concerns WS, as will become slowly apparent, is neither the YM's selfishness nor the world's loss, but his beauty – which is all WS *really* wants to write about, because he's falling in love with him. It's all very affecting. The Sonnets have to be read as a narrative of the progress of love. And sometimes love – especially the forbidden varieties – begins in denial. We're in for a lot of that. (None of this need contradict the 'commission' theory, of course; we just need to assume that they've already met.)

Still, I suppose there's some literal truth to it: the fact that beauty is mortal and evanescent is often a poignant aspect of our intense experience of it, but the wonderful thing about the human face is that – unlike sunsets and rainbows – you can sometimes copy it. And indeed vastly improve upon it. (I once showed a woman in a plane some pictures of my kids. She gave me a straight look and said '*Their mother must be very beautiful.*')

I'll nail my colours to the mast now, and declare myself a tepid Southamptonite: I think that the YM in the Sonnets was, at least some of the time, Henry Wriothesley, 3rd Earl of Southampton.

There's a bit of dodgy evidence in this poem: compare portraits of him with those of his mother, Mary, and note the same long, 3 sleek face. HW's beard, even as a 30-year-old (from a portrait made in 1603), was still clearly pathetic. Whereas the other main contender for the YM's identity, William Herbert, 3rd Earl of Pembroke – is portrayed as having very full a beard from a youthful age – plus he looks *less* like his mother, another Mary. Yeah, OK: it's not exactly scientific. The portraits are hardly reliable; but would you *really* compare a heavily bearded man to his mum? I think not. (And I'm already thinking ahead to the wispy-chinned young man in *A Lover's Complaint*.) It all depends from when you date the poems, though, and one perfectly respectable theory is that the procreation sonnets were indeed for the young, beardless, bookish Pembroke, commissioned from his favourite poet by a mother dismayed by his lack of interest in the opposite sex. This *doesn't* necessarily mean that the later sonnets were for the same YM, however, and WS may have been more than happy to add to the confusion, and keep their dedicatee vague.

l.4 *beguile*: trick, betray. The line is an error of rhetoric, if you ask me. *Thou dost unbless some mother, beguile the world* is the more natural and effective auxesis. But of course poets have to worry about other things, like rhyme. *You* try rhyming 'another'. However I sense he used the opportunity to then improvise on the idea of the YM's imaginary wife for the next two lines, which papers over the crack.

l.7 *fond*: (a) foolish or silly; (b) loving.

ll.13–14 If I was brave, I'd have it *But if thou'dst live remembered not to be.* It seems I'm alone in hearing the ellipsis in these lines as: *But if thou* (would) *live remember'd not to be,* (by all

means go ahead and) / *Die single*(:) *and thine image dies with*
3 *thee.* Otherwise it makes no grammatical sense. I'll settle for reading it with an expressive stress on *not*.

4

Unthrifty loveliness, why dost thou spend
Upon thyself thy beauty's legacy?
Nature's bequest gives nothing, but doth lend,
And being frank, she lends to those are free:
Then, beauteous niggard, why dost thou abuse
The bounteous largess given thee to give?
Profitless usurer, why dost thou use
So great a sum of sums, yet canst not live?
For having traffic with thyself alone,
Thou of thyself thy sweet self dost deceive;
Then how, when nature calls thee to be gone,
What acceptable audit canst thou leave?
  Thy unused beauty must be tombed with thee,
  Which usèd, lives th' executor to be.

This sonnet pursues the same idea through an extended metaphor about money-lending and inheritance. It's cleverly worked, but it's still a rather desiccated little poem. Some commentators mention that *spend* in l.1 also indicates 'masturbation', since it's a frequent synonym for 'discharge semen' (whose unfortunate survival or revival in contemporary English we can see in the phrase 'to spend one's wad'). Since an innuendo is to Stephen Booth what a banana is to a monkey (I mean this in the most respectful way), and he doesn't mention it at all – I'm inclined to think that secondary sense isn't all that strong, and that we should pass over it discreetly. Not least because the YM has spent, rather cack-handedly, upon *himself,* leaving a dry-cleaning bill to subtract from the *sum of sums*. In ll.13–14, if his *beauty* is *used*, it won't be entombed with him, but live on – to be, as it were, its own executor. From which we can jump to the sense: if you use your seed properly, your children can be your executors, in the literal sense of your estate and the metaphorical sense of your beauty; that way the future can enjoy your legacy.

Anorak alert: can I point out that if you accept that 'beauty' in l.13 can be read, in part, as meaning 'seed', it's an example of a specific-domain metonymy. Metonymy is a 'trope of relation', and usually draws on the attributes of a thing – or the secondary connotations of a thing that we all more-or-less agree upon – to stand for the thing itself, within the generic domain of our every-day language and culture. This might be anything from 'Downing St' for 'Prime Minister' (on the 'residence for resident' rule) to 'he drank the bottle' for 'he drank the bottle of beer' (on the 'container for contained' rule) and 'rhyme' for 'poetry' (on the 'part for whole' rule). Specific domains are a bit different, and have very limited and arbitrary concerns, and narrow rather than broad rules of substitution. So in the specific domain of 'the dog show', a spaniel's owner might be referred to merely as 'the spaniel', as in 'the judges are talking to the spaniel' (on the 'dog for owner' rule), or in a café, a diner might be referred to as a 'ham sandwich', in the classic textbook metonymy 'the ham sandwich wants his cheque' (on the 'order for patron' rule). Poems are one-off specific domains, and work in just the same way. Here 'beauty' works as a metonym for 'seed' only because it's already been forged within a very specific rule-based context, i.e. the tightly framed poetic theme of beauty and procreation; any mention of 'seed' or 'beauty' will connote, through a ghostly rule, 'beauty' or 'seed'. This is a good example of the way in which new metonymies can arise in poems that wouldn't and couldn't occur in the language otherwise. 4

(Just so I don't have to bring this up later: in conceptual terms, the deep distinction between metonymy and metaphor is that between intra-domain and inter-domain operations. Basically, a 'domain' is anything you can think of as more-or-less one thing, and is conceptually made up of lots of attributes, aspects, connotations and relations. So a domain could be anything from 'zebra', 'train-travel', 'French cuisine', 'epistemology' or 'irregular verbs'. The metonymy family of 'tropes of relation' operate *within* one conceptual domain, while the metaphor family of 'tropes of correspondence' operate *across* two conceptual domains. Calling a bullet 'lead' is intra-domain: you've swapped an attribute of the thing for the thing. Calling a train 'a bullet', on the other hand, is inter-domain, because you've linked two domains, trains and bullets, through the ground of a common attribute, 'speed'.)

l.4 *frank*: generous; *free*: (a) generous; (b) promiscuous.

l.5 *niggard*: miser. G. R. Ledger hazards a slang meaning of 'wanker'; a happy idea, but one for which I can find no support.

l.6 *bounteous* has two syllables: *bown-tyus.*

l.7 Don't try and shoehorn this line into the metre. *Profitless usurer* is a bold deviation.

l.12 Stress it *ACCeptable*, and it almost works. Failure to deliver 'acceptable audits' of assets were an imprisonable offence.

l.14 *th' executor*; an awkward elision. Say *theggsecutor*.

5

Those hours that with gentle work did frame
The lovely gaze where every eye doth dwell
Will play the tyrants to the very same,
And that unfair which fairly doth excel.
For never-resting time leads summer on
To hideous winter, and confounds him there,
Sap checked with frost, and lusty leaves quite gone,
Beauty o'er-snowed and bareness every where.
Then were not summer's distillation left,
A liquid prisoner pent in walls of glass,
Beauty's effect with beauty were bereft,
Nor it, nor no remembrance what it was.
  But flowers distilled, though they with winter meet,
  Leese but their show; their substance still lives sweet.

Hannah Arendt wrote, 'Poets are the only people for whom love is not only a crucial but an indispensable experience, which entitles them to mistake it for a universal one.' If this is true, and it might be, it's an alarming statement. 'Poet' is less a calling than a diagnosis, and the condition of 'poet' is, I'm convinced, only one aspect a complex of symptoms – only one of which is a special attunement to the weight and texture of language. It often comes with the inability to drive a car properly, a talent for all kinds of mental illness, and an excessive interest in movies and alcohol – in much the same way that dyslexia often comes with travel-sickness and first-rate business skills. I fear another facet of the poet's abnormal brain-wiring is their ability – if that's the word – to fall in love at the drop of a hat, or a glove. Many poets are love-junkies of the worst sort; by the worst, I mean the most selfish, often blind to the consequences their fleeting adoration has for the beloved. The condition of being-in-love often moves them to write, however, and poets who aren't writing are even more insufferable than those who are. So for all its torments, crazy love also brings an assuagement, at least on one arc of its vicious circle.

This rather tedious poem is at least easily enough understood . . . until we get to the turn. The metaphor is deeply confusing. However, it can be resolved if we know that this is a two-part poem and runs on into Sonnet 6. I think the salvation lies in the metaphor being second-hand. Look at this passage from Sidney's *Arcadia*, with which WS and his readers will have been thoroughly familiar:

> *Haue you euer seene a pure Rosewater kept in a christal glas; how fine it lokes, how sweet it smels, while that beautifull glasse imprisons it? Breake the prison, and let the water take his owne course, doth it not imbrace dust, and loose all his former sweetenesse, and fairenesse? Truly so are we, if we haue not the stay, rather then the restraint of Cristalline mariage.*

I think the *image* may have been stolen from Sidney, but not the metaphor. Sidney uses the crystal vial to represent the constraints of marriage that preserve the distilled sweetness of personal virtue. In this sonnet the vial, we assume, contains the distillation of the YM's beauty; so the vial can't be 'marriage'. Might it be the child, which preserves the essential beauty of the

YM? This makes even less sense. It's *outward* appearance of the
5 YM that WS has been obsessed with, not some essence.

There are two ways to resolve this. The first is probably wrong, but fun: the unspoken tenor is *WS's own poetry*. If we'd read this poem in the middle of the sequence, we'd unthinkingly jump to that conclusion. But perhaps this poem anticipates those later verses, where he credits his own verse with immortalising powers. The second was probably WS's intention, and it's to read these two sonnets as a 28-line poem. Even though the image of the glass vial and the perfume *occur* within the metaphor of 'time's winter' – try not to read the image metaphorically *just yet*, and merely as an anecdote or a riddle. We're not supposed to *quite* know where WS is going with this, until we get to . . .

6

Then let not winter's ragged hand deface,
In thee thy summer, ere thou be distilled:
Make sweet some vial treasure thou some place
With beauty's treasure ere it be self-killed.
That use is not forbidden usury,
Which happies those that pay the willing loan;
That's for thy self to breed another thee,
Or ten times happier, be it ten for one:
Ten times thyself were happier than thou art,
If ten of thine ten times refigured thee;
Then what could death do if thou shouldst depart,
Leaving thee living in posterity?
  Be not self-willed, for thou art much too fair
  To be death's conquest and make worms thine heir.

. . . this. Which proves the sestet of Sonnet 5 was indeed a riddle, the meaning of which WS then unpacks for us (a riddle is a metaphor which consist of a vehicle and a text-absent and often concrete tenor; see Sonnet 7 for a crash course in this stuff). He does this by laboriously repeating the image, but this time with an explanation of its meaning: the glass vial is a womb, which the YM might fill with his child, his distilled essence. Leaving aside the fact it now sounds like a sperm bank, this is a lousy metaphor so full of holes I don't know where to begin. (We'd already rejected this possible interpretation in the previous sonnet.)

6 Note how WS abandons the conceit – in embarrassment, I think – almost immediately, knowing the comparison can't be sustained for another half-line without even larger cracks developing. WS reaches quickly and all-too-easily for another off-the-peg moneylending riff, as he often does. But this, too, makes little sense. Its lack of logic is disguised in wretchedly neat parallel rhetorical effects and echoes. You can tell he's struggling. The 'commission' theory is gaining ground. This certainly *feels* like one; indeed the dosh-trope may have been suggested by his too-intense meditation on the cheque. (Although WS was a canny investor, as we'll see, and financial metaphors came naturally and readily to him.) Pad, pad, pad . . . 'Oh why not make ten of yourself? That would be, uh, ten times better. Because then you'd have ten children who could make ten images of you, and that would be, like, ten of you. Or maybe a hundred. I dunno.' The last line is a contender for the worst in all the sonnets, and certainly the most musically incoherent. I can almost *hear* WS say 'Oh christ – that'll have to do', and open the bottle.

So in Sonnets 5 and 6, we have two slack, windy poems where there should have been only one. Or less. Here I see more evidence for the argument that WS hadn't even *met* the YM yet when he turned in this effort: this is poetic hackwork.

l.6 *Which happies those that pay the willing loan*: given the fact that *pay* can mean 'pay out' or 'pay back' – i.e. both 'lend' and 'borrow' – he could be referring to the father's generous sperm-donation, or the mother's gratitude.

l.11 echoes the traditional marriage vows.

7

Lo, in the orient when the gracious light
Lifts up his burning head, each under eye
Doth homage to his new-appearing sight,
Serving with looks his sacred majesty;
And having climbed the steep-up heavenly hill,
Resembling strong youth in his middle age,
Yet mortal looks adore his beauty still,
Attending on his golden pilgrimage:
But when from high-most pitch, with weary car
Like feeble age, he reeleth from the day,
The eyes, fore-duteous, now converted are
From his low tract, and look another way:
So thou, thyself outgoing in thy noon,
Unlooked on diest, unless thou get a son.

Well, at least this straightforward and rather unconvincing poem allows us to look at the way an extended metaphor works. This will come up a lot, so let's nail it now. I mentioned that metonymy is a 'trope of relation'; by contrast, metaphor is the 'trope of correspondence', and in most of its forms has two parts that we generally refer to those as the *tenor* and the *vehicle*. The tenor is the 'real' subject, and the vehicle is the imaginary thing to which the tenor is compared or claimed to be, with which it's conflated, or which it's symbolised by. The way the metaphor is presented in the text gives rise to all its different species –

'metaphor', simile, symbol, allegory, riddle, and so on. What you
7 don't get told in school is that number of ways you can present a metaphor is infinite. (WS, for example, will often locate it in the verb – where it does all the usual interesting stuff, only with much more dynamic force and forward momentum.) What's *really* important in metaphor is not trivial distinctions between simile and allegory, and all that – but what's going on conceptually. All things that we distinguish as 'things' are made up of a bunch of attributes that we consider central to their definition. What a metaphor does is find overlaps between the sets of those attributes. (We often call this overlap the *ground*.)

Here, the two things that are compared are the life of the beautiful boy (the tenor), and the passage of the sun across the sky (the vehicle). It's a reasonable metaphor, because both things have within them the idea of the passing of time, and of something that is admired; this forms their ground. Where the ground of the metaphor is strong, or contains more than one attribute, the comparison can often be elaborated at length, and we get an extended metaphor or 'conceit'.

Usually it's *totally* unimportant for the reader to know *any* of this stuff. If the poem is a good one, the metaphor will be understood just by reading it, not analysis. But reading conventions change, and elaborate comparison was an Elizabethan specialty, so it's a small help, sometimes, to understand the mechanism. In this case, it also allows us to say why the metaphor isn't very good. It isn't good because the ground is overextended; the metaphor, in outstaying its welcome, has begun to creak. To say that 'human eyes, who once looked dutifully on the YM/sun, look away in the afternoon and evening of the YM's/sun's life' is actually true *only* of the YM, who will in all probability lose his beauty. Like me, you will have often admired the sun at four o'clock, or sat blissed-out and mind-blown before a gorgeous sunset. The claim that the ground of the metaphor contains the term 'something whose beauty fades after its halfway point' simply isn't true. 'Something whose light dies' might have proved more fruitful, but it's no more than suggested here. (WS may have simply taken over the idea from such contemporary proverbs as 'The rising, not the setting, sun is worshipped by most men', and a similar comparison elaborated in Book XV of Ovid's *Metamorphoses* – but we're entitled to expect a more penetrating interrogation in a poem.) The *sun/son* pun attempts to distract us but is actually – when you think about it – meaningless; although JK makes a good stab at a defence, with the *son* essentially becoming the new morning *sun*, and the YM's beauty being reincarnated. I think this is a bit sophistical, however, and the logical objection remains.

There's some evidence that WS had consulted Thomas Wilson's *The Art of Rhetoric*, which reprinted the long 'Epistle to persuade a young gentleman into marriage', by Erasmus; it's full of stuff like *Neither can he seeme to dye, that when God calleth him, leaueth a yong childe behind him.* One alternative to the 'commission' theory is that WS was using these early sonnets as a means of practising his craft, turning Erasmus into verse – rather like an apprentice piece he would make over and over again until he got it right. This would certainly account for the impression that these poems are less *felt*. I think he was doing both; cribbing from the Erasmus would've saved both time and imaginative expenditure.

(The poem also has an oddly elemental feel, and seems more directly concerned with the subject of Time than other poems in

the 'procreation' sequence. This may well be down to its numer-
7 ical position – 7 being a climacteric number, of which much more soon.)

l.6 *middle age* was definitely a bit earlier then than it is now, but it's unlikely that WS meant the same thing by the phrase as we do. Here it seems to refer to what we'd call the 'prime of life'.

l.9 *car*: WS has in mind Phoebius' chariot.

l.14 some commentators – not this one, I hasten to add – hear a rude pun on *diest*, and suggestions of spilt seed and solo masturbation, i.e. 'you will end your days wanking alone'. Let's at least hope his aim has improved since Sonnet 4.

8

Music to hear, why hear'st thou music sadly?
Sweets with sweets war not, joy delights in joy;
Why lov'st thou that which thou receiv'st not gladly,
Or else receiv'st with pleasure thine annoy?
If the true concord of well-tuned sounds,
By unions married, do offend thine ear,
They do but sweetly chide thee, who confounds
In singleness the parts that thou shouldst bear:
Mark how one string, sweet husband to another,
Strikes each in each by mutual ordering,
Resembling sire and child and happy mother,
Who all in one, one pleasing note do sing:
  Whose speechless song being many, seeming one,
  Sings this to thee: 'Thou single wilt prove none.'

WS often hears sweet music as melancholic or sad, and here the YM is shown enjoying the misery (*receiv'st with pleasure thine annoy*, where *annoy* means something like 'pain'). A cursory reading might leave you with the impression that the YM doesn't *like* music, and that his lovely shell-like is offended by *the true concord of well-tuned sounds* – but that isn't what's being said here at all. WS is talking about the strange fact that we're often addicted to the sadness that music produces in us. But what's *really* going on here, he suggests, is that the harmony is actively chiding the YM for his bachelorhood; his unhappiness doesn't

8 proceed directly from the melancholy music, but from the music *reminding* him of his singleness. (He's close to suggesting that the YM is *suppressing* this knowledge; a very modern idea.) In the end it warns him very explicitly, saying 'single, boy – you're nothing'. (Remember, if we hear WS falling in love, he'll want the YM to be as miserable as he is, since love insists on its symmetries.)

Sonnet 8 is where the early sonnets start to hit their stride, and this is the most effective and convincing conceit we've seen so far. It's a bit of a shop-bought trope, to be sure: a single line of music = a single life; whereas the harmony of several string = the harmony of a family. However no one had pushed it anything like as far before. *Mark how one string sweet husband to another*, I read here, refers to the coursed pairs of strings on the lute, but I strongly doubt it. It'd muddle the conceit, which is about 'parts', i.e. harmony, not the strings themselves. (*As* a conceit, it has a basic flaw, though: it's rather easily refuted. Is there *really* no future in the lovely unadorned melody?)

I can't resist quoting SB here: 'Sometimes Shakespeare's own sentences can be demonstrated to mean nothing at all – even where readers actually understand them perfectly.' We're going to see a lot of that. The lines *They do but sweetly chide thee, who confounds / In singleness the parts that thou shouldst bear* being a case in point. Perfectly clear and almost totally unparaphrasable, WS clearly means something like 'who suppresses, in his singleness, the roles that he should take on', but that loses all the magic of the full-masted galley of WS's language steering a perfect course through the confluent themes of human and musical relationships.

Not to mention the brilliance of that word *confound*. The rhyme will have suggested it, the bravery of his talent will have sanctioned it – but WS's transcendental skill with syntax and lyric weave allowed him to actually get away with it. Skipping the neuroscience, the default line-length in poetry universally defaults to something around three seconds long – the length of the human auditory 'present', which corresponds to what we can retain in our minds as a living instant: three seconds is the frequency of the carrier-wave of poetic sense. By the same rule, there are about three seconds or so on either side of a word in which it can be prepared for, or retrospectively sanctioned (unless it has a salient position, like a rhyme-word; these are noisier, and can be committed to memory then recalled several lines later). In the case of *confound*, *offend* in l.6 gets the ear ready for it, and soon the *g* in *singleness* weaves in what could have been the rogue hard *c*. This is all poet's lore, and is supposed to be registered unconsciously by the reader. *Confound* is employed in a very unusual way here – but so seamlessly has WS woven it in to his soundscape, he's practically fashioned it a new definition.

l.1 *Music to hear:* 'given that you are music to hear'.

l.14 Katherine Duncan Jones hears in the last line an allusion to Aristotle's 'one is no number' from the *Metaphysics*.

9

Is it for fear to wet a widow's eye
That thou consum'st thyself in single life?
Ah, if thou issueless shalt hap to die,
The world will wail thee like a makeless wife;
The world will be thy widow, and still weep
That thou no form of thee hast left behind,
When every private widow well may keep,
By children's eyes, her husband's shape in mind:
Look what an unthrift in the world doth spend,
Shifts but his place, for still the world enjoys it;
But beauty's waste hath in the world an end,
And kept unused the user so destroys it:
  No love toward others in that bosom sits
  That on himself such murd'rous shame commits.

'It is the thought of your future widow lamenting your death that keeps you single?' . . . I doubt it. But from that wholly dodgy premise, we move seamlessly to 'Aha! But if you die without issue, the whole *world* will weep like a bereaved wife. The whole world like a bereaved wife will weep, if you die without issue. But if you had a wife, I mean like a *real* wife, she'd have your kids to look at. Wouldn't she. And that'd be better, obviously. And while I'm thinking about money – a person who spends all his money at least keeps his money in the world. But beauty, that's another thing. If you don't use it, you destroy it. O – anyone who could commit such a murderous shame on himself has no love for anyone else.' Or, as heard once on a Dundee bus, 'See Tam: he's nae self-respect for other people.'

Oh, man: this is *rubbish*. More to the point, there's no *way* WS doesn't know it. Why might he reprint this stuff? Is it because their still-flattered recipient, nearly fifteen years later, is now coughing up the money for the Quarto? Not the wildest theory, especially if we decide it was William Herbert, assuming (a) he was the target of the procreation sonnets and (b) was Mr WH, and financed Thomas Thorpe's publication of the ms. Either way, this awful poem is the best evidence yet that procreation sonnets were work undertaken for hard cash. Helen Vendler has a theory that WS has obsessed over the (modest, frankly) symmetries of *widow* here, and scattered *w*s and *u*s and *v*s throughout the poem. Yep: there's certainly a lot of them.

10

For shame deny that thou bear'st love to any,
Who for thyself art so unprovident;
Grant, if thou wilt, thou art beloved of many,
But that thou none lov'st is most evident:
For thou art so possessed with murderous hate
That 'gainst thy self thou stick'st not to conspire,
Seeking that beauteous roof to ruinate
Which to repair should be thy chief desire.
O! change thy thought, that I may change my mind:
Shall hate be fairer lodged than gentle love?
Be as thy presence is, gracious and kind,
Or to thyself at least kind-hearted prove:
  Make thee another self for love of me,
  That beauty still may live in thine or thee.

Another dull one, and you don't need a gloss. It's all clear enough. 'Everyone loves you – but *you*, on the other hand, love no one, because . . .' etc., etc. Note that the poem isn't entirely free-standing, and assumes our knowledge of the nature of WS's accusation. Yeah, we're up to speed on this. He doesn't explicitly mention 'breeding' until the couplet.

The main point of interest here is that it's the first time WS declares his own interest in the outcome – *Make thee another self for love of me* – and uses this as emotional leverage. While this might, as most commentators insist, indicate WS's true feelings

beginning to surface, the request is still plausible even if we assume that the two men are yet to meet. Remember, WS already **10**
had a reputation in the early to mid-nineties. William Boyd, in an interesting BBC play on the Sonnets' composition called *A Waste of Shame*, convincingly pursues the idea that William Herbert's despairing mum commissioned the first seventeen sonnets, one for each year of his life. Herbert was a bookish lad, and here's the point – already a huge fan of WS's work; his mother's ploy was that he'd be flattered into taking WS's advice seriously. This, according to Boyd, was undertaken before the two had met; but *after* they'd met – Herbert's tastes being at least as versatile as WS's – the poems continued, but in a very different vein. Certainly if Herbert looked anything like the young actor who played him on the box, I can see WS's problem. (Although he almost certainly *didn't*, if we're to trust the portraitists of the time. Wriothesley, on the other hand, is clearly gorgeous. While I admit that playing a game of 'who'd you rather' at 400 years' distance does not, perhaps, represent the leading edge of scholarly research.)

Though here's a raunchier interpretation: I wonder if the whole performance had been conceived as a *seduction*, with WS gradually softening up the YM with a barrage of flattery, delivered courtesy of an apparently legitimate concern – before very slowly allowing his true feelings to become known? If we read the first as an act of deliberate self-restraint, it certainly makes them sexier, if not better poems.

Lest we get too carried away as we venture forth . . . this first sign of self-interest on WS's part is a good time to take on board CB's wise caution: 'In a period when sodomy was a capital offense, even if homoerotic affection was a deep element in literary and personal life, one needs to be very careful in arguing that

Shakespeare authorised the publication of homoerotic poems
10 dedicated to a member of the English nobility.' Well, one needs to be careful, but one might still go on to argue it; and the vast majority of the sonnets, for all their innuendo, are never *that* explicit. This leaves room for plausible deniability, and all sorts of alternative interpretations that could have been used by their author to prove that they were perfectly innocent affairs, if he'd had to. (Heaven knows all these readings *were* later deployed, for centuries, by his homophobic critics.) It's unlikely, though, that WS would ever have written like Rochester, even if the times had allowed it; suggestion is far more sensual, apart from anything else. And Rochester is great, but he's not sexy, just rude.

May I don my anorak again, and be the first commentator to point out that *beauteous roof* is a rare example of a metaleptic double metonymy? Thanks. Roof is a synecdoche for *house* (synecdoche is 'part-for-whole' substitution, and a subset of metonymy; this is a controversial remark in certain circles of anoraks, but trust me for now), and *house* is a metonym for the aristocratic family of which the YM is a member.

What else. *Unprovident* and *evident* are horrible rhymes, and too close. Unless they're functioning as feminine or triple rhymes – i.e. they're adding extra syllables to the length of the line – polysyllabic words tend to only rhyme well when the other rhyme word is monosyllabic, as we find the symmetry too strong when more than one stressed syllable is matched, or (as here) near-matched. This is why we tend to find *rime riche* inadmissible in English verse, e.g. rhyming *scene* and *seen* or *dye* and *die*; our unspoken and instinctive 'rule of rhyme' demands that we balance similarity with difference, and the coincidence of both stress *and* sound is too much for the Anglo-Saxon earhole.

(In French, the symmetry is less noticeable because their stresses
are relatively even, meaning that while there's just as much simi- 10
larity, there's less perceived coincidence.)

❧

11

As fast as thou shalt wane, so fast thou grow'st
In one of thine, from that which thou departest;
And that fresh blood which youngly thou bestow'st,
Thou mayst call thine when thou from youth convertest.
Herein lives wisdom, beauty, and increase;
Without this folly, age, and cold decay.
If all were minded so, the times should cease,
And threescore year would make the world away.
Let those whom nature hath not made for store,
Harsh, featureless and rude, barrenly perish
Look whom she best endowed, she gave the more;
Which bounteous gift thou shouldst in bounty cherish:
  She carved thee for her seal, and meant thereby
  Thou shouldst print more, not let that copy die.

As an occasional and graceless undertaker of commissioned work myself, my heart goes out to the author here. The prevalent emotion in this poem is, for me, nothing to do with the poem at all, but the unspoken frustration gathering behind it. He wants this wretched commission *over*. Where WS and I differ – one of many divergences, I should add – is that *his* resentful labour is nonetheless completed with real virtuosity. But even so . . . There are only two things worth pointing out here. The first is the extent to which this poem is not free-standing – you need to have read Sonnet 1, at least, to make any sense of *If all were minded so . . .* i.e. 'if everyone thought like *you*, humanity would die out by teatime'. The second thing is that the poem confounds our usual expectations: while the first twelve lines are a predictable yawn, the couplet shows a flash of genius, which is the last place we usually expect it in the English sonnet. 'Nature has carved her very seal upon you; and what a criminal waste, if you don't use it to stamp out more versions of yourself.' Lurking behind this metaphor is the rather interesting idea of the future child as unformed molten wax, a tabula rasa upon which the looks and character of the parents are stamped. But that's the only naked-eye star in this otherwise dull constellation.

12

When I do count the clock that tells the time,
And see the brave day sunk in hideous night;
When I behold the violet past prime,
And sable curls all silvered o'er with white;
When lofty trees I see barren of leaves,
Which erst from heat did canopy the herd,
And summer's green all girded up in sheaves
Borne on the bier with white and bristly beard:
Then of thy beauty do I question make,
That thou among the wastes of time must go,
Since sweets and beauties do themselves forsake
And die as fast as they see others grow,
  And nothing 'gainst Time's scythe can make defence
  Save breed to brave him when he takes thee hence.

In the midst of this increasingly knackered conceit, WS conjures – well, not the corker some claim it to be, but a pretty good poem. 'It will always be one of the finest sonnets in the history of language', claims GRL. I don't see it. It's not bad, but far from perfect. For starters, in l.1 *the clock that tells the time* is a redundancy that its rhetorical gambit doesn't justify, and the alliteration in l.8 is annoying as hell, and serves no purpose. The numerical position of the sonnets often turn out to be a little meta-pun, providing more justification for the belief that we can read the author's hand in the arrangement of the sequence.

(Publishers and editors just don't pay that much attention: ask
my authors.) Anyway – here we have the twelve hours of the 12
clock. The poem itself has an eerily inevitable, regular syntax, and measures itself out with pendulum-like monotony. It's also a rather second-hand old thing, and is seriously indebted to Arthur Golding's version of Book XV of the *Metamorphoses*, ll.199–216.

As KDJ points out – the absolutely convincing picture WS paints of time's all-consuming destruction, and the fleeting nature of the beauty that soon lies withered and crushed before its onslaught, almost serve to nullify his argument: l.12 holds out little hope for the survival of beauty in *any* form. But the couplet is a much more sensibly tempered than usual, and all the more convincing for it. *Breed* does not defeat Death here, but it does at least *brave* him when he snatches the YM away; *brave* here in the sense of 'defy', in distinction – but not necessarily in contrast; I see no evidence of that – to the sense in l.2. Nonetheless, time and death will win. Thanks to them, we're all soap-bubbles on the wind. It has a contemporary feel, this one. The literature of the last forty years has shown a steady move back to the idea of time as less a dimension than a force.

l.8 *bier* is clever, and serves a double function, making a metaphor out of what was apparently just a meditation on literal instances of time passing. It means both 'wheelbarrow', of the sort you'd use for harvested grain, and the more familiar sense of 'the movable frame on which the coffin is placed'. The white-bearded wheat does the same job too, and is meant to make us think of a grizzle-chopped corpse. Kabbalists take note: l.8 contains WS's only use of the word *bristly*, within which you'll find the phonetic pronunciation of *Wriothesley*. Significant? Nah.

12 l.11 *sweets and beauties*: sweet things and lovely things, i.e. not profiteroles and Jean Seberg.

❧

13

O that you were yourself – but, love, you are
No longer yours, than you yourself here live;
Against this coming end you should prepare,
And your sweet semblance to some other give:
So should that beauty which you hold in lease
Find no determination; then you were
Yourself again, after yourself's decease,
When your sweet issue your sweet form should bear.
Who lets so fair a house fall to decay,
Which husbandry in honour might uphold
Against the stormy gusts of winter's day
And barren rage of death's eternal cold?
O none but unthrifts, dear my love, you know:
You had a father; let your son say so.

I suppose we can detect a more tender note, here; the argument is less logically than emotionally forceful, and we begin to sense the ghost of . . . something else. A feeling not entirely professional. WS's address is also far more intimate than before – he's switched from *thou* to *you* – and the two men now seem closer in their acquaintance. WS may indeed be contemplating the YM's future decrepitude, however far-off, but he does so with more of a sense of personal loss: 'how could *my* beautiful love ever fall to decay?'

From WS's perspective, I suspect the real heart-stopping

moment here was the risk taken in his addressing the YM as 'love'
13 – twice. In the couplet, the apparently throwaway *Dear my love* contains far more of WS's real intent here than the silly circular argument of *You had a father; let your son say so.* For me, though, the poem's real sadness lies in its bizarre position. Think about it: WS, like most Elizabethans, was numerologically sensitive in a way we can barely comprehend. The first open declaration of love (albeit one quiet as he could make it) is in l.13 of Sonnet 13. Does WS believe his love foredoomed? Probably. How could it be otherwise?

(Incidentally, the only suggestion of 'love' between WS and the YM prior to this was l.13 of Sonnet 10. Until then, as SB points out, we've had no reason to refer to the YM as 'the beloved' at all.

ll.1–2 are interesting. *O that you were yourself* is something you might say to a sick man (as in 'he's not himself'), almost as if the YM's decay were already seeded within him, as a result of his choice to remain childless; but the sense is wholly altered by what follows, essentially 'you are yourself for no longer than your span'. So we can see that an alternative sense of the first phrase is something like 'O that your were a permanent feature on this earth'. This is elaborated in ll.6–7, which clarifies WS's intention to the point of clumsiness.

l.6 *determination*: a legal term for the expiry of a lease, of the sort that might occur after the last male heir to an estate has died.

l.13 *unthrifts*: foolish prodigals.

14

Not from the stars do I my judgement pluck;
And yet, methinks, I have astronomy,
But not to tell of good or evil luck,
Of plagues, of dearths, or seasons' quality;
Nor can I fortune to brief minutes tell,
Pointing to each his thunder, rain and wind,
Or say with princes if it shall go well
By aught predict that I in heaven find;
But from thine eyes my knowledge I derive,
And, constant stars, in them I read such art
As truth and beauty shall together thrive
If from thyself, to store thou wouldst convert:
  Or else of thee this I prognosticate,
  Thy end is truth's and beauty's doom and date.

This sonnet unfolds in a thoughtful way, gracefully and effortlessly turning at the sestet. 'I might not be an astrologer, but I do have a kind of astrology: no, I can't look to the heavens and tell you about the all cataclysmic events that fate has in store for us, nor can I tell fortunes and read the changing weather of mood, of anyone's minute-to-minute luck; but I can read the stars of your eyes. I can see that truth and beauty would thrive together, if only you would turn your attention from yourself, and focus on the business of making provision for your future (*If from thyself, to store thou wouldst convert*). Otherwise, I predict: your end will

14 be the end of all that.' Sweet, isn't it? Then again I wept yesterday at the end of *Hotel for Dogs.*

HV takes this poem *way* too seriously: 'The shaping of this sonnet into impregnable fortune-telling parallels is the formal equivalent of a conviction that inner moral prognostication is an art as secure in its procedures as astrology; in view of Shakespeare's perennial scepticism, we may find the speaker's believability impugned by his very syntactic confidence.' Vendler's planetary brain is wasted on this bagatelle, this baguette, this lucky-bag, and she's spent too long with it. It's like watching a neurosurgeon dissect a hamburger.

l.5 since 'second' was not yet in use to indicate a division of time, *brief minutes* were as brief as you could have.

l.6 *Pointing*: 'appointing' is the accepted gloss here. Got to be.

l.8 *By aught predict that I in heaven find* . . . if we accept the Q, we have 'by way of frequent predicted-stuff based on what I find in heaven' – meaning *oft* is an adjective qualifying the noun *predict*; the only time in the entire history of the English language that *predict* has been used a noun. Prompting SB to observe that 'the perversity of the diction . . . and the awkwardly elliptical syntax suggest the pompous obfuscation of a smug hack'. Ouch! You wouldn't catch HV saying something like *that.* I think they're both losing it, one in denial and one in despair, and who could blame them. But while *predict* is just affected, there's no way it's *oft.* Someone's misread something. KDJ accepts Charles Gildon's correction to *aught predict*, which certainly makes more sense, though I can't really see the justification for it. In the absence of a better suggestion, let's go with that.

ll.9, 12 note the shift back to *thou*, as if he feels the previous sonnet had risked overfamiliarity.

❧

15

When I consider every thing that grows
Holds in perfection but a little moment,
That this huge stage presenteth nought but shows
Whereon the stars in secret influence comment;
When I perceive that men as plants increase,
Cheered and checked even by the self-same sky,
Vaunt in their youthful sap, at height decrease,
And wear their brave state out of memory:
Then the conceit of this inconstant stay
Sets you most rich in youth before my sight,
Where wasteful Time debateth with decay
To change your day of youth to sullied night:
  And all in war with Time for love of you,
  As he takes from you, I engraft you new.

This is an odd one, falling within the procreation sonnet sequence, but with no explicit mention of the p-word. However 'time decays all, even *you*, sunny Jim – so what are you going to do about it?' has been so many times and has so much momentum, we hear it without needing to hear it – just as a melody repeated often enough will persist in the ear when we hear only the harmony that accompanied it. Nonetheless if this poem had occurred in twelve sonnets' time, I doubt you'd have batted an eyelid, and the shift in theme from immortality-through-procreation to immortality-through-deathless-verse continues

apace. Building on Sonnet 13, it's a bolder declaration of love
15 than ever. (Though yet again, it's in the doomed 13th position.)

l.4 SB says this line 'asks to be pronounced as a twelve-syllable, six-stress line, and sounds good when pronounced that that way'. It certainly doesn't, and it certainly doesn't. I think WS's intention was that we read it *Whereon the stars in secret in-flince comment.*

l.6 shows a very Shakespearian touch, where a shared sound is used to bring two antonyms together, creating a little sensual paradox: here it's the alliteration of *cheered* and *checked*. *Pace* SB, I don't think it's *cheerèd*, which is ametrical; I think *cheered* is a monosyllable, and the line is acephalous.

l.14 'as time takes your life, I give you a new one' – through the horticultural process of engrafting, i.e. taking a cutting from the YM that will flourish and live on in WS's poetry. JK rules out a pun on the Greek root *graphein*, 'to write' – but surely there's a more obvious one on *engrave*, neatly uniting his men-are-plants conceit and his own memorialising pen. SB claims that the burden of the previous sonnets is now so well-established we'll likely hear this as 'As time wither you, I renew you by joining you to a wife', but I'm a bit sceptical.

16

But wherefore do not you a mightier way
Make war upon this bloody tyrant, Time,
And fortify yourself in your decay
With means more blessed than my barren rhyme?
Now stand you on the top of happy hours,
And many maiden gardens, yet unset,
With virtuous wish would bear you living flowers,
Much liker than your painted counterfeit:
So should the lines of life that life repair,
Which this, Time's pencil or my pupil pen,
Neither in inward worth nor outward fair,
Can make you live yourself in eyes of men:
  To give away yourself keeps yourself still,
  And you must live drawn by your own sweet skill.

This is rather amusing: as if he'd merely *forgotten* the procreation bit in Sonnet 15, WS continues from where he left off in an attempt to gloss over the fact, and presents us with a 28-line poem. Whether this was always his deliberate intention or whether it's a mildly desperate attempt to correct this error, we can't know. It certainly *reads* like the latter, as if WS had been temporarily distracted from his task in Sonnet 15 by his own rising infatuation. Somewhere in the lacuna between the two sonnets it seems to go [*. . . there. Hang on . . . did I miss out something? Damn! Erm . . . no, I've got it:*] 'But why not fight this bloody

16 tyrant Time a stronger way, and fortify yourself in your old age with something better than my rubbish poems?' And with one bound, we're back on track again. 'You're at the very top of your game in the pleasure department, and many maidens would love to be planted with your seed and bear your living flowers – and these replicas would be much better likenesses of you than any artful counterfeits. Like this one.'

As for the next four lines – they're so muddy, involuted and ambiguous that SB picks them out for especial treatment to demonstrate the impossibility of definitive interpretation in certain passages of the Sonnets. I, for one, am totally convinced. Anyway I'll give you my own gloss, as far as I can make sense of 'em: 'Thus should the bloodlines of life renew that very life of yours – that life, which neither time's pencil (which created lovely you), nor my student-of-time's pen (which attempts to depict lovely you) has the power to make you live again in the eyes of future men – whether in terms of your inner virtue or outward beauty.' My head hurts.

The couplet's rather clever, though. 'To give away a part of yourself actually allows you to *remain*; you'll depict yourself by your own hand (i.e. preserve your image by your own will).' He will draw this image with his big man's *pencil*, of course, in which WS sees no shortage of lead.

l.6 note the use of 'unset' for 'unplanted', supporting my paranoiac-critical theory of 'setting forth' in the dedication.

17

Who will believe my verse in time to come,
If it were filled with your most high deserts?
Though yet, heaven knows, it is but as a tomb
Which hides your life, and shows not half your parts.
If I could write the beauty of your eyes,
And in fresh numbers number all your graces,
The age to come would say 'This poet lies;
Such heavenly touches ne'er touched earthly faces.'
So should my papers (yellowed with their age)
Be scorned, like old men of less truth than tongue,
And your true rights be termed a poet's rage,
And stretched metre of an antique song.
  But were some child of yours alive that time,
  You should live twice: in it, and in my rhyme.

The last of the procreation sonnets. Everything starts to look up from here. So why did WS even bother to include these seventeen poems? With only a couple of exceptions, they're no better than weak-to-average, and there's a good argument that the true sequence, a 108-poem cycle (in imitation of Sidney; I'll talk about it at Sonnet 108), starts on Sonnet 18. Possibly there's a coming-of-age theme here – it certainly seems like the poems themselves have to come of age before the mature sequence can begin. The poem itself is nothing to shout about – although we can, perhaps, detect a sweetening intimacy in its tone: 'If I really *could* sing your praises, when they read it in the future – who'd believe me? They'd just say "such angelic features *never* appear on the faces of men", and dismiss my poem as a crazy inspiration, a poet's frenzy.' And whaddye know: *But were some child of yours alive that time, / You should live twice: in it, and in my rhyme.*

The last line has a *right* old ugly tune, with half the consonants nasals, and most of the vowels all either 'ih' or 'aye' (/ə/ or /ɪ/ or /aɪ/), giving it a horrible whiney noise. You can almost say the line with your nose alone. I'll bet WS was disgusted with himself with writing it, and probably knew it was high time to stop. *But* in this line he proposes the possibility – albeit in a negatively stated way – that there might be *another* way for the YM to achieve immortality: through WS's verse. This is an idea WS seems to have planted in his own mind right here, and when it's more positively and self-consciously stated in the next sonnet (and combined with an open declaration of love), it turns into something imaginatively potent. One's *own* literary immortality makes for a more compelling subject, apart from anything else.

l.2 *If it were*: even if it were to be; *deserts*: things deserved, here 'merits'. Though I wish I could stop seeing a knickerbocker glory every time I read this line.

l.6 *numbers* was a frequent metonymy for 'poetry' among the writers of the age, and it's interesting to see which term WS chooses, depending on his emphasis. *Numbers* means 'verses, or lines of verse', but refers specifically to metrical feet and musical measures, and so specifically to the metre-and-music-making, technically adept aspect of his composition. Here, it allows WS to play on the word too.

l.11 *a poet's rage:* the poet's inspirational frenzy, the *furor poeticus*; probably all goes back to Delphi and Delos, when the prophetesses spoke their crazy poetic talk, half-mad with the fumes. By WS's time it was a cliché, and had lost much of its force.

l.12 *And stretchèd metre of an antique song*: 'Which by the by will be a capital Motto for my Poem, won't it?' wrote Keats to J.H. Reynolds in 1817. And indeed the line appears on the title page of *Endymion*. Which I've never understood, really, as here it refers to the implausibility of a hypothetical poem, one which *really* numbered all the YM's graces, and was found (a) garrulous (b) barking (c) affected and strained; so it was hardly intended as a compliment. *Stretchèd* sounds long and windy, and *antique* was probably as much 'antic' as 'old' – i.e. odd, crazy, bizarre. Perhaps Keats's use of the line was self-deprecatingly wry. No idea.

l.14 There's no punctuation in the Q after *twice*, leaving open the possibly that what WS meant was 'you should live a second time in it (i.e. in your child), and (a third time) in my rhyme' – but if this was WS's intention, it's very clumsily expressed. I don't buy it. Let's whack in a colon.

18

Shall I compare thee to a summer's day?
Thou art more lovely and more temperate:
Rough winds do shake the darling buds of May,
And summer's lease hath all too short a date;
Sometime too hot the eye of heaven shines,
And often is his gold complexion dimmed,
And every fair from fair sometime declines,
By chance, or nature's changing course untrimmed:
But thy eternal summer shall not fade,
Nor lose possession of that fair thou ow'st,
Nor shall death brag thou wander'st in his shade,
When in eternal lines to time thou grow'st.
  So long as men can breathe or eyes can see,
  So long lives this, and this gives life to thee.

Far and away one of the most famous sonnets, and easily the best so far, joyously breaking free of the increasingly tiresome procreation theme. Read within the context of the sequence, it also contains a moment of heartbreaking drama, of which more in a minute. The next eight poems fall very much within the honeymoon period, and see WS make open declarations of his love, while simultaneously becoming intoxicated with his own poetic power; we also hear intimations of his future suffering. WS firmly moves away from the conceit that only progeny will the YM to win the immortality his beauty deserves, and turns instead to his own poetry as a means of accomplishing this. Maybe he was just getting bored with it; maybe the commission is complete. But look at what happens between l.12 and l.13.

I'll bet he was sorely tempted at l.13 to write yet *another* couplet banging on about why the YM should marry and breed; indeed this turn in his argument has become so habitual he seems to have unconsciously or deliberately cued himself up for it, with that lurking genealogical pun on *eternal lines*. But he quite deliberately steers the poem away, and invests his *own* lines, not the YM's bloodline, with the immortalising gift. (To be quite honest, I'm convinced he wrote a 'procreation' couplet, scratched it out, and wrote this instead, his heart pounding.) And what a faith to declare in yourself! It's a hubristic gesture – but it's also one of great self-empowerment; by contrast, in the two previous poems he specifically mentions the *inadequacy* of his verse. (Folk don't always realise how much sheer *brass neck* this job takes.) But more to the point: he stops praising the YM as a way of convincing him of the necessity of reproducing; he praises him for the sake of praising him, and openly declares his own interest. He's in love. There's no ulterior motive any more.

Here, we also sense the other poets WS felt himself to be in competition with, a theme he'll return to frequently, and far more explicitly. One reading is 'Shall I make a boring or facile simile of the sort that the rest of you unimaginative buggers would make? Nah. I could do, but even the very best simile would fall short, because my beloved is incomparable. I'll show you.' HV talks about how WS has searched here for the *summum bonum*, the toughest competition he can find – dawn and roses and rainbows would have been way too easy – and *still* proves it inadequate and inferior to his love. But he doesn't just show how the summer's

18 day is a poor comparison; in enumerating all the *ways* in which it's poor – a summer's day is changeable, it passes, it's intemperate – he provides a negative litany of his love's real qualities.

This lovely poem has suffered much yawnsome parody of the 'Shall I compare thee to a cheese soufflé?' variety. It sounds pretty cool in Klingon, though: *qaDelmeH bov tuj pem vIlo'choHQo'? / SoH 'IH 'ej belmoH law', 'oH belmoH puS . . .*

l.1 Only bad actors use the expressive stress on *shall.* Don't you: it's crude. Not because it goes against the metre – which is often mandatory for a properly expressive reading, and just what WS expects of you half the time, as we'll see – but because it simply isn't the question. It isn't *will I / won't I?* The poet isn't indecisive. He *is* going to compare him to a summer's day, goddammit, and promptly does so, to the great detriment of the poor summer's day. The expressive rise should be on *day*. Note that whenever, as here, WS gets into an elaborate comparison, an expressive reading will contain a lot of contrastive emphasis.

Many actors – especially the metre-deaf variety – have a special 'arbitrary stress' which they use when they don't understand something; but they do understand that the emphasis of some word *IN* the sentence, however random, will give the superficial impression *OF* an expressive and consequently 'meaningful' cadence. If you don't believe me, go listen to (the normally magnificent) Ben Kingsley read 'Ozymandias'. It's a pretty bold trick, to cover your ignorance by loudly declaring your superior understanding – but acting is a bold profession. It does, though, require a very gullible or trusting listener. It's all a bit like the use of expressive *rubato* with certain classical musicians, which always mysteriously coincides with a bit that's hard to play in time.

l.3 is very famous, not just because of H. E. Bates: it's the way

WS has drawn the whole comparison down on such a specific, 18
minutely observed detail. The vowels are fat, which inflates the line, but also carefully varied, which means it's great fun to wrap your mouth round, and enact the distinct shape and sense of each word in turn.

l.11 Psalm 23 was surely in the back of WS's mind here.

19

Devouring Time, blunt thou the lion's paws,
And make the earth devour her own sweet brood;
Pluck the keen teeth from the fierce tiger's jaws,
And burn the long-lived phoenix in her blood;
Make glad and sorry seasons as thou fleet'st,
And do whate'er thou wilt, swift-footed Time,
To the wide world and all her fading sweets:
But I forbid thee one most heinous crime,
O carve not with thy hours my love's fair brow,
Nor draw no lines there with thine antique pen;
Him in thy course untainted do allow
For beauty's pattern to succeeding men.
  Yet do thy worst old Time: despite thy wrong,
  My love shall in my verse ever live young.

WS continues with his theme of Verse vs. Time. There are two things I love about this rather slight poem. The first is its bravado, its bolshiness: rather than standing cowed before time, the poet says *do thy worst*, and indeed urges it on with a series of imperatives – a rather meaningless gesture to display before an ineluctable blind force of nature, you might think, but still. Some of the details are brilliantly imaginative: *And burn the long-lived phoenix in her blood* is a great line. The Phoenix was self-renewing and stood against time, but here she's finally roasted, like a turkey. Delicious. Phoenixburger, anyone? But with a loud

But at the turn, the poet turns Canute, and affects to forbid Time to age the youth: *carve not with thy hours my love's fair brow . . .* then realising that time's juggernaut will plough on regardless, gives up in the couplet: because the poet knows he'll have the last laugh. *Do thy worst* – because *My love shall in my verse ever live young.*

The second thing is that, for all the earlier *intimations* of love, this is the first time *my love* is used so unequivocally. (He airs the phrase in Sonnet 13, but hesitantly and awkwardly.) Previously his feelings could have been read – wilfully read, but read nonetheless – as mere admiration. The next sonnet *really* goes for it. I hear a sudden emotional bravery, here; his heart must've been in his mouth writing that last line, as if the real purpose of all the poem's mock-bravado had simply been to steel his nerves, ready to make one of the bravest declarations we ever find ourselves making in this life.

20

A woman's face with nature's own hand painted,
Hast thou, the master mistress of my passion;
A woman's gentle heart, but not acquainted
With shifting change, as is false women's fashion:
An eye more bright than theirs, less false in rolling,
Gilding the object whereupon it gazeth;
A man in hue all hues in his controlling,
Which steals men's eyes and women's souls amazeth.
And for a woman wert thou first created;
Till Nature, as she wrought thee, fell a-doting,
And by addition me of thee defeated,
By adding one thing to my purpose nothing.
  But since she prick'd thee out for women's pleasure,
  Mine be thy love and thy love's use their treasure.

'Dude', as Aerosmith sang with such vacant gusto, 'looks like a lady'. OK: this is as good a place as any to clear this up. I feel I will scarcely be believed, but this poem has been often cited as *evidence* of WS's non-homoerotic intent. No: really. As levels of denial go, this is right up there with the heath-benefits of Marlboros. KDJ describes it as 'famously puzzling', but in this regard, if no other, my generation is a little more enlightened, and the puzzle has pretty much evaporated; not because it was solved, but because it wasn't a puzzle. Homosexuality is no longer considered either unnatural, deviant, outré, exotic, pathological or wicked, except by stupid and backward people, and is about as controversial a human attribute as left-handedness. (I'm utterly embarrassed to find myself obliged to rehearse this stuff, but needs must.) This change of attitude has cleared the way for the heterosexual imaginative empathy to be fully engaged – at which point the text's alleged 'problems' evaporate, having been revealed as largely a product of our own intervening prejudices. It doesn't help, though, that SB, our native guide, says that 'this sonnet has been carelessly cited as evidence of its author's homosexuality'. Well – I'm citing it, but I don't think I'm being particularly careless. While I'm here, let me also carelessly cite the wider context of this poem, i.e. its being one of 126 love-poems dedicated to a bloke. (Let me also cite the recently-unearthed portrait of Wriothesley which the Cobbe family – in whose possession it had been for 300 years – had assumed was of a female ancestor. Not only had nature painted Wriothesley as a damn fine-looking woman, some unknown artist of the early 1590s had too, with rouge and lipstick.)

It also raises the sonnets to a new and somewhat heartbreaking level, if you can ignore WS's knee-jerk misogyny. I don't think a paraphrase is necessary, as the sense is clear enough, if you read it plainly. The *master mistress of my passion*; does a fine job of both androgynising *and* feminising the subject (to which WS is thrall), depending on whether you read *master/mistress* or *master-mistress*. l.3: *acquainted* might well have been heard, especially in this context, as *a-quainted, quaint* being an Elizabethan alternative to 'cunt'. *An eye . . . less false in rolling* is a slyly equivocal compliment: note WS doesn't say the YM's eye *doesn't* roll. I think l.7 means something like 'a man in appearance, all appearances in his controlling' – he still looks a bit like a bloke, and his

stunning looks allow him to control the expressions of all who
20 gaze upon him, an idea unfolded in the next line.

We have a bit of a problem with the hammy capitalisation and italicising of *hues* in the Q – 'A man in hew all *Hews* in his controwling' – like a big fat clue. Inevitably, this hath detained us o'ermuch. Is it a bloke called Willie Hughes? Is he the Mr WH of the dedication? (The theory was first put forward in the 18th century by Thomas Tyrwhitt, and later pursued in Wilde's 'The Portrait of Mr. W. H.', where Willie Hughes is a young actor in Shakespeare's troupe who specialised in female roles.) I think it's very unlikely.

However . . . HV, our kabbalist-in-chief, observes that the poem appears to have been constructed so that the letters of the word *hews* appear in nearly every line. This is, I'm afraid, deeply unremarkable, and HV's 'random checking of a few' other sonnets to ascertain that this doesn't happen elsewhere is hardly reassuring. Firstly, there are many sonnets where you'll find the very common letters *h-e-w-s* in most of the lines – I just plucked out Sonnet 82 at random, and gave up counting after the first five lines – and secondly there will be other sonnets where many *other* 'significant' words will be similarly and accidentally buried. Organising factors as basic as tense, grammatical mood, theme and sound-patterning make this quite inevitable. Thirdly, *h-e-w-s* is missing from l.11: given that, as cryptograms go, it's one of the least demanding for the author to construct, there can be no good reason for this. Other than the fact it just ain't there.

The sestet is where most of the intrigue resides, though. *And for a woman wert thou first created* is a nice ambiguity – both for the *use* of a woman, and *as* a woman. But nature fell for her own creation, and being female, gave him a prick. By this addition, the

YM's alteration to masculinity, WS is defeated; nature has added *one thing to my purpose nothing*. Oh for god's sake, man: use your imagination. Now this is precisely where interpretations will differ, but me, my gaydar is going off like the four-minute warning. All I hear in this line is someone hastily distance himself from an accusation he has done *everything* to invite. The idea that the *prick* was for a woman's entertainment alone is an idea that an imagination like WS's could only wilfully or disingenuously sustain, even if he'd been straight. (Leaving aside the obvious third beneficiary. I'm reminded of an Irvine Welsh short story, where a woman watches a man drop his shorts on their first date, to be confronted with something less than wholly impressive. 'Who'd ye expect to please wi' *that?*' she asks. 'Masel,' he replies, reasonably.)

Although . . . the last line has such a resigned nobility, such a note of noble self-denial in the face of such an insuperable social taboo, that you can't but weep for the guy. In reading this poem as an act of sincere distancing from any accusation of anything but a pure and platonic love for another man, certain critics are strenuously foregrounding a few lines while gleefully ignoring the emotional tenor of the whole poem. Putting aside more mundane observations, like . . . I have a deep love for many of my male friends too, but there's no way I'm writing 126 sonnets for one of 'em. Even the dead ones. Oh *come on*, people. The guy's in love with a bloke. Since when was homosexuality all about sex? Besides, why do we feel we have to except *Shakespeare's* love of this guy as uniquely pure and non-sexual, when we'd never dream of making that argument elsewhere, faced with the same evidence? Because he occasionally *says* it's so? Since when did we ever take an author at their word? It's a desperate tragedy that WS was forced into this disavowal of the nature of his own desire.

Whether it was sincere or not, who knows. I suspect he was at

20 least sincere in his self-delusion.

HV sums up the whole sorry mess rather neatly: 'The couplet's defiant final scission of love from intercourse will determine a good deal in the later YM sonnets. Once one has separated love from the act of sex, love can – indeed must – eventually stand alone, hugely politic, inhabiting the realm of the Forms. It certainly no longer inhabits the realm of the flesh, though it pervades the emotional and erotic *imaginative* life entirely.' Indeed. Better to murder an infant in the crib, and all that. On the other hand, *without* that frustrated desire, and its compulsory translation from the sexual to the imaginative realm, the Sonnets wouldn't have existed at all.

21

So is it not with me as with that Muse,
Stirred by a painted beauty to his verse,
Who heaven itself for ornament doth use,
And every fair with his fair doth rehearse,
Making a couplement of proud compare
With sun and moon, with earth and sea's rich gems,
With April's first-born flowers, and all things rare
That heaven's air in this huge rondure hems;
O let me true in love but truly write,
And then believe me: my love is as fair
As any mother's child, though not so bright
As those gold candles fixed in heaven's air:
Let them say more that like of hearsay well,
I will not praise, that purpose not to sell.

An attack on the simile of which William Carlos Williams would have heartily approved; he too thought a thing should be as sufficient unto itself as WS thinks his beloved. (WCW thought this should apply to *everything*, though, and is our prize exhibit when we demonstrate the ways in which a huge talent can transcend some pretty daft theories, and indeed thrive on them.)

l.1 presents some confusion. Firstly, *Muse* is a metonym for *one-inspired-by-his-muse*, i.e. a poet, as becomes swiftly clear. However *So is it not* is just an inversion of *it is not so*, i.e. 'it *isn't* the same with me as with that other poet'. The sense immediately makes

this clear. It does *not* also mean, surely, 'Isn't it the same with me
21 as with that other poet . . . ?' This is a possibility SB feels obliged to explore, though this ambiguity simply isn't confirmed by the text.

All the poem says is 'I'm not like that poet stirred by *his* tarted-up beauty into song [miaow! contrast with the unadorned beauty of Sonnet 20, *painted* only by nature's fair hand] – who will drag out heaven itself, and every beautiful thing in god's earth to ornament his description or to use as a simile. [*couplement*: a linked pair.] O let me, as one true in love, write truly: believe me, my ladis as good-looking as the next guy [one plain sense of *mother's child*, but it's a clever phrase, as the child is *everything* in the mother's eye]. But I'm not going to say something as patently stupid as "he's as bright as the stars in the sky".' By which WS simply means that no comparison can add (and by implication can be adequate) to his beauty; and that *false compare,* a theme we will return to with deadening frequency, doesn't do right by anyone. Compare Sonnet 130 for the nasty version of the same argument.

The couplet's more of a problem. That word *hearsay*: gossip and rumour? Things we only hear, not see or confirm, so perhaps he's referring to the over-inflated and unverifiable descriptions of the other poets? The hyphenation of *heare-say* in the Q makes it clear WS enjoyed the repetition of 'say', and I think the line might represent a triumph of music over sense. l.14 alludes to, or rather inverts, a well-known proverb 'he praises who wishes to sell'. My guess is that the lines intend something like 'Let the folk who enjoy that kind of thing (the poets) keep on yapping; me – I'm keeping shtum, because I'm not selling anything.' i.e. I'm keeping it to myself, and not reducing its value by its misrepresentation.

(And perhaps he's being literal: might he mean the commission's
behind him, and he's now just writing this for himself and his 21
beloved?)

However I'm more interested in the question this sonnet poses and leaves unanswered. If all these comparisons are inadequate or unseemly – when we do speak of the incomparable beloved, what *do* we say? Love must speak. Nothing isn't an option. We're forced into similes precisely *because* we feel our love to be inexpressibly strong, yet can't stay silent: it's a doomed project, but it's all we have.

22

My glass shall not persuade me I am old
So long as youth and thou are of one date;
But when in thee time's furrows I behold,
Then look I death my days should expiate:
For all that beauty that doth cover thee
Is but the seemly raiment of my heart,
Which in thy breast doth live, as thine in me;
How can I then be elder than thou art?
O therefore love be of thyself so wary
As I not for myself, but for thee will;
Bearing thy heart, which I will keep so chary
As tender nurse her babe from faring ill.
    Presume not on thy heart when mine is slain;
    Thou gav'st me thine not to give back again.

'As long as you're young, so am I, because we're one – we've exchanged hearts; keep yourself safe, and I'll look out for you too.' That's pretty much the first twelve lines. All beautifully expressed, but as a *sentiment* . . . it's about twelve years old, with all the emotional sophistication of 'best frendz 4ever' broken heart necklace. (OK: *Bearing thy heart, which I will keep so chary* [carefully] / *As tender nurse her babe from faring ill* is quite nice, I agree.) Then again, the *entire emotional landscape* of the sonnets is adolescent – which isn't necessarily to criticise it at all; that was the time in our life when we felt those infatuations most intensely and most frequently, and WS often physically re-engages us with that old, mad, stomach-churning can't-sleep-can't-eat-can't-think-about-anything-else stuff. Once in a while, the Sonnets are 'adolescent' in the simple sense of 'not grown-up', but it's a price worth paying. Essentially, the Sonnets present us with the thrilling prospect of a hyper-articulate thirty-something writing with the emotional intensity of a man half his age. Usually these kids can't *speak.*

Pleasingly, the couplet isn't the usual redundant coda: this time, it's a catastrophe in its own right. WS has freely mixed the literal and metaphorical, which must have seemed a good idea at the time. 'When my heart's dead, you can't have yours back – you gave me it for ever.' Now think about it: what the hell is the YM going to do for a blood-pumping organ in his remaining years? SB says 'the wit of these lines derives from seeming to take a metonymy literally'. ('Heart' for 'love' can be both a literary symbol, which is a form of metaphor, *and* a metonym, whose formula here is 'place for tenant'.) But I just don't think it's *witty*, exactly, and besides – it doesn't actually *mean* anything: is he taking the YM's heart with him? Is it dying with him? Why would he be such a bastard anyway, and play keepers when he doesn't need it any more? How will he do any of that when he's dead? Oh, it's too daft. By far the most charitable way to read the couplet is to ignore the sense and just going with the emotional tone – which has suddenly turned dark, sexy, vampiric, 'if I can't have you, no one will'.

Give me Sidney's 'The Bargain' any day:

My true love hath my heart, and I have his,
By just exchange one for another given:

I hold his dear, and mine he cannot miss,
There never was a better bargain driven:
My true love hath my heart, and I have his.

His heart in me keeps him and me in one,
My heart in him his thoughts and senses guides:
He loves my heart, for once it was his own,
I cherish his because in me it bides:
My true love hath my heart, and I have his.

l.4 *Then look I death my days should expiate*: then I anticipate death will extinguish my days. It's hard to convey just how easy it was to rhyme back then. To simplify, but not *that* much: all you did was move the word you needed to the end of the line. The consequent mangling of the syntax (this is the best bit) serving only to *enhance* the rhetoric; switching the parts of speech out of their conventional sentence-position might make things sound a bit weird – but that weird was perceived as a desirable attribute of a heightened poetic diction. (Exactly the same procedure worked for fixing up the metre.) Talk about cake and eat it. Ah, the days those were! The poets easy had it. I think poetic diction *will* make a comeback, but right now we're in a bit of an after-you-Alphonse impasse. At some point, though, one reckless soul will barge through the door, and we'll all follow. But the sad and banal truth is people liked poetry a lot more when it *sounded* like poetry.

23

As an unperfect actor on the stage,
Who with his fear is put beside his part;
Or some fierce thing, replete with too much rage,
Whose strength's abundance weakens his own heart;
So I, for fear of trust, forget to say
The perfect ceremony of love's rite,
And in mine own love's strength seem to decay,
O'ercharg'd with burden of mine own love's might:
O! let my looks be then the eloquence
And dumb presagers of my speaking breast,
Who plead for love, and look for recompense,
More than that tongue that more hath more expressed:
  O learn to read what silent love hath writ:
  To hear with eyes belongs to love's fine wit.

A very sweet poem on the depth of silent love, and how a love too strongly felt can silence or tie the tongue. Again – I'm convinced of its sincerity, though neither of the general truth of the statement, nor of the author's ability to honour it. Yes, sometimes love *is* carried silently in the breast, carried to bursting-point; but there are other loves, equally as strong, that just can't shut up. WS's seems the latter sort. KDJ seems to suggest our man may have had in mind Sidney's beautiful *Dumb swans, not chattering pies, do lovers prove; / they love indeed, who quake to say they love.* (*chattering pies*: magpies, of course, not what happens in Greggs after night fall.)

23 An interesting and indeed crucial crux is l.9, *let my looks be then the eloquence . . .* if the Q is allowed to stand, we have *let my books be then the eloquence.* Replacing *books* with *looks* changes the sense rather dramatically. The poem is then nothing to do with real 'writing' whatsoever; we can just read it as WS's plea to be judged not by his speech but by his deeds, by his lovestruck demeanour. *let my books be then the eloquence* inclines us to read l.13 *O! learn to read what silent love hath writ* much too literally. Going against my elders and betters, my hunch is that it's definitely *looks.* Apart from its superior lyricism, echoing the consonants of *eloquence,* (and putting aside the fact that there are close *b*s in the text to explain the eye-skip) – it allows l.14 to expand naturally on l.13 – 'learn to read the looks written by my silent love; to hear with your eyes is a feature of love's intelligence' – rather than learning l.14 as what *silent love* had actually written, which is clumsy as hell. Changing *books* to *looks* also simultaneously explains a second problem with the text, while introducing a rather clever allusion. *Presagers* means very little: how can his books be the *presagers*, the foreshadowers of his speaking breast? They foreshadow nothing; they just substitute for it. However *looks* could certainly be presagers of the speaking breast, in the way they foretell the great, as-yet-unarticulated love WS carries within him; especially so, if we read *dumb presagers* as alluding to the brief mime-shows that introduced and summarised the spoken contents of an act in early Elizabethan theatre. This leaves only the problem of the repeated word *look* in l.11, which sounds almost cleverly deliberate, if we assume its subject to be *dumb presagers.* (I think it's a goof, actually, but a minor one.)

Moreover, I'd point out that all three quatrains now neatly

alternate, in couplets, between the subjects of the 'acting' metaphor in ll.1–2, and the 'raging beast, whose passion is so 23
great it renders him dumb' image introduced in ll.3–4.

l.1 *unperfect*: not line-perfect.

l.2 *is put beside his part*: forgets his lines.

l.11 *look for recompense*: look for reciprocation.

l.12 *more hath more expressed*: has more often expressed more.

24

Mine eye hath played the painter and hath steeled
Thy beauty's form in table of my heart;
My body is the frame wherein 'tis held,
And perspective it is best painter's art;
For through the painter must you see his skill,
To find where your true image pictur'd lies,
Which in my bosom's shop is hanging still,
That hath his windows glazed with thine eyes.
Now see what good turns eyes for eyes have done:
Mine eyes have drawn thy shape, and thine for me
Are windows to my breast, wherethrough the sun
Delights to peep, to gaze therein on thee;
  Yet eyes this cunning want to grace their art:
  They draw but what they see, know not the heart.

The bulk of the reader's time – at least this reader's time – is going to be spent hacking his way through the mangrove-swamp of the conceit and its syntax towards the plain sense. Whether we'll have the energy left to *think* about that sense, or just fall down gratefully at its feet – we'll see. Let's attempt a working paraphrase. SB, very helpfully, says 'the sonnet is carefully designed to boggle its reader's mind . . . but some sanity may be retained if one holds on to the idea of two people looking into one another's eyes'. Fine, but it's going to be a bumpy ride.

The first three lines are easy enough. The Q's *steel'd* is usually corrected to *stell'd*, from *stell*, 'to depict'. There are arguments for *styled* and *steeled*, but they're weak. OK: 'My eyes have played the painter, and have painted your beauty on the tablet of my heart. My body's the picture-frame.' So far, so good.

But l.4 is a nightmare. *No one* knows what it means. This is bad, as I'm pretty certain that WS *intended* a single meaning, or at least an uppermost one. What does the 'it' refer to? To the noun *perspective*, making *it* a redundant emphasis, so it means 'and perspective is the painter's greatest skill'? Or does *perspective* modify *held*, making it an adverb (Elizabethans would freely employ nouns and adjectives as adverbs; might the weird stress *PERspecTIVE* flag this use as a different part of speech, the way we stress, say, 'alternate' differently, depending on whether we use it as a verb or an adjective?); or might *perspective* even qualify *frame/body*, and mean something like 'clearly proportioned'? Beats me.

Winging it for a moment, I'd point out that it all makes a bit more sense if you read a bunch of erroneous or unhelpful punctuation into the Q, and insert a full stop after *held*. This way ll.1–3 sound more elegantly reasoned, and l.4 sounds far less of a free-standing and apropos-of-not-much statement, because l.5 immediately explains it, through its pun on the Latin root of *perspective* ('see through') – especially if we accent *through*. So we get the marginally more intelligible

And perspective it is best painter's art,
For through the painter must you see his skill
To find where your true image pictured lies;
Which in my bosom's shop is hanging still,
That hath his windows glazed with thine eyes.

24 (There are plenty of Shakespearian sentences starting with 'And', by the way.) So we get *perspective* as an etymological pun: 'and clarity, transparency, is the painter's greatest art, because this allows you to apprehend [through the clear-eyed painter, i.e. WS's eyes; see l.1] his skill, and this will lead you to your true image, hanging in the workshop/studio of his heart, its [his] windows being *your* eyes'. Though I confess this is very far from satisfactory. If the YM's eyes are the studio's windows, are they missing from his *true image*?

The sestet is better, sweeter, and a little more easily understood, but still poses a thousand questions: if the conceit is 'two pairs of eyes looking at each other', why are the YM's eyes now looking at WS's breast? They can't be, so 'breast' must be metaphorical – i.e. the YM's eyes are windows not to *his own* soul but WS's. But if the octave is consistent, and the YM is also *looking* into WS's breast – what *with*, given those very eyes also form the windows of his heart's studio, where the (possibly eyeless) portrait of the YM hangs? Oh for heaven's sake.

At least the couplet's plain enough. 'Yet my eyes are short of one skill that would grace the others: they only draw what they see, but they don't see into your heart.' A pretty nervous conclusion, after all that.

However I've no earthly idea where anyone's bosom, eye or heart is any more. (A contemporary diagnosis – or at least mine, if this were a class I was teaching – might say this poem has lost control of its deictic centre.) But maybe WS is *enacting* a confusion between lover and beloved. There's a very sweet Jimmy Webb song, where he says '*I was looking in the mirror, and I though your eyes were mine*'. But this is far too charitable. While we often attempt to instil 'the emotion of the poem' in the reader,

confusion and boredom can't count; the poem might just be confusing or boring. It's far too *easy* to design a poem to 'boggle the 24
reader's mind'. All it takes is a bit of incompetence. WS is the least incompetent writer who ever lived, but if ever a poem died a fashion-victim to the Elizabethan conceit, this was it.

So: does our limited understanding of the plain sense of the poem, towards which we have so manfully and womanfully laboured, enlighten us as to how the beloved is depicted or beheld, or shed any light on the nature of human beholding? I have two answers: (a) don't know; (b) don't care. I think this is the sort of poem I have in mind when I talk about the ratio between investment and reward. Me – I'm overdrawn. At some point, we simply have to conclude that something is badly expressed, or written in a form or style more complex than the idea it expresses, or written for very different fashions and tastes. Here, I suspect, we have all three.

25

Let those who are in favour with their stars
Of public honour and proud titles boast,
Whilst I, whom fortune of such triumph bars,
Unlooked for, joy in that I honour most;
Great princes' favourites their fair leaves spread
But as the marigold at the sun's eye,
And in themselves their pride lies burièd,
For at a frown they in their glory die.
The painful warrior famousèd for might,
After a thousand victories once foiled,
Is from the book of honour razèd quite,
And all the rest forgot for which he toiled:
  Then happy I, that love and am beloved
  Where I may not remove, nor be removed.

After the torments of Sonnet 24, we turn with some relief to this blessedly straightforward number. The argument runs: 'You can keep the honour and titles of the great, the favoured, the well-starred: their pride and glory depends on favour, and favour comes and goes; it rises and fades just the way the marigold opens and closes to the sun. A noble warrior can win a thousand victories – but one big loss, and his name *is from the book of honour razèd quite. My* joy, *my* pride, *my* honour come from a different and far less fickle source. I love, and I am beloved; and this love is so strong and sure, I can neither remove myself from it, nor be removed.'

There's a lot of feeding the metre with these stressed -èd endings, though, which gets wearing.

l.4 *Unlooked for*: ignored, unregarded. I disagree that the phrase refers to both *I* and *joy*, as most commentators note; the second requires us to read it as 'unexpectedly', or twist the verb *joy* to a noun. A pun's one thing, but words tend not to like being two parts of speech at once; that's *no* fun. Besides, I don't see the need for that sense anywhere in this poem, and the pun's laborious. I'll bet WS would've read it with a comma, so I'll slip one in.

l.9 *Painful*: enduring pain. The Q has *worth* as the rhyme-word, which is clearly a slip on WS's or the printer's part. We tend to charitably assume the latter (though I fear it may be the former), then play detective, working from 'quite' in l.11 to figure out the original. Clearly it's *might* or *fight*; most commentators have *fight*, but I think *might* is right. 'Mighty warrior', but also it avoids the ugly triple alliteration *famousèd for fight*; WS's louder sound-effects usually pull in more sense.

26

Lord of my love, to whom in vassalage
Thy merit hath my duty strongly knit:
To thee I send this written embassage,
To witness duty, not to show my wit;
Duty so great, which wit so poor as mine
May make seem bare, in wanting words to show it,
But that I hope some good conceit of thine
In thy soul's thought, all naked, will bestow it:
Till whatsoever star that guides my moving,
Points on me graciously with fair aspect,
And puts apparel on my tattered loving,
To show me worthy of thy sweet respect;
  Then may I dare to boast how I do love thee;
  Till then, not show my head where thou mayst prove me.

Another oft-overlooked gem, rarely anthologised these days. We see the familiar – or at least soon-to-be familiar – trick of WS claiming his incompetence in the most exquisitely competent way possible; but his felicities have an added piquancy here, occurring as they do within stern rhetorical constraints. It's the first of seven poems which introduce the subject of WS's suffering and torment, and after that it all goes to hell in a handcart. Which is grand. They have great poems in hell.

The conceit here is that this sonnet is an *ambassage*, a formal letter, an ambassadorial message. Within the self-imposed limits of this near-officialese, WS finds a way to demonstrate both his strength of feeling and imaginative invention: the poem is primarily a performance, but it's a mightily impressive one. It may also be read, as KDJ points out, as a dedicatory epistle, as if this were itself the start of a poem-cycle. That might be precisely WS's intention: there are now exactly 100 poems to go in the YM sequence. However it can also be read as an envoi to the first 25 poems, putting a seal on the whole courtly love shtick. Either way, its placing seems a significant formal marker.

(There are similarities between the language here and the dedication to *The Rape of Lucrece*, leading some to interpret this poem as evidence for Southampton being the intended recipient; he was the dedicatee of the earlier poem. But there's really nothing in the claim. Both merely happen to use the language of formal dedication.)

The poem's easier to paraphrase than gloss: 'Love, I am your humble servant; your virtue compels me to serve you with unshakeable loyalty. I send this message to bear witness to my devotion, not to show off my wit as a writer; indeed I'm so incompetent, I may even succeed in making my monumental devotion to you look like a small, poor thing. I totally lack the words to do it justice. Nonetheless, I hope that some imaginative leap on your part will bestow some meaning on my meagrely expressed love. When the star that guides me looks down on me graciously, and allows me to clothe my tattered love in fine words, and shows me worthy of your sweet respect . . . *that's* when I'll dare to proclaim my love. Until then, I won't risk showing my face anywhere you can test me.'

Does he mean it? I'm pretty sure the answer has to be yes and no. It's too easy to read *too* much slyness in here, I think; it's

26 perfectly possible for someone both to write something that is sleekitly manipulative of its reader, and yet believe every word of it. There's a difference, incidentally, between WS saying he's a bad writer – he knows he's a brilliant one – and a writer whose skill just can't do justice to the cask-strength love he feels towards the YM. When he claims the former we *should* be sceptical; the latter, far less so. (However, such is WS's need to believe in the *perfection* of his love, its inexpressible nature – its constant betrayal by common language becomes a matter of contractual obligation; to find a satisfactory and worthy form of words to express it would simply imply that his love had decayed.)

To be controversial . . . the Sonnets form a poem-sequence that's not much use, I'd contend, if you're actually *in* love. There are few poems that handily articulate anything like 'common emotions'; WS's experience is too singular, and he's too weird a bloke. However, in a way he's done something even more remarkable: he's written a poem that, when you intone it, when you inhabit it, can make you physically *feel* like you're in love again. You remember? *Love*, in all its derangement, fatal hope, excessive caution, recklessness, sleeplessness, nausea, delirium, euphoria, terror, in all its strange superstitions and propitiations . . . it all comes roaring back, and you feel, to quote C. K. Williams, 'the old heart stamping in its stall'.

❧

27

Weary with toil, I haste me to my bed,
The dear repose for limbs with travel tired;
But then begins a journey in my head
To work my mind, when body's work's expired:
For then my thoughts, from far where I abide,
Intend a zealous pilgrimage to thee,
And keep my drooping eyelids open wide,
Looking on darkness which the blind do see;
Save that my soul's imaginary sight
Presents thy shadow to my sightless view,
Which like a jewel hung in ghastly night
Makes black night beauteous, and her old face new.
  Lo, thus by day my limbs, by night my mind,
  For thee, and for myself, no quiet find.

Yawn . . . I was half asleep when I read this, or fell asleep while reading it – and was momentarily convinced that I was leafing through one of the Georgian anthologies. Fredegond Shove. Or maybe a bit earlier. I dunno. Dowson. (Dowson was the first to record the word *soccer* in written English. 'I absolutely decline to see socca' matches.' Not a lot of people know that.) Anyhoo . . . I mean this as a diss to WS, not a compliment to the late Victorians. There's something facile in its mimsy, prettified tone, something prissy and tame in its too-regular scansion. All it really says is 'I work all day – and you keep me up all night. At least the night's less ugly and scary for your jewel-like apparition.'

27 SB points out that the *jewel* alludes to the belief that some precious stones could glow in the dark. It's worth bearing in mind that the Elizabethans assumed a kind of broadcasting intent on either side of the beholder–beheld divide, and conceived of the gap between eye and object as a conducting medium, with eyebeams firing out, and objects sending back little optical simulacra of themselves. What lay behind this (and here I crib from my friend Eric Langley's own research) was a view of their sensory and emotional landscape as working on deep principles of transmission, infection, contagion, sympathetic resonance, and ultimately the porosity of both body and soul, which were always primed to harmonise or dissonate with anything the world might send their way. (Plenty of that stuff would have come via Plato, but I sense it riding on an MS-DOS of pagan hylozoism and pantheism.) Either way, it's a lot more fun than *our* reality, which is terrifyingly passive on all sides. Think about it: apart from us, and our words, nothing means anything, in every sense.

When things we rationally know can have no agency *are* claimed to 'mean something', we usually diagnose paranoia, religion, or artistic license. (It's to be hoped that emergence theory offers us a way out of this, and permits us the rational science to compliment our wonder at the fact that the biosphere and the universe are *plainly* alive with self-organised creativity.)

Where were we. This poem works with a traditional theme, and it certainly feels a bit tired and worn-out. HV hears a 'splendid nocturne'. I beg to differ. It's *OK*, but it lacks anything much in the way of dramatic proposition. It's a fine subject for a poem – who among us has not known this delicious torment, tossing and turning before the luminous eidolon of the beloved? – but it's hard for any poet to get too excited by a trope that's been trotted out by a hundred other poets. You only get fired up by the ones you make up. Not a bad couplet, though: it's summary, sure, but it's pithy and punchy. And anyone who doesn't hear a *decidedly* non-Platonic infatuation in all this, I propose, a damn fool. 27

l.2 Since *travel* and *travail* aren't distinguished in Elizabethan spelling, we're free to choose, since we've lost the pun anyway. I'll go for *travel*, and keep the metre tight.

l.3 *journey* is a clever pun, and plays on the French *journée*, a day, or a day-long task; though obsolete now, 'journey' was long used in this sense in English, and seems to have been an agricultural word similar to *darg* in Scots. So a night-journey is a nice paradox.

ll.9–10 *Imaginary sight* doesn't mean he imagined it – just that it was a sight possible through the action of his imagination. *Shadow* here is 'image', and a Neoplatonic term. Of which much more later.

l.12 *black* has the strong connotation 'ugly', for WS – something that finds its full and wretched expression in the Dark Lady sonnets.

ll.13–14 'I find no quiet for myself because of you'. Though the double meaning of that first *for* (you can just about read it as 'I find no quiet – for either you or me') makes the YM's shadow sound restless too, as if he'd been dragged from his bed by WS's feverish imaginings.

28

How can I then return in happy plight,
That am debarred the benefit of rest?
When day's oppression is not eased by night,
But day by night and night by day oppressed,
And each, though enemies to either's reign,
Do in consent shake hands to torture me,
The one by toil, the other to complain
How far I toil, still farther off from thee.
I tell the day to please him, thou art bright,
And dost him grace when clouds do blot the heaven;
So flatter I the swart-complexioned night,
When sparkling stars twire not thou gild'st the even.
  But day doth daily draw my sorrows longer,
  And night doth nightly make grief's length seem stronger.

This is a *cracking* wee poem, and very unfairly neglected. It can be classed as 'accountably overlooked', however, being flanked by two duffers. No one seems to have much to say about it. It runs on from the previous sonnet, and focuses and intensifies its insomniac rage to terrific rhetorical effect. Try reading the poem aloud, and feel how the very syntax itself (which is brutally chiastic, with night and day working in hideous, unnatural parallel where one would expect a rhetorical antithesis) conspires to crucify the poor poet at its centre. Of course it's all crazy overstatement; but in the guy's defence, he's crazy. You'll find that you want to raise the entire pitch-floor of your voice up a bit – this poem is such a *wail.* I love the lines *And each, though enemies to either's reign, / Do in consent shake hands to torture me.* The natural foes of night and day nonetheless conspire to torment their common enemy, WS, and seal the deal between them.

The sestet takes an interesting turn, and WS tries to buy off the day and night with the YM himself – essentially asking *how can you torment me with something that is your own adornment?* Whether he's sincere in this or not is irrelevant; he's just trying to stop the torture. But it's to no avail. Every day draws out his grief even longer, while all he can do at night is watch his misery deepen and strengthen. Again, it's so viscerally evocative of that wretched lovelorn state, it almost makes you feel you're in its throes again – and then mightily relieved that you aren't.

l.1 *plight* was still neutral. So *happy plight*: good condition. HV posits a fiction where WS receives a letter from the YM which says something like 'I hope you will return in happy plight', in which case you would use the expressive stress on *can*, i.e. 'How *can* I then return in happy plight . . . ?' although *then* now makes little sense. It's an interesting reading, though I suspect WS just intends the rhetorical question 'How am I supposed to get up in good enough nick to face the day . . . ?'

l.14 is sometimes emended to *And night doth nightly make grief's strength seem stronger*, which strikes me less ill-advised than totally deranged, though SB is more tolerant. But *length* makes absolute sense, and conveys an image of the poet lying on his couch, his whole body nothing but two yards of pain.

29

When in disgrace with fortune and men's eyes
I all alone beweep my outcast state,
And trouble deaf heavén with my bootless cries,
And look upon myself, and curse my fate,
Wishing me like to one more rich in hope,
Featured like him, like him with friends possessed,
Desiring this man's art, and that man's scope,
With what I most enjoy contented least;
Yet in these thoughts myself almost despising,
Haply I think on thee, and then my state,
Like to the lark at break of day arising
From sullen earth, sings hymns at heaven's gate;
  For thy sweet love remembered such wealth brings
  That then I scorn to change my state with kings.

As Shakespearian arguments go, 'whenever I feel awful, I think about you and then I feel much better' isn't up there with his most sophisticated; but it's a sweet enough poem, I suppose. It's really no more than flowery periphrasis, though. There's very little here to lift it out of the mundane. And very little to gloss; its sense is perfectly transparent. I referred to this sonnet as a 'duffer' a moment ago. I'm obliged to tell you that this has not been the popular consensus, and this sonnet has often been placed among the very greatest. There really is no accounting for taste. It's fluff. *Like to the lark at break of day arising / From sullen earth* . . . is a sentimental and poor metaphor, because instead of coming up with an interesting 'objective correlative' – an image that expresses his feelings, basically – he's taken an off-the-peg one, and just coloured it with his own emotion. The dark earth isn't *sullen* to the lark, in which case it would've been admissible: it's only sullen to WS. That's cheating. If you interfere with the internal consistency of the vehicle and start altering it to fit your metaphor better, the whole trope falls apart and has no power, unless you're a sentimentalist. (The rule is: qualify the tenor as much as you want with the alien attributes of the vehicle, but if you start qualifying the vehicle with the alien attributes of the tenor, the metaphor loses all naturalism, all plausibility, and smacks of a fix. My fragrant love might be like a rose, but my love can't be like a sexy rose.) But then the Victorians, especially, loved that sort of thing, and they'll have loved this. It took Ezra Pound to purge us of this stuff, for which all poets should remain eternally grateful.

(I had a bet in with myself just there that Coleridge, too, had marked it as a favourite of his: he had too. STC was a genius, of course, but his tastes run to the smoothly gloopy something terrible.)

Such little interest as the poem provokes is biographical: *why* is he so wretchedly miserable? The reasons seem to have nothing directly to do with the YM here; but without some means of dating the poem, it's all pointless speculation. There's nothing in the poem to indicate the source of his misery – a bomb at the Globe? A port hangover? The death of his son Hamnet? Or is he just indulging his Olympic-standard talent for self-hatred and self-pity? Who knows. We never will. My own particular problem is that as a Scottish Calvinist (United Free Atheist), stains, blots, disgraces, bootlessness and the whole massed firepower of WS's

self-directed ordnance prompt no intrigue whatsoever. Self-
29 hatred is our resting state. Blots my meat, stains my drink, and
disgrace the air I breathe. He sounds fine.

❧

30

When to the sessions of sweet silent thought
I summon up remembrance of things past,
I sigh the lack of many a thing I sought,
And with old woes new wail my dear time's waste;
Then can I drown an eye (unused to flow)
For precious friends hid in death's dateless night,
And weep afresh love's long since cancell'd woe,
And moan th'expense of many a vanished sight;
Then can I grieve at grievances foregone,
And heavily from woe to woe tell o'er
The sad account of fore-bemoanèd moan,
Which I new pay as if not paid before;
    But if the while I think on thee, dear friend,
    All losses are restored, and sorrows end.

A simple poem, in its way, but it has a very pretty music that's deeply wedded to its subject, full of moany Os and sighing sibilants: the torments of memory, and the fact that we never really get over *anything*, so long as we can bring it back to mind. Yes; best not to remember at all, if we've already managed to call a halt to our mourning. The memory is a repository of endless pain and regret. Give us the time and the silence to indulge them, and we'll just relive all those griefs and grievances afresh.

This is one of those sonnets that suffer from the 'irrelevant' variation of Redundant Couplet Syndrome, and ends at l.12.

30 The couplet is tacked on, and brings us back (somewhat too conveniently) to WS's grand theme. But I don't buy it, personally. It's too facile, and it sounds like Patience Strong. Read it up to l.12, and stop there. Works just great.

Throughout this poem WS uses metaphors drawn from financial and legal language (*sessions*, *summon*, *cancelled*, *expense*, *tell* and so on), reinforcing the idea that he's taking meticulous account of his grief – and adding an unhealthy dose of guilt to the proceedings. WS rarely uses anything so crude as a completely straightforward metaphor of comparison or identification, but will instead delegate the metaphor to many single parts of speech, so that it slips into the reader's brain almost unnoticed. Here, the metaphor is everywhere, and the poem is hooked up to it like a drip.

l.2 *I summon up remembrance of things past*: from Wisdom of Solomon, a book in the Old Testament Apocrypha. 'For a double griefe came upon them, and a groaning for the remembrance of things past.' In other words, a perfect and beautiful allusion. The English title of C. K. Scott Moncrieff's translation of Proust's wrist-sprainer took the line from this sonnet, however.

l.6 *death's dateless night*: 'dateless' is more legalese. A chilling phrase, is it not.

l.11 I love that *fore-bemoanèd moan.* It's a quiet little flourish, as flourishes go, but another sign that WS casually ignores the received rules of the English language, in much the same way someone like Thelonious Monk casually ignores the received rules of piano-playing. This is the poetic equivalent of deliberately hitting a crack, and still sounding cool.

❧

31

Thy bosom is endeared with all hearts
Which I, by lacking, have supposed dead;
And there reigns love, and all love's loving parts,
And all those friends which I thought burièd.
How many a holy and obsequious tear
Hath dear religious love stol'n from mine eye,
As interest of the dead, which now appear
But things remov'd that hidden in thee lie:
Thou art the grave where buried love doth live,
Hung with the trophies of my lovers gone,
Who all their parts of me to thee did give;
That due of many, now is thine alone.
  Their images I loved, I view in thee,
  And thou (all they) hast all the all of me.

The main point of interest in this rather insipid effort is WS's development of the metaphor of 'dead' love. When love's dead, we tend to mean 'dead' in the restricted metaphorical sense of 'finished', perhaps with a strong hint of 'unable to feel anything'; but here WS takes it so far, we're almost tempted to read him literally – especially after the previous sonnet, where we encountered *precious friends hid in death's dateless night*; but there he was referring to dead friends, not lovers. Here I think it's more likely he's just indicating old ex-lovers, not old dead lovers.

31 The first two lines are tricky, but if we omit the Q's unhelpful comma in l.1, we get something like 'Your bosom is made precious with all hearts – which, because I don't carry them in my own bosom, I have supposed long dead.' In other words: 'You now have the love of all those who used to love me; and because they don't love me any more, nor I them – I assumed they were dead.' The YM is now the receptacle and reliquary for all things love and loverly, all the love WS ever felt. But WS *will* elaborate the conceit. He weeps as he would at a funeral, or in remembrance of the dead. The sestet pushes it further, though too far for me. Yes, we know the YM is where all WS's former loves now reside, but comparing him to a mass grave isn't quite as romantic as WS seems to think. This walking charnel-house, brimful of the living dead, KDJ rather generously reads as a 'spacious memorial chapel'. Huh? With *zombies*? This conceit is out of control. Lock up your similes. The poem ends with the usual happy conflation of everything: they're all in you, I'm all in you, and we're all back together again. Yay.

This poem echoes little in my own experience. It may in yours; I know folk who love *everything* again in love. But I've always found that the newly beloved tends to put even more distance between . . . you and your amorous past, not less; old lovers are called to mind less frequently than ever. So is this *felt*? Or is it just a rhetorical exercise? Or is it a deliberately mixed message, just to keep the beloved on his toes?

SB finds much sexual innuendo here – *parts*, *holy*, *things*. Yeah: *things*.

l.5 *obsequious*: here, it means 'dutiful', and was closer to 'obsequy' than the word is now.

1.8 the Q has . . . *in there lie*, which works, just about, if we
read *there* as referring to 'bosom'; but it's a strain. I've accepted 31
the standard emendation to *thee*.

32

If thou survive my well-contented day,
When that churl death my bones with dust shall cover,
And shalt by fortune once more re-survey
These poor rude lines of thy deceased lover:
Compare them with the bett'ring of the time,
And though they be outstripped by every pen,
Reserve them for my love, not for their rhyme,
Exceeded by the height of happier men.
O then vouchsafe me but this loving thought:
'Had my friend's Muse grown with this growing age,
A dearer birth than this his love had brought,
To march in ranks of better equipage:
  But since he died and poets better prove,
  Theirs for their style I'll read, his for his love.'

'If you survive me, and one day happen upon these rough verses again . . . compare them to the finer things the poets are writing in that better age; but though my poems are outstripped by these happier and more gifted poets – preserve them: not for their great literary style, but for the love in them. Think this, for my sake: *if he'd lived in that more sophisticated age and developed a style equal to it – true, he'd have written better poems: good enough to allow him to march in the ranks of these other poets. But since he died, and there are better poets than* him *to read – well, I'll read them for their style, and him for his love.*'

Again there's been a tendency to read this as a simple ironic inversion of what WS is *really* saying, but I wouldn't be too quick to call this poem insincere: there's some ingenuity in the argument here, as WS subverts the compliment-fishing 'my poems are rubbish: here's another pretty good poem' routine, and proposes that there's an advantage to the very *failure* of his style. When set beside the works of better poets and found wanting, what will nonetheless sing out clear from his verse is the raw strength of his love – the depth of which will, indeed, be all the *more* intensified by the contrast.

Again, SB finds more double entendre in *con*-tented and *pen*. He may be right. I find it very hard to care. I mean where do you end with this stuff? Look and ye shall find. Besides, the trouble with slang is that there's often no written record of it; there was no Elizabethan equivalent of that estimable contemporary resource, *Roger's Profanisaurus*. Maybe *muse* really meant penis, as *mowse* was Elizabethan for banana. So l.10 starts to look *decidedly* oo-er missus, if you really want it to.

l.12 is a rather odd military metaphor; against what, exactly, are the massed ranks of these poets/poems marching? But that isn't his intention, and my clumsy paraphrase can't reflect this. I think we're supposed to map this military image to the ranked lines of the well-drilled poem, in which his love will be the more efficiently expressed. KDJ helpfully points out that he may have had in mind a sentence from Sidney's *Defence*, in 'England: A Hard Stepmother To Poets', where he lays in to those poets who write the first thing that pops into their heads, 'never marshalling it into any assured rank, that almost the readers cannot tell where to find themselves'.

❧

33

Full many a glorious morning have I seen
Flatter the mountain tops with sovereign eye,
Kissing with golden face the meadows green,
Gilding pale streams with heavenly alchemy;
Anon permit the basest clouds to ride
With ugly rack on his celestial face,
And from the forlorn world his visage hide,
Stealing unseen to west with this disgrace:
Even so my sun one early morn did shine
With all triumphant splendour on my brow;
But out alack, he was but one hour mine,
The region cloud hath mask'd him from me now.
　Yet him for this my love no whit disdaineth:
　Suns of the world may stain, when heaven's sun staineth.

Oh, there's a chill in the air and a change in the weather coming. Sonnets 33 and 34 form a pair, and should be read together. If we give them a biographical reading (and it'd be almost perverse not to), what's clearly happened is that the YM has, in some sense or other, turned away from WS. Who hasn't felt, when unexpectedly slighted by the beloved in this way, that the sun – or indeed the face of God – has turned from them? Repeated pain always creates a logic; and poor WS has been forced again into another bout of Barthesian rationalisation (I'll talk elsewhere on the similarity between the Sonnets and

A Lover's Discourse). This is probably all the more tortured because he's keenly aware of the small size of the offence, and the disproportionately huge suffering it has caused him.

'The morning sun never lasts a day' was proverbial, and the octave of the poem elaborates this incontrovertible observation. (Note that this sonnet wouldn't work in the Spanish. Our rubbish weather provides a plethora of handy analogues and metaphors for the fickleness of the human mood that our Mediterranean colleagues just don't have access to. Scant consolation for sleet in August, but hey.)

As they say in Crit. Anal. 101, 'the sun is anthropomorphised here'; but then we should always ask: as whom? We're clearly supposed to map this to the YM, so it's going to be telling. Well . . . For a sovereign, the sun is very generous and beneficent: it kisses and it flatters. Usually sovereigns expect someone to flatter *them*. But it *permits* an *ugly rack* (a mass of wind-driven cloud) to pass before its face, and is *disgraced*, the principal meaning of which here is 'disfigured'. This is very passive, and it sounds like WS is making excuses for the YM's volte-face. As you do: the last thing the lover wants to think is that the beloved has turned away in *deliberate* slight. The *region cloud* (region: heavenly, and so 'clouds of the upper air') has merely masked him. No blame, and one of the occupational hazards of being so damn high and empryean.

But what might that literally *mean*? Just that the important business of the day came between the YM and WS, the way clouds come between kingly suns and us, their lowly subjects? (Note that this reinforces the Wriothesley/Herbert theories a little – the YM is being described in terms of high rank; I'm not so sure. To me this whole poem sounds like the neurotic and obsessive interrogation of 'I'm ironing my ruff tonight' – as it may well have been; though what the YM was *really* up to is hinted at in Sonnet 35. Either way, we should never be fooled into thinking that noble art always has some commensurately noble inspiration behind it. The ends may be adult, but the means are often adolescent. (Bob Dylan wrote 'When the Ship Comes In' after a hotel clerk took exception to his unwashed appearance.)

But WS's is a contrived and false comfort. He knows only too well that his love *could* have come out to play that night if he'd really wanted to, if WS was important enough to him. It's not enough to say 'well – if we allow the *sun* to be so fickle and unreliable – we have to accept that other celestial bodies will behave in the same way'. Again, through the desperate need to maintain the illusion of the beloved's perfection, WS has turned what might have been the occasion for a big '*screw you*' into a supreme compliment.

But he *knows* that his conceit is starting to creak. Look closely at the last two lines. *Suns of the world* is a pun, and a beautifully contradictory one. It can be read as 'great men' – but lurking behind it is 'sons of the world' – i.e. mere terrestrial mortals, in all their low corruptibility. Here WS weakens, shifts and then subverts the divine comparison; suddenly that *disgrace* is looking less like 'disfigurement' and more like 'shame', and *stain* less the passive result of the passing cloud – and more like 'sin'. There's a rising note of the sun's culpability, of the author's accusation. This is sounded far more clearly in the next sonnet, but you can sense WS's thoughts start to curdle in this line, and lose faith in the false comfort of his conceit.

Incidentally, here's a nice piece of carbon-dating to support the theory that the first sixty sonnets date from the mid to late 1590s. Listen to Prince Harry's speech in *1 Henry IV*, I. ii:

Yet herein will I imitate the sun,
Who doth permit the base contagious clouds
To smother up his beauty from the world,
That when he please again to be himself,
Being wanted, he may be more wonder'd at
By breaking through the foul and ugly mists
Of vapours that did seem to strangle him.

33

This was written around 1598. A litte recycling going on here?

34

Why didst thou promise such a beauteous day,
And make me travel forth without my cloak,
To let base clouds o'ertake me in my way,
Hiding thy brav'ry in their rotten smoke?
'Tis not enough that through the cloud thou break,
To dry the rain on my storm-beaten face,
For no man well of such a salve can speak
That heals the wound, and cures not the disgrace;
Nor can thy shame give physic to my grief;
Though thou repent, yet I have still the loss;
The offender's sorrow lends but weak relief
To him that bears the strong offence's cross.
  Ah, but those tears are pearl which thy love sheds,
  And they are rich, and ransom all ill deeds.

You can tell this is going to be a fine poem from the first line: it's all in the scansion. Such is his strength of feeling, WS is doing battle with the pentameter from the start, and using it to flag his distress. Normally the disagreements between speech-rhythm and metre don't begin until the rhythm has bedded down and the argument is properly under way – but here there's no time. Passions are too high. '*Why* didst thou promise such a beauteous day?'

This poem elaborates the previous conceit, but the poet seems to have become suddenly conscious of his own growing suspicion, which we heard buried in 33's closing couplet. The tone here is very much 'Actually – let's forget all that "*Yet him for this, my love no whit disdaineth*" stuff. To hell with you, you unfeeling bastard.' The remarkable thing is that WS manages to say all this while being completely faithful to the existing weather-conceit. He still compares the YM with the sun, but no longer to flatter him. The sun's lost its sovereignty.

This poem shows a good deal more self-knowledge than the last. It should be no surprise to anyone that WS – capable of entering the minds of monsters, of ventriloquising individuals we'd rather not even *think* about – is shaky when it comes to knowing himself. (WS had the ability, I suspect, to *vanish* his ego like a magician, to render it virtually negligible through his almost infinite capacity for human empathy. If ever a man had overactive mirror neurons, it was WS.) But do you see how the more honest feeling gives rise immediately to far better poetry? The presence of strong, undiluted and direct feeling is the best argument for writing – sometimes, at least – from experience, rather than imagination: maybe it's the only one. And nothing writes more articulately than anger, sad to say.

The clouds are still *base*, but seem nearer the ground; they've overtaken WS, not just the sun. *Rotten smoke* is terrific. (Elizabethans thought clouds carried the plague.) 'It isn't enough that occasionally you deign to break through the cloud and dry the rain on my face [for which we quickly read "tears"]; that won't heal the *disgrace*.' Again *disgrace* means primarily 'disfigurement', perhaps here in the sense of a lasting scar. (Note how *face* and *disgrace* occur on exactly the same lines in Sonnets 33 and 34.) But by the end it's 'Who's crying now? Ha. You are. It wasn't enough that you dried my tears: I want to see you suffering

for the suffering you cause *me*.' A plausible touch of sadism, here.
34 Pearl was used medicinally by the Elizabethans, who believed it had curative properties, and WS cleverly elaborates the wound/cure/physic metaphor introduced earlier in the poem. Primarily, though, the YM is just buying forgiveness with his tears' value.

l.2 alludes to a bit of proverbial advice not taken: *Although the sun shines leave not your cloak at home*. As I've mentioned, 'travel' and 'travail' were spelled identically in Elizabethan English, and modern readers lose the pun here.

ll.5 and 7 the rhymes would have been almost full in WS's Warwickshire accent, both rhyming with 'lake'.

l.13 *sheeds* in the Q, but even then the form was archaic. Was WS straining for a rhyme? Kerrigan thinks this shows the poet's especial difficulty, here, in bringing the poem round to a 'last-minute restitution'. But I don't hear much restitution; just a barely concealed and sexually fuelled enjoyment of the YM's distress. It's as well the camera cuts away at l.14. I can sense it getting all a bit post-watershed.

A bit of a textual quibble, for your amusement: the Q has *loss* at the end of l.12, duplicating the rhyme on l.10, and the standard emendation is *cross*. KDJ is queasy on the grounds that it introduces the theme of the speaker as a Christ-figure – an unforgiving one, at that – absent elsewhere. But the case for *cross* is strongly reinforced by the presence of *bear*; *a cross to bear* was already a commonplace. SB says the 'repetition might possibly be purposeful' but he doubts it, and so do I. The second *loss* seems more likely a printer's eye-skip, and it's too cheap a trick: the gesture of repeating the word would be too loud, and drown any other sense it might conceivably carry. (The retention of *loss* can only be justified by the argument that the repetition might communicate a sense of *intensified* loss – but no one would *feel* that intensification on a first reading; they would just notice the repetition. I know this sounds like a small point, but it does illustrate a good rule: if you can only establish the presence of an effect by retrospective analysis, you didn't feel it when you read it the first time – meaning that in a very straightforward sense . . . it just isn't there. What you've found is not an 'effect' but either a misfire on the poet's part, an invention on yours, or most likely a bit of both.) There's also the presence of *ransom*: Jesus dies on the cross to *ransom* us from our fall into sin. Gotta be *cross*. There's also something of Peter's denial of Jesus, too, in the YM's earlier rejection of WS.

35

No more be grieved at that which thou hast done;
Roses have thorns, and silver fountains mud;
Clouds and eclipses stain both moon and sun,
And loathsome canker lives in sweetest bud.
All men make faults, and even I in this,
Authorizing thy trespass with compare,
Myself corrupting, salving thy amiss,
Excusing thy sins more than thy sins are:
For to thy sensual fault I bring in sense;
Thy adverse party is thy advocate,
And 'gainst myself a lawful plea commence:
Such civil war is in my love and hate
  That I an accessary needs must be
  To that sweet thief which sourly robs from me.

What an elegantly balanced poem. It starts off in a rather pedestrian manner: 'we all make mistakes, even the best of us; there's good and bad in everyone'. Which sounds a little clichéd and proverbial, and indeed it is – but if we don't know the phrases WS is alluding to, we lose a dimension: l.4 is supposed to put the reader in mind of '*canker soonest eats the sweetest bud*'. That 'soonest' is a nuance missing from the poem, but present in the allusion. (You can bring it out by leaning on *sweetest* a little.)

All this is just a beautifully timed bit of flannel. The poem turns into something much more conflicted and interesting at the line *All men make faults, and even I in this*; in other words: 'I'm erring as I write this, condoning *your* sins with all these fancy comparisons of mine, by which I seek to excuse you; they're surplus to requirements. All I'm trying to excuse is *a sensual fault*, a slip of the body; and all this rational reasoning is a greater expense of intellect and a more energetic defence than your behaviour actually requires. Look at me, stood here playing both advocate and defendant, pleading your case against my own. In my warring confusion, I'm just an accessory to another crime – to your theft of my time and energy.'

Aha: so he *wasn't* ironing his wig that night after all. There *was* some *sensual fault*, which we're entitled to interpret as the YM having, y'know, strayed a little. You might think that WS is being as self-deluded as ever, and downplaying his own terrible jealousy here, and find his forgiveness unconvincing. Surely there's nothing worse for the lover than the knowledge that the beloved has committed some 'sensual fault' with another? But WS has either been reassured, or is consoling himself with the thought that it *wasn't* an act that threatened their love; that would have been intolerable. It was just sex. (I doubt this will strike anyone as an earth-shattering revelation, but sex and love are sometimes less closely linked in the mind of the human male than in the female. In heterosexual relationships this reality might have to be denied or suppressed by the male party – if it's a relationship the male wants to survive. I'm obliged to make the observation that my gay male friends – whose desires are male first, and homosexual second – often *do* make just this distinction in their relationships; I sense WS is quite sincere. With heterosexual men, it's often different: they'll regard a sexual betrayal as a greater offence than an emotional one. With many heterosexual women, we can reverse all that again. What a mess.)

35 Note how the language turns legalistic in the sestet, quietly introducing a courtroom metaphor. Everyone says that *authorizing* should have its stresses on the second and fourth syllables. Maybe it should – but to perform it like this sounds ridiculously pedantic to the modern ear, and a little anachronistic unmangling of the prosody here seems justified. Try reading the line as starting with a strong stress, and swallow the second syllable, i.e. as *AUTH'rizING.*

36

Let me confess that we two must be twain,
Although our undivided loves are one;
So shall those blots that do with me remain,
Without thy help, by me be borne alone.
In our two loves there is but one respect,
Though in our lives a separable spite;
Which though it alter not love's sole effect,
Yet doth it steal sweet hours from love's delight.
I may not evermore acknowledge thee,
Lest my bewailèd guilt should do thee shame,
Nor thou with public kindness honour me,
Unless thou take that honour from thy name:
But do not so; I love thee in such sort,
As thou being mine, mine is thy good report.

If we're to believe the previous sonnets, the blot was largely on the YM's side, and WS's worst offence has been to construct some over-elaborate conceits – the monster; so it's hard to work out what the hell he's on about here. Indeed it's been suggested that such is the masochistic self-flagellation of the speaker, WS is actually ventriloquising the YM in this poem, and taking advantage of the conceit in Sonnet 35, where he acts as the YM's representative in the legal muddle he has constructed. I think that's wrong, but WS really does push the whipping-boy routine to extremes, here. The sestet says 'I don't want to bring shame on

36 you with my public wailing; and nor should you show me any *public kindness*; that might just take honour from your own name. That's something I have a stake in: since we're the same person [here we go again], your *good report*, your reputation, is mine too.'

We can't help but hear in that first line one heartbreaking allusion: while their love might be undivided, they cannot be 'one flesh' (as man and wife are described in *Ephesians*). ll.6–8 are very sad, too: regardless of the *separable spite* (something like 'the terrible vexation that keeps us apart') our love is unchanged; but it steals hours that we might have spent together.

This is one of the very few sonnets, incidentally, which Coleridge regarded as of the first water – at least according to the tatty envelope bearing the scribbled notes I made from STC's (borrowed; cheerfully defaced) copy of Anderson's *The Works of the British Poets* at Grasmere library. STC had a point-system, and awarded what he deemed the best of the sonnets – a fraction of the whole – marks out of four. Only eight gained top marks. His choices are utterly bizarre, and do tend to reveal his alarming taste for smooth numbers and the smoothly sentimental, and explain why he thought so highly of William Bowles. But I like this one too.

ll.1–2 you can read these lines with the expressive accent on *twain* and *one*, but I prefer to stress *loves*, as it enacts a more telling contrast – between 'two' as in 'bodies', and their united love. In a poem with many compare-and-contrasts, performing your understanding of the sense in your reading is especially important. But remember – the more subtle and layered the poem, the more alternatives you tend to have; there will be more than one correct performance. This, incidentally, is why the Sonnets are *not* (as some have claimed) a 'dramatic poem'. That's not to say the same few lines of dramatic writing can't receive a number of different and equally plausible deliveries; but you choose one, because there's an audience. In a poem, you don't always have to. Your performance changes in the dynamic flow of your rereading and deepening understanding of the poem; each new interpretation will demand a different delivery.

l.5 *respect*: consideration, or motive.

ll.13–14 are repeated at the end of Sonnet 96, which looks a bit shabby, at first, until you realise they're being used to very different effect.

❧

37

As a decrepit father takes delight
To see his active child do deeds of youth,
So I, made lame by Fortune's dearest spite,
Take all my comfort of thy worth and truth:
For whether beauty, birth, or wealth, or wit,
Or any of these all, or all, or more,
Entitled in thy parts, do crownèd sit,
I make my love engrafted to this store:
So then I am not lame, poor, nor despis'd,
Whilst that this shadow doth such substance give
That I in thy abundance am sufficed,
And by a part of all thy glory live.
  Look what is best, that best I wish in thee;
  This wish I have, then ten times happy me.

The storm's over, and WS puts his recent troubles behind him for a few poems. 'Stocktaking' some commentators call this poem, though 'marking time' or 'treading water' would be more accurate. Right from the off, we have a wretchedly weak second syllable in the first line, which doesn't bode well for the dramatic robustness of the poem, and so it quickly proves. The 'lame' conceit, developed with no conviction whatsoever, is exactly that (some literally minded critics hear a crippled WS, here; dear god no), while the old Neoplatonic binary of 'substance' and 'shadow' is thrown in as a bit of window-dressing.

(SB hears a witty reversal in that *shadow* brings forth *substance.* I hear a prayer for the invention of television.) In fact the whole poem turns out to be a shoddy patchwork of ideas and effects WS has developed or will develop elsewhere, and has no thematic coherence whatsoever. There's an impotence riff in all this somewhere, though, with the usual boring puns scattered throughout to massively enervating effect. One wants to end the poem with *Private Eye*'s standard editorial gloss (*you've done this already – Ed.*)

In the list of *beauty, birth, or wealth, or wit, / Or any of these all, or all, or more, / Entitled in thy parts, do crownèd sit,* KDJ hears a humour, almost – 'as if the addressee is being mocked for his superabundance of gifts, rather than praised for them'. Me, I think it's exhaustion: it's the poet's trick of trying to revive a knackered brain and a collapsing pudding of a poem by pumping in the hyperbole. The great thing about hyperbole is that it takes no longer to write than anything else (try it: time yourself to scribble the words 'eternity', then 'Bovril' – you'll find there's little difference in either the physical effort or the imaginative expense), and it can momentarily leave you with the happy impression that you've come up with something really substantial with minimal effort. The opposite is always the case; your poem couldn't be smaller if you tried. And in terms of the light it sheds on the larger situation . . . this sonnet's batteries are dead. HV points out that the poem is patterned round *th* sounds, although there's little to read into this but WS's default lyric riffing. She also finds no 'couplet tie', remarking that 'such is the force of the graphic liaison in *th* that no verbal liaison is needed'. This is beyond parody, to be honest with you. And also pretty funny, given this poem is screaming out for a verbal liaison of *any* kind.

37 l.1: *As AY decrepit father* . . . – i.e. giving the indefinite article its (unjustified) emphatic pronunciation – is the only reading that can save the line. 'A' is normally toneless, and is very unhappy in an exposed strong-stress position.

l.7: 'having the right and title, sit throned like a king among your good qualities' (JK)

❧

38

How can my Muse want subject to invent
While thou dost breathe, that pour'st into my verse
Thine own sweet argument, too excellent
For every vulgar paper to rehearse?
O give thy self the thanks, if aught in me
Worthy perusal stand against thy sight:
For who's so dumb that cannot write to thee,
When thou thy self dost give invention light?
Be thou the tenth Muse, ten times more in worth
Than those old nine which rhymers invocate;
And he that calls on thee, let him bring forth
Eternal numbers to outlive long date.
  If my slight Muse do please these curious days,
  The pain be mine, but thine shall be the praise.

After the last poem, this is rather amusing. 'How can I lack inspiration while you are alive?' is less the airy rhetorical question it might seem. Under his breath WS seems to add . . . *and still manage to write so badly*. However 'lack of inspiration' is, perversely, a subject a poet can get quite animated about; at least this poem has some identifiable centre of gravity.

'O give yourself the credit for anything half-decent you see in my work.' An ugly accidental chime on *argument/excellent*, and then a felicitous couple of lines: *For who's so dumb that cannot write to thee, / When thou thy self dost give invention light?* 'For

38 who's so unresponsive that he can't write about you, when you provide the very spark of creation?' And then it all goes off the boil again. 'You could be the tenth muse, you could,' etc. – but at least his real muse flared, momentarily. The couplet says 'if my little inspiration pleases those demanding readers in the future . . . well, the labour involved will have been mine, but the praise shall be yours'. However the use of 'muse' as a synonym for 'inspiration' in in l.13 is dreadful. Only a few lines before, he'd elevated his capital-M Muse, the YM, to goddess-like status. So to hear the word suddenly qualified by 'slight' is bizarre – until you realise he's using the word in a different sense. Dear me.

l.4 gives us a big trope-hunter's tick: in *vulgar paper*, 'paper' is a metonym for 'literary production written on paper', but by this WS really intends a *further* metonym, 'those who compose literary productions written on paper', i.e. 'poets' – giving us a lovely doubled trope, or metalepsis. So he means 'too excellent for common poets to describe'. Trainspotting, I know, but you have to get your thrills somewhere.

39

O how thy worth with manners may I sing,
When thou art all the better part of me?
What can mine own praise to mine own self bring,
And what is't but mine own when I praise thee?
Even for this, let us divided live,
And our dear love lose name of single one,
That by this separation I may give
That due to thee which thou deserv'st alone.
O absence! what a torment wouldst thou prove,
Were it not thy sour leisure gave sweet leave
To entertain the time with thoughts of love,
Which time and thoughts so sweetly doth deceive,
 And that thou teachest how to make one twain
 By praising him here who doth hence remain.

Back on track again. This is effectively a companion piece to Sonnet 36 (*Let me confess that we two must be twain*), and one of several extemporisations on the proverbial theme 'a friend is one's second self'. Why are these two good poems separated by two indifferent ones? To enact their theme of separation? Was it just an editorial error? Either way, they're better read together, as a double sonnet. HV beat me to an analysis of their near mirror-image rhyme pairs of *twain/remain*, *one/alone*, *thee/me*, though being a poet, I'm always keenly aware of less noble reasons for doing things. It's entirely possible that WS separated the poems so that we wouldn't notice he'd recycled his rhymes.

39 A relief, though, after the last two poor efforts, to be faced with this seamless composition, a proper song. I think its initial proposition may have more logical than emotional truth – 'if we're one, then any praise of you is also self-praise – and therefore conceitedness on my part'. As neat as that is, I doubt WS actually *felt* that. (A sentence, I suspect, that I will find myself typing with some frequency.) This kind of epistemic asymmetry – where the mind gives a false account of the emotional truth of the situation, because the shape of its logic is just too damn attractive – is endemic to the poetry of the time. It also accounts for about half of my deeply unfashionable misgivings about John Donne, whom I'd like to like much more than I do. Felt experience, in my experience, rarely accords with such ferociously balanced equations. It might in yours.

Anyway . . . WS develops the idea that through the couple's separation he will distance himself from his own charge of self-aggrandisement, and any praise he gives will now be the YM's alone. I don't buy this either, but the emotional reality behind it seems plain enough: this is a desperate attempt to put a positive spin on an intolerable enforced separation. It's all rather beautifully expressed. (And l.6 has such a sad echo. The only couples who have *name of single one* are married.)

And there's no mistaking the sestet as anything but wholly sincere. 'Your absence would be an insufferable torment, if it didn't afford me the leisure to indulge so many sweet thoughts.' We've all been *there*. The one and only compensation for the beloved's absence is that you get to think about them deliriously – which you can't do when they're present. (I can recall situations where I've been positively *annoyed* by them, and couldn't wait for them to leave so I could get back to daydreaming about them again. In our infatuations, it's love we love, not the beloved. See Sonnet 56 for a very amateur stab at a neurological explanation.) And the couplet is summary, but it's magisterial. His lover's absence is teaching him how to divide his love, as of course it must. And he adduces this sonnet as *proof* of his earlier argument; it's praise untainted by self-interest, composed while the YM has been removed elsewhere.

40

Take all my loves, my love, yea take them all;
What hast thou then more than thou hadst before?
No love, my love, that thou mayst true love call;
All mine was thine, before thou hadst this more:
Then if for my love thou my love receivest,
I cannot blame thee, for my love thou usest;
But yet be blamed, if thou thyself deceivest
By wilful taste of what thyself refusest.
I do forgive thy robb'ry, gentle thief,
Although thou steal thee all my poverty:
And yet love knows it is a greater grief
To bear love's wrong, than hate's known injury.
  Lascivious grace, in whom all ill well shows,
  Kill me with spites; yet we must not be foes.

The next three sonnets seem to refer to the same incident as Sonnets 133 and 134 from the DL sequence, told from the same apex but along a different side of the love-triangle. (See Sonnet 144 for an overview of the whole sorry mess.) For all the potential intrigue, the jury's out as to whether this sonnet is worth the bother, but persist with it; there's an awful desperation in WS's relentless invoking of 'love', here, and the word occurs a full ten times. Its constant incantation is almost a spell to ward off love's *failing*, as WS finds himself rapidly becoming the gooseberry in this hideous affair. It's a very monosyllabic poem, saved from the nail-gun effect by its lovely varied and rich vowels, and would make a fine if incomprehensible song.

I'll gird my loins, and attempt a working paraphrase. 'Take all my loves, my love, take them all; and what do you have then, that you didn't have before? Nothing you could call true love, anyway: you *had* my true love, before you had this additional stuff. If, out of affection for me [though *for my love* could also mean, more sinisterly, "in place of my love"], you enjoy my mistress [I know, I know] – I can't blame you, because it's still *my* love/mistress that you're taking advantage of. But nonetheless you should be blamed if you deceive yourself – by lustfully testing out what you yourself refuse/hold back.' (Judiciously oblique, but I prefer the interpretation 'if you cheerfully make love to one person, but you refuse to make love to me'.)

Then on to the sestet: 'But I do forgive you, gentle thief, even though you've taken even the little I have left. Yet every lover knows it's much harder to take a wound from a lover than it is from someone who hates you – where you expect such things. You – whose very *lust* looks graceful, who makes bad look good – go ahead, kill me with your spiteful hurt; yet we mustn't become enemies.' Isn't that last line pathetic? It comes out of nowhere, and has little to do with the rest of the argument. It's so shamelessly *pleading*.

I've rather breezed over l.5, even though SB gives *seven* different possible interpretations, hinting darkly that there may be more. This is not good. That's too many, and it takes us past the point where the poem can be said to be a worthwhile game for the reader. The poem is an unstable sign: it's always forcing itself into original expression, so it can say things that aren't usually amenable to representation in speech. Original expression very

often demands an *interpretation*, as it obviously has no con-
40 sensual meaning yet. Interpretations will vary wildly. Poets know all this, and one aspect of the art of poetry is controlling the bandwidth of interpretative ambiguity. Too little, and the poem has no wider suggestive dimension; too much – as here – and no consensual interpretation can ever be reached: the text is incapable of confirming or confounding your sense-hunch. Anyway I'm not going through them all. It's not why I got into this game. Nor you, I suspect.

l.13 The only phrase that displays much in the way of real verbal innovation here is the near-oxymoron *lascivious grace.* As HV rightly points out, it's remarkable that such an odd phrase should fall so rightly on the ear; however the reasons she gives for this are erroneous. HV claims its natural fall comes from the ear being prepared by the earlier 'amphibrachic' rhyme words *receivest/deceivest* and their – / – stress-pattern; but I doubt this. In English we can retrospectively *identify* all sorts of mad feet, but pretty much all we *hear* and can retain are vague impressions of runs of duples and triples, and isolated deviations from those patterns – and that's your lot. The only exceptions are overdetermined metres, where, for example, the poem is performed in a way that makes the syllables conform to an unusual stress-pattern – think Edith Sitwell – or where the poem is deliberately written to the rhythms of a well-known song that the reader recognises. (Incidentally, see the note to Sonnet 10 as to why that pair of rhymes just don't satisfy: they're too close to *rime riche*, as the stressed syllable – from which the ear measures the rhyme – leaves us with *see-vest/see-vest.*)

Anyway – the perverse sweetness of *lascivious grace* lies firstly in its semantic foreshadowing of an even bolder oxymoron – the *ill well* later in the line – and in its component sounds. First, it incorporates both the motivic global consonants of *love*, and the 40 *sssss* that seeps through the poem like a gas leak; it's also woven in locally through the l/r liquids in ll.12–13, and through *grace*'s repeating the initial sounds of the earlier *greater grief*. More pertinently, however, it works through the repeated assonantal pattern of *injury* and *-ivious grace* (*ih-uh-ay* and *ih-yuh-ay*, to spare you the IPA). These rich vowel-meadows are an unconscious landscape for the reader, but they're where the most deeply registered symmetries often lie. All this, it should go without saying, will have been arrived at by WS quite instinctively. Suffice to say this poet has one hell of an ear.

41

Those pretty wrongs that liberty commits
When I am sometime absent from thy heart,
Thy beauty and thy years full well befits;
For still temptation follows where thou art.
Gentle thou art, and therefore to be won;
Beauteous thou art, therefore to be assailed;
And when a woman woos, what woman's son
Will sourly leave her till he have prevailed?
Ay me, but yet thou might'st my seat forbear,
And chide thy beauty and thy straying youth
Who lead thee in their riot even there
Where thou art forced to break a twofold truth: –
  Hers by thy beauty tempting her to thee,
  Thine by thy beauty being false to me.

Not much to see here, folks. Sonnet 40 was weirdly moving, if deranged, and Sonnet 42 is much more fun, but this is just so much preamble. The octave says 'I know I can't be on your mind 24/7, and it's quite natural that you should play the field – god knows, with your youthful beauty, you have plenty opportunity; and what red-blooded male *wouldn't* take advantage of all these women hurling themselves at you?' – more or less. Then the sestet takes a different tack: 'But you might have left *her* alone, at least: in tempting her with your beauty, you break her fidelity to me – a beauty which causes *you* to be false to me too.' Refreshingly, he's annoyed enough to use the couplet to further press his accusation, not as an opportunity to turn it into a compliment, or contrive some kind of reconciliation.

It doesn't save this dull little poem, alas. Again, it's unlikely to find much echo in our own experience – and even in the event that you *are* a married man in love with your best mate, and have just discovered he's sleeping with your bit on the side, I doubt this poem will bring you much in the way of solace or elucidation. You need a therapist or a hit-man, not a poet. Other than its famous backward acrostic, spelling out the name of the tavern in Southwark where all three would gather – it's just versified moaning, too occasion-specific to be of any interest to anyone other than to its author. This isn't really poetry as public art, but I suppose if you can enjoy it at the level of a sort of verse-soap – be my guest.

l.1 *liberty*: freedom, so the line means 'those sweet little infidelities you commit when you're at large'.

l.8 *sourly*: ungraciously.

l.9 *my seat*: my place, here more specifically 'the place where I have sexual rights'.

OK, I was joking about the erotic.

42

That thou hast her it is not all my grief,
And yet it may be said I loved her dearly;
That she hath thee is of my wailing chief,
A loss in love that touches me more nearly.
Loving offenders thus I will excuse ye:
Thou dost love her, because thou knowst I love her,
And for my sake even so doth she abuse me,
Suff'ring my friend for my sake to approve her.
If I lose thee, my loss is my love's gain,
And losing her, my friend hath found that loss;
Both find each other, and I lose both twain,
And both for my sake lay on me this cross:
  But here's the joy; my friend and I are one;
  Sweet flattery! Then she loves but me alone.

Let's remind ourselves what a singular and thoroughly unrepresentative individual we're dealing with here. The parts of his brain that dealt with sex and empathy were hideously over-wired. Had there *been* a third alternative, WS would have been a trisexual, trust me. But would you have it any other way? Would you have our greatest writer *normal*?

'It's not just that you have the woman I love that hurts me: it's that she has the man I love. You pair of rotters . . . anyway here's how I'll rationalise it: you love her because you know I do; she puts up with your lovemaking [*approve her* means something like "to test her sexually"] because she knows how I feel about you. If I lose you, she wins; if I lose her, it's your gain; you both find each other, and I'm doubly bereft. But – aha! Since you and I are one, she loves only me!'

And so – by some very dodgy algebraic sleight-of-hand – the equation is balanced again, WS's torment briefly assuaged, and the wobbly equilibrium restored. But he *knows* how mad this all is. 'Sweet flattery' means something like 'Happy consoling delusion'. As the Irish say, he's caught himself on. But what an awful sadness lies behind all this brave wordplay.

But as I was saying – while we'll certainly identify with the broad emotion, the truth is that very little here is likely to chime with our own experience; this is one of those sonnets that those starry-eyed lovers who allegedly constitute the Sonnets' core readership will skip right over. Rightly too. More than a few unusual circumstances obtain here: the author is bisexual, and his two loves are now sexually involved, something which causes him understandable grief. (And apart from anything else – isn't this, like, the worst luck *ever*?) However, via a remarkable logical contortion, he decides that it's really all about *him*. While not a great poem, this sonnet does tell us a great deal about the solipsism of love, and while WS reveals a lot of self-knowledge in that *Sweet flattery* . . ., the bit he's blind to is the extent to which he's made this whole scenario all about *himself*. The possibility that the two lovers don't give him a second's thought has to be immediately dismissed: the notion that we might be irrelevant to those we're obsessed with is perfectly intolerable.

43

When most I wink, then do mine eyes best see,
For all the day they view things unrespected;
But when I sleep, in dreams they look on thee,
And darkly bright, are bright in dark directed.
Then thou, whose shadow shadows doth make bright,
How would thy shadow's form form happy show
To the clear day with thy much clearer light,
When to unseeing eyes thy shade shines so?
How would (I say) mine eyes be blessed made
By looking on thee in the living day,
When in dead night thy fair imperfect shade
Through heavy sleep on sightless eyes doth stay?
  All days are nights to see till I see thee,
  And nights bright days when dreams do show thee me.

The first of a few poems which take a strange inward turn, prompted, in seems, by the YM's absence. The leave-taking is taking its toll, but see how WS's comfort is conjured from the very *source* of his agony. In other words, it's moving from a dubiously rationalised comfort to a pathologically rationalised one. This is a febrile and tormented poem about lying in the dark, alone, consoled only by the beloved's image – their radiant spectre summoned all the more intensely by the physically acute sense of their absence.

Bold antitheses – sight/blindness, day/night, asleep/awake,

light/dark – underpin the whole awful-yet-exhilarating paradox. In those *bright/bright, shadow/shadows, form/form* repetitions 43
KDJ identifies something called 'polyptoton', which sounds like it should require a minor procedure; but I'd say the *trope du jour* here was more properly 'antanaclasis', when a word is repeated in a different sense.

Now let's look at the troublesome lines 4–6. Yikes. l.4 is something like . . . 'and [my eyes] shining brightly in the dark are directed towards that which is bright-in-the-dark [remember the Elizabethans believed in the eye-beam, and thought that eyes emitted light]'. Well, that's the best I can do, though the line's real effect lies less in its sense than its shape, in its semi-coherent, oxymoronic, horribly inverted madness. ll.5–6 are something like 'then you, whose image the darkness makes bright – how would your body [the body is the *shadow's form*] shape a joyful spectacle / show a happy form'. The first sense is more pleasing as it repeats *form* antanaclastically – but l.7 seems to demand we read *show* as a verb, not a noun, making 'show a happy form' correct, and leaving *form* as the same noun twice. This is unprofessional advice, but you'll get a lot more out of this poem if you just wing it. WS's syntactic madness is just enacting his own.

It's hard not to be put in mind of Plato's cave – especially in ll.7–8, when the YM's image takes on such an incandescence, the thought of its appearance as a *real* form in broad daylight beyond seems unthinkable, a blessing so fiery and fierce it might not be able to be borne. The couplet is strong: 'All my days are nights until I see you; but when I see you in my dreams, my nights are as bright days.'

l.2 *unrespected*: ignored, as well as 'not respected'.

43 l.11 *imperfect shade*, meaning an image which is deficient, less-than-whole because unreal. Though *shade*, here, sounds as much 'ghost' as 'image'.

❧

44

If the dull substance of my flesh were thought,
Injurious distance should not stop my way;
For then, despite of space, I would be brought,
From limits far remote, where thou dost stay.
No matter then although my foot did stand
Upon the farthest earth remov'd from thee,
For nimble thought can jump both sea and land
As soon as think the place where he would be.
But ah, thought kills me, that I am not thought,
To leap large lengths of miles when thou art gone,
But that so much of earth and water wrought,
I must attend time's leisure with my moan;
  Receiving nought by elements so slow
  But heavy tears, badges of either's woe.

I'm really fond of this one. WS describes a very common fantasy – but one so naff and adolescent most writers have been embarrassed to set it down. Sci-fi, really: what would it be like if we could defeat physical law and move and travel at the speed of our thoughts? Why am I trapped inside this gravity-bound, dull vessel, and why can't I just beam myself down at your side? Cioran, completely misremembered (I really did look): 'To bear the curse of consciousness is painful enough, but to also drag this *corpse* round for seventy years is just a bad joke.'

I've always said that the major design flaw of this universe – by which I mean the strongest evidence of its non-design – is the 44 *stupid* amount of distance it places between stuff. (Well, that and the male genitals, although there we might at least divine a sense of humour.) Yet it's not the distances between the stars you feel most acutely, it's the distance that opens up between you and the beloved – which might as well be interstellar, since there's no way of traversing it when you need to, i.e. *right now*.

It's a very clear poem, too, and requires little glossing. ll.11–12: 'Except that I'm made of so much earth and water [and by implication too little fire and air], I'm condemned to wait on leisurely unfolding Time. While complaining. [With the sense "I have nothing to do but fill the long hours of your absence with my moaning."] And all I get from these slow elements are tears.' *Heavy tears* are *badges of either's woe*, in their earthly weight and watery wetness. SB thinks it also carries the additional sense 'your woe and mine', but I don't. Although the last line is a bit lame: *badges* drives headlong against the metre for no good reason, and there's an ugly chime, both in the pointless *badges/either's* assonance (/æ/ə/ then /aɪ/ə/), and in their repeated /z/ sounds.

45

The other two, slight air, and purging fire
Are both with thee, wherever I abide:
The first my thought, the other my desire,
These, present absent, with swift motion slide.
For when these quicker elements are gone
In tender embassy of love to thee,
My life, being made of four, with two alone
Sinks down to death, oppressed with melancholy,
Until life's composition be recured
By those swift messengers return'd from thee
Who even but now come back again assured
Of thy fair health, recounting it to me.
  This told, I joy; but then no longer glad,
  I send them back again, and straight grow sad.

Ah, how could WS have resisted this? Having discussed the two heavy elements in Sonnet 44, he now explains where the remaining pair have gone. Air is his thought, and fire his desire, and these have been sent away in *tender embassy* – leaving him with just the two gravity boys to constitute his entire being. What a sweetly worked and emotionally convincing conceit.

Far and away my favourite lines here are . . . *Who even but now come back again, assured / Of thy fair health, recounting it to me*: which gives the impression of happening in real-time, as WS is writing the poem: the YM has sent word, through a messenger or

letter, to reassure him. It gives us a scenario suddenly deepened
45 in its intimacy, and its sense of a lived life. These irruptions of reality might be just rhetorical tricks, of course, but they're effective ones. (You didn't *really* believe all that stuff about the Person from Porlock, did you?) Those of you old enough: think back to the time when love's business was still conducted this way. Remember those long mornings watching the letterbox, your stomach in knots, holding out for something in the second delivery? (Remember the second delivery?) Like most of the non-optional hardships of one's youth, it's tempting to suggest the agony was somehow character-building, but the truth is things are much better now that cyberspace has narrowed the distance between us. You *know* when you're being ignored, or you're tenth on someone's list of priorities.

l.4 Sidney, in *Astrophel and Stella*, says 'O absent presence, Stella is not here', but that has the merit of being fairly clear. *These present-absent with swift motion slide* is much less so, but I'm pretty sure that, as well as the quantum-jump, their gone-now-back-the-next-moment movement of these fleet messengers, WS also means to encapsulate the paradox of something which is banally and literally *within him* (his thought and his desire) being in an emotionally true but non-literal sense *away with someone else*, the beloved.

The final couplet is almost so bare it shouldn't work, but its plainness rhymes a simple truth. No sooner has the lover been reassured, than all his worries assert themselves anew – and once more, he's waving goodbye to his lighter elements.

❧

46

Mine eye and heart are at a mortal war
How to divide the conquest of thy sight;
Mine eye my heart thy picture's sight would bar,
My heart mine eye the freedom of that right.
My heart doth plead that thou in him dost lie,
A closet never pierced with crystal eyes;
But the defendant doth that plea deny,
And says in him thy fair appearance lies.
To 'cide this title is empannellèd
A quest of thoughts, all tenants to the heart,
And by their verdict is determinèd
The clear eye's moiety, and the dear heart's part:
As thus: mine eyes' due is thine outward part,
And my heart's right, thine inward love of heart.

The first of a pair of sonnets where the eyes and the heart fight it out over which has rights to the YM's true image. It's a common conceit in the literature of the era, but what's most interesting about it – and I really don't mean this to sound facetious – is my total indifference towards the speaker: it's a situation wholly alien to me. It makes no damn sense at all. Why on earth would the eyes and heart *be at war*, unless there was something contradictory in the information they were getting? If the eye is custodian of the image, and the heart of feeling, where's the contradiction, and where's the competition? Assuming the

46 author is not lying, and he's *genuinely* detained by this, it must point to a belief-system entirely unfamiliar to us. If so, this rather frivolous conceit is riding on something far deeper: the Neo-platonic belief that there really *was* such a thing as an essence, as distinct from an outward appearance – and that substance and shadow were not just important distinctions to make but necessary ones, between the phenomenal and the ideal. Therefore the eye naturally defends the phenomenal truth it delights in, while the heart claims its ideal truth as the *true* truth. It's hard, however, to summon much contemporary sympathy for the conflict.

As it develops, the poem is increasingly couched in the language of the courtroom. It might help to make a quick gloss: 'My eyes and heart are locked in a fight to the death over how they should have rights over [*divide the conquest* is something like "share out the spoils of war"] your image. Each wants to bar the other from access to the image it has formed. My heart says that your true image lies with him, somewhere eyes can't go [i.e. an ideal form]; but my eye [initiate courtroom sequence], the defendant, rejects that claim, and says your beauty is *his* business. To settle this, I've enlisted a jury of my thoughts [*empannelled a quest*: assembled a jury in court]; all these thoughts pay their rent to the heart. And they've delivered a verdict on which portion [*moiety*] is the eyes', and which the heart's . . .'

. . . And at this we pause to observe that if the jury is stacked in favour of the heart, then they should surely all find one way: but the end isn't as triumphantly victorious as we might expect: 'The eyes are awarded the outward part, and the heart that part which resides in both my heart and your heart.' (*thine inward love of heart* suggests both.) This is a deeply unsatisfactory conclusion, if you ask me. It sounds just like the eyes and heart have ended up with more or less what they started with. So what was *that* all about. 46

l.4 *the freedom of that right*, having essentially the same sense as *thy picture's sight would bar* in the previous line, is a bit close to what Fowler would have sneeringly dismissed as an 'elegant variation'.

47

Betwixt mine eye and heart a league is took,
And each doth good turns now unto the other;
When that mine eye is famished for a look,
Or heart in love with sighs himself doth smother,
With my love's picture then my eye doth feast,
And to the painted banquet bids my heart;
Another time mine eye is my heart's guest,
And in his thoughts of love doth share a part.
So either by thy picture or my love,
Thyself away, art present still with me:
For thou not farther than my thoughts canst move,
And I am still with them, and they with thee;
  Or, if they sleep, thy picture in my sight
  Awakes my heart, to heart's and eyes' delight.

All fine now. Amicable and out-of-court settlement. The YM may still be absent (l.10, the only micro-frisson you'll get from this wretched poem), but now the eye and the heart are doing *good turns* for each other, sharing thoughts and images when one or the other is running a bit short in the image or thought department. Throughout, both eye and heart blithely ignore the fact that the conceit has gone way past 'largely meaningless' and entered the realm of 'totally ridiculous'. How can you share a thought with an eye? An image with the heart? You can't, unless by 'thought' he means summoning an image then beheld

in the mind's eye, and by 'image' he also intends the feeling that
accompanies it. But he doesn't say that. This wee poem is so thin, 47
you want to wrap it up and feed it soup.

l.1 *league*: alliance. As in 'League of Nations', not the measurement of distance.

l.5 *With*: on.

l.6 *painted banquet* is the one lonely flash of verbal invention here. JK hears an echo of Zeuxis' famous *trompe l'oeil* bird-fooling grapes. However no one seems to have mentioned the obvious point (I wonder why) – which is that perhaps the painted banquet doesn't refer to the imperfect and false feast conjured by the YM's summoned image, but simply to a literal portrait; which again might be read as evidence for YM's aristocratic credentials.

48

How careful was I, when I took my way,
Each trifle under truest bars to thrust,
That to my use it might unusèd stay
From hands of falsehood, in sure wards of trust;
But thou, to whom my jewels trifles are,
Most worthy comfort, now my greatest grief,
Thou best of dearest, and mine only care,
Art left the prey of every vulgar thief.
Thee have I not locked up in any chest,
Save where thou art not, though I feel thou art,
Within the gentle closure of my breast,
From whence at pleasure thou mayst come and part;
  And even thence thou wilt be stolen, I fear;
  For truth proves thievish for a prize so dear.

This begins a little series of poems where it all gets rather pessimistic; WS looks into the future, and sees it all end in tears. This is another poem that's better than it first reads (I know; it's a bit close to 'Wagner's music is much better than it sounds'), but our expectations have recently been lowered. Have a careful look at this, though. Even if it's not exactly chock-full of original phrasemaking, there's a pretty flawless and powerful conceit at work here. 'I was careful whenever I travelled to lock up my pathetic treasures, under the very strongest locks – so thieves couldn't get near them. But you, next to whom my jewels are trifles indeed – you my greatest, my dearest dear, are now my greatest sorrow and concern, because you're left wide open to any common thief. I haven't locked you in any chest other than a place where . . . you're not, really, I just *feel* you are – my own bosom, from where you can come and go at your own pleasure; but I fear you'll be stolen from even *there*, because even an *honest* person would turn criminal to get their hands on such a prize.'

Fairy stories and folk-tales are full of jealously hoarded and locked-up beloveds. At times our instinct might be to do exactly the same, and then we remember it's illegal. But then . . . what an irony we're faced with: while we bolt the doors and set the alarms for our rings and necklaces, iPods and TVs, the thing we treasure infinitely more than *any* of these things is permitted to wander freely in the world, where *anyone* might take them. And not just thieves: who wouldn't be tempted? (A further paradox: it might seem an *insult* to the beloved to think otherwise. *Not* to be jealous devalues them.) The sweetest part is l.10 where WS says he's locked the YM up in his breast, while adding . . . *though not really*. It's just an empty metaphor. It'll offer no security or protection. This is a heartfelt and honest little sonnet, and lying unspoken behind it is a complete lack of trust in the YM. The tension of the metaphor (the opposite of the 'ground', i.e. the *difference* between tenor and vehicle) in that 'jewels aren't men'; it's that 'jewels don't have individual will like men' – a will that our Will will not trust as far as he can throw it.

l.4 *in sure wards of trust* is a neat pun; *wards*, both 'guardians', and the technical name for an inner part of a lock.

l.5 A generous performance of this line will have to give an expressive rise on *are* to convey my suggested reading, 'you, next to whom my jewels are trifles *indeed*' – which is the only way to

48 explain the frankly dodgy repetition of the word *trifles*. The pitch of the voice should also fall on *trifles*, in de-emphasis.

l.14 'The prey entices the thief' was then proverbial.

49

Against that time, if ever that time come,
When I shall see thee frown on my defects;
When as thy love hath cast his utmost sum,
Called to that audit by advised respects;
Against that time when thou shalt strangely pass,
And scarcely greet me with that sun, thine eye;
When love, converted from the thing it was,
Shall reasons find of settled gravity;
Against that time do I ensconce me here,
Within the knowledge of mine own desert,
And this my hand, against my self uprear,
To guard the lawful reasons on thy part:
  To leave poor me, thou hast the strength of laws,
  Since why to love I can allege no cause.

A dry but ultimately rewarding sonnet. WS looks in his crystal ball, and it's all bad. Then he figures out a way to deal with his future in the present. The poem is built round the lovely unresolved anaphora of *Against that time* – which you have to hear three times before WS tells you *what*, exactly, he's going to balance against the awful vision of his beloved's abandonment.

It's a dense little number, though: 'In anticipation of that time, if it ever comes, when I'll see you frowning at my shortcomings, a time when your love has made its final accounts [i.e. "done its best to balance its books, and failed", I think], called in to be

audited by "considered motives" [*advis'd respects*]; anticipating
49 that time when you'll walk past me as a stranger, hardly lifting the sun of your eye to meet mine; when your love has changed, and turned a grave and sober thing – anticipating that time, I'm ensconcing myself here, I'm digging in [*ensconce* was then a little closer to its root-word, meaning "fort"], in the full knowledge of what I deserve, and my hand [by which he means also his handwriting, i.e. this poem] I raise in testimony against myself, to act as defence in the legal arguments that will prove your case: if you left me, well: that makes a sound sense. Because I certainly can't advance a good reason for you loving me.'

The trouble with being loved by someone you worship is that it doesn't make sense, and you can never quite believe it. Love overcharges our empathies; but if you *know* you're not the beloved's equal, with none of their charm, beauty, pureness of spirit (and hard cash), well: here's one place your empathy can't actually go. *You* wouldn't love you, if you were them. No, you can't identify with that at all, and what they see in you's a mystery. Here's where the books surely can't be balanced, and it all falls apart. It's a matter of time. But at least you can forgive them, if they *do* end up dumping you. Which is just what poor WS is setting *against* that dread day: at least it won't catch him surprised. It's an open acknowledgement and acceptance that the YM's desertion of him would be understandable and, hell, *correct* behaviour – no more or less than *poor me* deserves. Pretty good poem, isn't it? No one ever reads it. ll.7–8, in particular, are quite gorgeous.

The Elizabethans were *really* crazy for astrology, and the climacteric years – an ancient belief that the body altered in its fundamental constitution on multiples of seven, and sometimes nine years – were a particular obsession. We still make a song and dance about twenty-one; forty-nine was a big deal too (seventh sons of seventh sons were thought to have powers of healing, for one thing), but the most important and scary year was sixty-three, 63 being 7 x 9. Elizabeth's surviving of her 'grand climacteric' was thought no certainty – though seeing sixty-three in the first place amounted to a very decent innings back then. Eighty-one, as 9 x 9, would have been an even bigger landmark, but almost no one made it. The 49th, 63rd and 81st sonnets certainly have death and finality at their heart, but so do many others, so I really don't know how much we can read in here. KDJ's argument is that the true YM sequence is 108 poems long, in imitation of Sidney's sequence – with which WS knew he was in competition, like every other sonneteer of the day. Sidney's, too, is a multiple of nine (though 108 is also a big number in Pythagorean harmony). The whole sequence of 154 poems is a multiple of both 7 and 11 – 22 x 7 and 14 (sound familiar?) x 11 – and can be thought of as twice 7 x 11, or as composed of two sequences of two other 7 multiples: the YM sequence of 126 (7 x 18) and the DL sequence of 28 (7 x 4). (126, incidentally, is double the grand climacteric of 63, and 28 double the sonnet's line-count of 14.) Either way the last two poems are making up the numbers, and perhaps literally so.

If one regards the whole poem as a giant sonnet, by the way, the 'turn' would occur between Sonnet 88 and Sonnet 89 – bizarrely, a Fibonacci number, and therefore strongly emblematic of the golden section, the natural ratio that influences the division of octave and sestet (or at least *I* think so). Cryptomaniacs might want to have a closer look round there, though. I note also that the aforementioned key numbers 4, 7, 11 and 18 form part of the series of consecutive Lucas numbers, from which we can derive

the Pythagorean triangle 72, 170 and . . . 154. I wonder if there's
49 anything in those first two numbers, given WS was well aware of Pythagorean harmony in the Hermetic tradition (there are a couple of places in *The Merchant of Venice* where he alludes to it specifically).

. . . This is rubbish, by the way. Lucas wasn't born until the nineteenth century, and Pythagorean triangles have bugger all to do with Pythagorean harmony. I include this idle nonsense only as a self-generated example of the sort of deranged numerological speculation that has sprung up round the Sonnets. Trust me – compared with some of it, this is a model of sanity. But it's too easy to do, and you see how quickly it can all get out of hand. The trouble is, it's likely some of the numbers really *are* significant; but this kind of metatextual play on the poet *and* the reader's part is almost never, ever worth it, as it inspires or pursues just the wrong sort of intrigue, and takes us further and further from the poems. To which we will now return, and try to confine ourselves.

❧

50

How heavy do I journey on the way
When what I seek, my weary travel's end,
Doth teach that ease and that repose to say,
'Thus far the miles are measured from thy friend.'
The beast that bears me, tirèd with my woe,
Plods dully on to bear that weight in me,
As if by some instinct the wretch did know
His rider loved not speed being made from thee.
The bloody spur cannot provoke him on
That sometimes anger thrusts into his hide,
Which heavily he answers with a groan,
More sharp to me than spurring to his side,
  For that same groan doth put this in my mind:
  My grief lies onward, and my joy behind.

What a splendidly convincing little poem. Journeys which are made *away* from our beloved are wrong in a way no other journey can be. WS makes a miserable journey on horseback (feel free to speculate, but I see him making a grudging trip back from London to Stratford to remind his wife and bairns what he looked like). Even the horse has come out in sympathy, and miserably drags his hooves as a vast, aching chasm opens up between WS and his beloved. (Lying behind this is the conceit that the whole world is suffering with him, and his pain is less reflected in than *felt by* every sentient thing; never has the fallacy been more actively pathetic.)

50 ll.3–4, unless I'm hearing them wrong, contain one of the few examples of open sarcasm in the Sonnets: 'Fantastic. As soon as I get there at least I'll have the leisure to lie and think about how *awful* I feel.' *The bloody spur cannot provoke him on, / That sometimes anger thrusts into his hide* is a muscularly forceful account of the event, and great fun to wrap your chops round. The spur is already *bloody*, note – so the poem begins in medias res, at the midpoint of WS's anguished journey. I love that he still has the human pity to call the beast *wretch*, the poor horse he's taking out his anger on, as he enacts a kind of awful physical paradox – *hurrying* away from his beloved, not tarrying. If we have to go, let's get this goddamn thing *over* with. But horse and man are one, and the id of the beast won't be forced by WS's superego – and its groans are WS's, only serving to deepen the grief of the miles, the long miles to go before he sleeps. (Amazingly, SB diagnoses no innuendo in the last line. Boo.)

l.6 in the Q gives *duly*; 'dully' is the uppermost sense, so we tend to correct to that, but 'duly' – i.e. dutifully – lies close behind, and would've lain even closer when the spelling of the two words wasn't differentiated.

l.8 SB points out that being made from thee – especially given the author's recent elemental obsessions – can also be read as 'being composed of the same material as the beloved'. So as well as 'I didn't like the speed I was making away from you' we have 'I hated the speed, given I'm *of one thing* with you' – but it's a pretty contrived pun. If he meant it, I'm not sure I want to know. SB also complains about the empty syllables in l.13, but *that same* enacts his sudden reconsideration of the horse's groan in the light of his own grief, and *doth* is a near-consonance for *that*, so you

barely notice it. Sometimes you need empty syllables for timing,
and the trick is to have no one notice them. I'm all for scholarly 50
readings, but they can sometimes be unsympathetically *slow*, and
things which otherwise would have passed unnoticed or uniden-
tified have to be called to account for themselves. Things like
delivery-speed and reading-speed can affect the sense quite pro-
foundly, and shouldn't be left out of the equation.

51

Thus can my love excuse the slow offence
Of my dull bearer when from thee I speed:
From where thou art why, should I haste me thence?
Till I return, of posting is no need.
O what excuse will my poor beast then find,
When swift extremity can seem but slow?
Then should I spur, though mounted on the wind,
In wingèd speed no motion shall I know;
Then can no horse with my desire keep pace;
Therefore desire, of perfect'st love being made,
Shall rein no dull flesh in his fiery race,
But love, for love, thus shall excuse my jade:
Since from thee going he went wilful-slow,
Towards thee I'll run, and give him leave to go.

A rather superfluous continuation of Sonnet 50. WS must've felt the conceit was worth milking , but I'm not so sure. 'This is how my love for you excuses *the slow offence of my dull bearer*: "Why should I hurry away from you? There's no need to race [*posting*, like a letter delivered by a horseman] until I'm returning."' There's really nothing here that wasn't already sweetly implicit in the previous sonnet. Although having said that, the way WS describes the return journey is quite brilliant: *In wingèd speed no motion shall I know* – i.e. no matter how fast I travel it'll feel like a standstill, because it won't be fast enough. Also worth noting is the double sense of the last line *Towards thee I'll run, and give him leave to go*, which you might take to mean either giving his horse *leave to go* as fast as he likes (rather contradicting the fact he was digging his spurs into the froward jade only a minute ago, but anyway), or I'll *literally* run like Billy Whizz, and forget about the useless horse.

The clearly wrong *perfects* in the Q is usually corrected to *perfect* or *perfect'st*. Bewilderingly, HV rejects the emendation on the grounds that WS's intention was to have the (non-existent) key word 'slow' in the third quatrain, i.e. perfectS LOve. I'm certain it wasn't. As SB points out, the difference in sense between *perfect* and *perfect'st* is minimal, so if we're correcting, let's just call it on taste. WS uses the phrase 'perfect love' several times elsewhere, so that'll do. Having said that I'm pretty certain his intention was *perfectst*, as it seems a bit unlikely the compositor would have imported the *s* from nowhere; but frankly his error has allowed us the latitude to correct the phrase to the more natural one.

The tougher crux is what on earth was intended by the Q's *Shall naigh noe dull flesh in his fiery race.* There are two schools of thought – (a) it's just grand, or (b) it needs fixing. I think the arguments to leave it alone are weak; *shall neigh no dull flesh* is awful, and repunctuations such as *Shall neigh, no dull flesh, in his fiery race* hardly help. (JK defends the latter rather brilliantly by pointing out that the now-equinated desire is neighing to counterpoint the groaning nag of the previous sonnet.) If we remove the word, we would surely interpolate a sense of something like *carry*, *use*, *need*; and on those contextual grounds, *weigh* or *rein* are a common corrections. I might tentatively advance *haigh*, as an alternative spelling of *hie* (OK, the OED doesn't list it as variant but it does give *heigh*), as in 'to hasten, speed'; *h* is easily

mistaken for *n*, especially if you have horses in mind anyway. As
51 WS uses the spelling *hie* elsewhere, this seems a long shot, though. Beats the hell out of me. HV goes for *weigh*, SB for *neigh*, but his astonishingly ingenious defences of the Q's many clear balls-ups leave you suspecting that SB has been paid off by the compositors' union, or possibly the Templars. Haigh hoe . . . I'll pick one: *rein*, where *naigh* has been conceivably misread for *raign* . . . which also seems to assume WS confused the words *reign* and *rein*, so it definitely isn't that either – but at least it reads passably well.

❧

52

So am I as the rich, whose blessed key
Can bring him to his sweet up-locked treasure,
The which he will not every hour survey,
For blunting the fine point of seldom pleasure;
Therefore are feasts so solemn and so rare,
Since, seldom coming, in the long year set,
Like stones of worth they thinly placèd are,
Or captain jewels in the carcanet.
So is the time that keeps you as my chest,
Or as the wardrobe which the robe doth hide,
To make some special instant special-blest,
By new unfolding his imprisoned pride.
  Blessed are you whose worthiness gives scope,
  Being had, to triumph; being lacked, to hope.

Initially this conceit looks like a ten-car pile-up, but it's a very neat pile-up. It sends us back to the 'stolen jewel' conceit of Sonnet 48. 'I'm like a rich man, with the key to a treasure – one which he resists checking every hour because he doesn't want to blunt the pleasure he gets from it.' You might think this referred to WS deliberately not thinking about the YM too much, so as not to erode the piquancy of the thought from overuse – but no, as it transpires. 'That's why feast-days are so rare; they're strung out like jewels in a crown.' Well, that still fits the first reading. Rare pleasures are the more acute pleasures. But then: 'Similarly,

52 the time that keeps you [i.e. keeps you away from me, keeps us apart] is my treasure chest . . .' Huh? Then you see that the first quatrain isn't referring to a voluntary restraint, but an enforced constraint; it's not about WS thinking about the YM and then not thinking about him, but seeing him and then not being able to see him. In other words, it's yet another poem trying to turn a torment into a blessing. (You may have read this correctly from the start, but I confess – being incapable of reading any book by the route gently suggested by its pagination – I failed to keep in mind the theme of this run of sonnets. Of course, it fits neatly into 'absence'.) 'This time apart is like a closet which hides a beautiful robe – and makes what would be a special occasion anyway even *more* special, by opening to reveal a splendour anew [i.e. both the splendid moment, and the YM's glorious self].' The couplet, which is direly contorted, says 'Blessed are you, sir, whose worth is such that those who are in your presence feel triumphant – and those who are not with you feel the anticipation of that triumph.' Oh, he's a walking win-win situation, this kid. I don't buy a word of this.

l.5 *solemn*: ceremonious; awe-inspiring. SB points out that there may be an etymological pun here on the Latin root *sollemnis*,which was believed to derive from *sollus*, whole, and *annus*, year, though that's now thought highly doubtful. After ll.5–6 we might see something very deliberate in the numbering of this sonnet. On the other hand, maybe the number *itself* suggested the annual theme. Alas this year-stuff, together with appearance of the word *key*, has prompted several folk to go off in search of the keys, dates, names, places and god knows what else that might lie buried in the poem. Knock yourself out.

l.10 note that the *robe* is quite literally hiding in the *wardrobe.*

l.14 *had*, as now, had a sexual meaning. Although I think WS 52
might be *being had* in an another way too. Poor guy.

53

What is your substance, whereof are you made,
That millions of strange shadows on you tend?
Since everyone hath, every one, one shade,
And you, but one, can every shadow lend.
Describe Adonis, and the counterfeit
Is poorly imitated after you;
On Helen's cheek all art of beauty set
And you in Grecian tires are painted new;
Speak of the spring, and foison of the year:
The one doth shadow of your beauty show,
The other as your bounty doth appear;
And you in every blessed shape we know.
   In all external grace you have some part,
   But you like none, none you, for constant heart.

The first of four songs of unadulterated praise, this poem has, for me, the most beautiful opening lines in all the sonnets. Behind them lie two key terms in Renaissance Neoplatonism, *substance* and *shadow*. We can read these as something like 'idea and image' or 'form and reflection'; they allude to the belief that the images that constitute the external world are just shadows of a true inner reality, where the true essences and forms of things reside. In other words, this world is just a distorted dream of a divine and immortal reality. (Well, they got it half right. Anyone out there who thinks this *isn't* a distorted dream needs to read a little neuroscience. The dream, alas, extends to the invention of such mad ideas as Platonic forms, and all other supernatural guff. It's all one big mad human dream . . . Ach well – at least there'll be another one along in a minute, if you don't like this one.) The line is rather wonderful in that its apparent mystery, when unpacked, is even deeper and more extraordinary: the YM's inner being is an ideal form so rare and so complex, that a million images have to attend on, to converge upon his outer form to do it justice; the explanation does the opposite of 'explain away'. Those shadows might be images, or shadows, or the ghostly forms of others. WS is deliberately ambiguous.

ll.3–4 have caused some confusion, but they're worth a quick wrestle. WS has sacrificed clarity for music here. The first problem is how you read the first *every one.* I far prefer to read it as 'everyone', i.e. *not* really referring to the *strange shadows* of l.2; *shadows* having a *shade* seems a bit redundant. So 'everyone has, each one of them, one ghost or appearance'. *And you but one* – 'and you, though you're only one individual' – *can every shadow lend* . . . again, this is open to interpretation, but I'm (gulp) going to go against SB, here. I don't think the verb is transitive, and that it takes *shadow* as its object, i.e. 'you share in/supply/manifest every shadow'. I think, looking at ll.5–6, that *lend* might be intransitive, and mean 'have the ability to lend to every shadow'. ('Can lend it new and beautiful attributes', as it turns out.)

The rest of the poem is clearer. Describe Adonis, and it's a poor likeness of you (of course WS had already depicted him in his own *Venus and Adonis* – dedicated to young Master Wriothesley, by the way); paint Helen, and it's you in Grecian attire. (And a dress. Cough.) Your essence surfaces in the world whenever anyone depicts beauty in any form.

Now I'd like to point out that the comparisons after the turn
53 are *not* that negative; ll.9–10 are often understood as 'speak of the spring and the harvest (*foison*, abundance), and the first is just a weak reflection of your beauty' . . . But shadow needn't be weak; in the context it can just mean, neutrally, reflection – and l.11 says no more that the harvest is as his beauty appears. WS is just strongly privileging the natural over the man-made: artistic representations fall short, but natural comparisons will do just fine. (Rather contradicting earlier poems in the sequence, of course.)

ll.12–13 are plain in sense: 'I see you in every lovely thing.' Lionel Ritchie could sing this bit. But he has a line left over, and in l.14 can't resist paying some huge compliment to make the YM incomparable after all. 'But there's none like you for constancy of heart.' It prettily echoes the syntax earlier in the poem – look back to ll.3–4. But hang on: the last line is ambiguous. What if 'like' is a verb? 'But you – you don't like anyone for their constant heart.' I dunno; I think this reading, while fun, is wrong. It's too late in the day for that kind of turn. And given that I'm certain WS had full control over the ordering of the Sonnets, *had* that been his intention – I reckon he would have followed this up immediately with a sonnet pursuing this new idea; he always does. Sonnet 54 compares the YM rather lamely to a rose. So let's drop that idea: this is the first of a short run of chirpier sonnets. (However there's one more alternative: *But you like none, none you, for constant 'eart.* The dropped *h* in WS's pronunciation of *heart* might be a deliberate pun, I think, and at least gives the line a little artful interest. Me, I'm reading the poem with my finger over the couplet again.)

Millions of Strange Shadows, incidentally, is one of Anthony

Hecht's finest books. A student once bravely tackled Hecht on
his affectedly English accent; flustered, he replied 'I read a great 53
deal of Shakespeare as a young man.'

54

O how much more doth beauty beauteous seem
By that sweet ornament which truth doth give!
The rose looks fair, but fairer we it deem
For that sweet odour which doth in it live;
The canker blooms have full as deep a dye
As the perfumèd tincture of the roses,
Hang on such thorns, and play as wantonly
When summer's breath their maskèd buds discloses;
But for their virtue only is their show,
They live unwooed, and unrespected fade;
Die to themselves. Sweet roses do not so;
Of their sweet deaths are sweetest odours made;
    And so of you, beauteous and lovely youth;
    When that shall vade, my verse distills your truth.

Did I say 'lame'? Oh, I take it back. I'm quite fond of this poem. The YM is compared with a rose again, and the poem doesn't say much, but says it very sweetly. 'How much more beautiful is beauty when it's accompanied by truth and integrity.' At the end of the poem, this inner integrity is described as a perfume, which the *canker* rose (either a dog-rose or a red poppy) lacks. 'Oh these are pretty flowers, but they're all show. No one really wants them, and they win no respect. They'll die alone.' Here, the vehicle gets the better of the tenor, frankly, and the metaphor is a tad overextended. (There's another rude sense, by the way: they'll just have to masturbate – *die*, as in *petit mort* – as no-one want to make love to them. This is worth recording, as it's the only occasion KDJ beats SB to an innuendo.) This seems an excessively harsh judgement on the other youth, whose only crime was to tart themselves up, and lack the great pure soul that's the sole birthright, it would seem, of the YM. I feel we have a straw man here, all rouged and bewigged and powdered, wheeled on just to make the YM look even lovelier.

'And in the end my poetry, like a bottle of scent, will distill and seal that lovely inner fragrance, the essence of your *sweet death* long after you've faded away.' You know: I believe him, a bit. I don't get much sense of the YM's looks or personality in the poems, but the sonnets *do* have an utterly distinct fragrance that could only have been distilled from living reality, from real love. Wonder what we'd call it. *L'Amour Interdit. Lunacy. Avon Calling. Éternité pour homme.*

l.1 I don't think we should overinterpret *seem*: I hear no doubt. He just means 'appear'.

l.2 To call truth a 'sweet ornament' seems a mistake, if WS – as he seems to – means something more essential.

55

Not marble, nor the gilded monuments
Of princes, shall outlive this powerful rhyme;
But you shall shine more bright in these contents
Than unswept stone, besmeared with sluttish time.
When wasteful war shall statues overturn
And broils root out the work of masonry,
Nor Mars his sword, nor war's quick fire shall burn
The living record of your memory.
'Gainst death, and all oblivious enmity
Shall you pace forth; your praise shall still find room
Even in the eyes of all posterity
That wear this world out to the ending doom.
  So, till the judgment that yourself arise,
  You live in this, and dwell in lovers' eyes.

WS's boast about the longevity of his poetry is hardly misplaced. Here we are, poring over it four hundred years later. But isn't it ironic – or tragic, or amusing, or something – that WS really has *failed* his subject, whose *name* we don't even know with any certainty? And where are all the poems of such meticulous physical description that we can conjure the YM forth from the shadows, and through this *living record* see him before us again, as promised? WS spends a lot more time promising than delivering. The poems have survived just fine, but their human subject has gone, and is now only a cipher, the vanishing point that represents the focus of the poet's love.

Most of this is down to the fact that WS's 'subject', half the time, isn't his subject at all: more often than not, the poems are as much about something else – time, love, memory, poetry, fame, death – as the thing they claim to be. In poetry, 'subject matter' is often just a pretext. What this poem is *really* about, or at least *more* about, is the power of verse to survive in the human mind, even when our human talent for destruction and mayhem has trashed and reduced every other great and beautiful monument. Note that WS uses 'rhyme', here, as his metonym for 'verse'. Rhyme is, of course, the most effective means of committing a poem to memory. Is that line *true*, that the YM 'dwells in lovers' eyes'? Lovers have eyes only for each other. There are other YM-inspired sonnets of WS's that lovers will intone sweetly to each other, but it's unlikely to be this one. This is a poem about the poetry's power to keep something in the mind over time, *regardless* of the something it makes immemorial. And can anyone really doubt that WS had anything but the clearest intention to see these poems in print, after reading this?

I should confess, though, that I'm no great fan of this sonnet; I've never quite understood why it's so frequently anthologised, other than to save our most beloved writer from the ignominy of his own false prophecy. I find it a bit crude and mildly hysterical. And I *hate* the fourth line. It's almost impossible to speak without slavering over the phonetic car-crash of *unswept stone* . . . and it's ugly in its sibilance, which pulls little sense along with it. To call time 'sluttish' is revealing, though, even allowing for its slightly different Elizabethan nuance. Let's not go there. I maintain that Wendy Cope's splendid parody beginning: *Not only marble, but the plastic toys / From cornflake packets will outlive this rhyme* is the superior work, and by some distance.

55 The boast itself would have been inevitably influenced by the conceit and music of the final passage of Book XV of Ovid's *Metamorphoses* (in Arthur Golding's version, the one WS would have known):

Now have I brought a woork to end which neither Joves feerce wrath,
Nor swoord, nor fyre, or freating age with all the force it hath
Are able to abolish quyght . . .
. . . And tyme without all end
(If Poets as by prophesie about the truth may ame)
My lyfe shall everlastingly bee lengthened still by fame.

– genius to write it in fourteeners, which gives it a cracking momentum.

ll.12–13 WS is referring to the Last Judgement. While as near to a practising atheist as it was possible to get at the time (my strong impression is that while he was a conforming Anglican for the sake of appearances and a quiet life, he didn't believe a word of it), WS nonetheless assumed, like most of his contemporaries, that human history was, and would continue to be, a narrative of decline.

l.13 the decision to use 'that' for 'when' was probably a musical one.

❧

56

Sweet love, renew thy force; be it not said
Thy edge should blunter be than appetite,
Which but today by feeding is allayed,
Tomorrow sharpened in his former might:
So, love, be thou; although to-day thou fill
Thy hungry eyes, even till they wink with fulness,
Tomorrow see again, and do not kill
The spirit of love with a perpetual dulness.
Let this sad interim like the ocean be
Which parts the shore, where two contracted new
Come daily to the banks, that when they see
Return of love, more blest may be the view;
  As call it winter, which being full of care,
  Makes summer's welcome thrice more wished, more rare.

A lovely, wretchedly undervalued poem on a too-little-mentioned twist in love's awful narrative. What happens when the drugs wear off? Well: no one shrugs philosophically. You start to realise how addicted you were – *not* to the beloved, but to the feeling of being-in-love; and realise that, for all its hideous side-effects, you want it back – raw, uncut, full-strength, and damn the consequences. By *sweet love* WS means love itself, the real subject of the Sonnets.

What *are* love-drugs? In this poet's case, my money's on a whole bunch of dopamine. It's the neurotransmitter you get high

56 on when you anticipate a reward for something undertaken. Note 'anticipate'; we used to think that the dopamine kicked in on receipt of the reward, but the test-monkeys show it peaks soon after they embark on the work which they have learned will *guarantee* the reward; the reward itself produces nothing. This means that all the fun really *is* in the anticipation. But here's the horrible twist: when you adjust the experiment, and the monkey learns that pulling x lever will only result in a reward exactly 50 per cent of the time – i.e. when he's working under conditions of a perfect statistical *maybe* – guess what happens? The dopamine goes *through the roof*. In other words – add will he/won't he? to the equation, and you have the recipe for the perfect high. And as soon as you know she *will*, or he *will* . . . the risk has gone, and the thrill begins to wane. So many of the Sonnets are work undertaken with an uncertain conclusion – and WS knows these are the best, most excited and thrilling circumstances in which to perform that work.

When WS says *be it not said / Thy edge should blunter be than appetite*, I suspect he means *both* hunger and lust, which work in much the same way; briefly sated and swiftly sharpened. Would that love were like that. But here's the tension in the metaphor: love is not an appetite. This kind of love *doesn't* answer a physical need, like lust or hunger; it's prompted by a beloved – for all the cipher they might eventually become – and some folk go their whole lives without knowing it.

It's poems like this that make the argument for reading the Sonnets as an Elizabethan version of *A Lover's Discourse*. If you haven't read the latter, do; Roland Barthes's masterpiece is possibly the only truly *beautiful* book to come out of poststructuralism, and belongs to a genre of literature that we might identify, to completely misappropriate Richard Rorty's term, as 'post-philosophy': works whose truth-value lies as much in their style as their logic, under which we now might place Wittgenstein's *Tractatus* and Eliot's *Four Quartets*. *ALD* is, to be honest, a more reliable source of solace for the intelligent tormented lover in the 21st century than the Sonnets. Our cultural metaphors have changed, and we no longer think in terms of the deep symbols of token, message, contagion, substance and shadow that formed the lens through which literate Elizabethan lovers were obliged to observe their own behaviour. However, in poems like this WS demonstrates a Barthesian keenness of insight into love's effects, even if we remain for ever ignorant of their cause; and it offers us exactly the same kind of solace, a camaraderie which we can summarise as: *my situation may have seemed to me insane and wholly exceptional – but at least I see now that it's one others have suffered in an identical fashion.*

ll.5–8 say 'Have your fill, hungry eyes, but don't gorge yourself into a state of lethargy'. And then we switch conceits, with a heartbreaker: 'Let our sad separation be like a body of water [ocean needn't mean *ocean*] where two newly-wed lovers [argh! it's too much! compare the *contract* of the early sonnets when WS was entreating the YM to marry; or in the back of his mind, might he mean two gay men trapped in heterosexual marriages?] come to the opposite shores every day – and when they catch sight of one another, behold something blissful. Or [switching conceits again] call our time apart *winter* – which being so miserable, makes summer three times more wished for, seem three times more rare.' WS is again trying to salvage some comfort from the very source of his pain, almost unaware that he's moved the goal-posts. The poem *was* about the waning of love in a time of

56 separation; it's become about the separation itself – and you sense that by the end, he's talked himself back into it, has scored another fix, and is feelin' the love almost as keenly as ever. A remarkable little poem, and the journey it makes is all the more fascinating for only being half-conscious.

❧

57

Being your slave what should I do but tend
Upon the hours and times of your desire?
I have no precious time at all to spend;
Nor services to do, till you require;
Nor dare I chide the world-without-end hour,
Whilst I, my sovereign, watch the clock for you,
Nor think the bitterness of absence sour,
When you have bid your servant once adieu;
Nor dare I question with my jealous thought
Where you may be, or your affairs suppose,
But, like a sad slave, stay and think of nought
Save, where you are, how happy you make those.
  So true a fool is love, that in your will,
  Though you do anything, he thinks no ill.

Oh dear. Another turn for the worse. A good, miserable sonnet depicting a situation which the morbidly infatuated will recognise all too well. This is not an equal relationship. (The great irony is that *both* parties often feel like this.) All WS does is *wait*, in both senses. The only time that exists for the enslaved is on the master or mistress's clock; there's nothing for the slave to do, other than twiddle his thumbs until his next hour of service. Nor dare he question his master's other allegiances, or enquire into his business; he's too afraid of offending the beloved, and losing the little wretched attention he has. The hideous irony is

57

that such enslavements are voluntary – I mean no one is *making* you do this; but it sure as hell doesn't *feel* voluntary. In short, it's a pretty masochistic arrangement.

But this inequality can't persist without a terrible brewing resentment. About halfway through the poem you become aware of the acidic sarcasm in every line. He's merely *affecting* an attitude of subservience. The couplet shows his full awareness of his situation; a *true* fool wouldn't have this perspective on the extent of his self-duping. Note the pun on *your will* – i.e. *your Will*; it has a capital in the Q – for once pulling some real weight. Look back to Sonnet 26, and you'll hear someone far more cheerfully resigned to his *vassalage*. Not any more.

ll.1–2 *tend / Upon*: wait for.

l.2 *times of your desire*: both the times of your choosing, and the times when you're overtaken by lust.

l.5 'As it was in the beginning, is now and ever shall be, *world without end*', meaning 'everlasting'. So *world-without-end hour* is the endless hour of the clock you watch when you're waiting for the beloved to arrive; the hands are frozen. On the plus-side, your soup's coming to a nice boil.

l.10 a happy anachronistic misreading of *affairs* is 'sexual affairs', but alas it didn't mean that yet, just 'activities'. Although you can almost hear WS begin to innovate the newer sense.

58

That god forbid, that made me first your slave,
I should in thought control your times of pleasure,
Or at your hand th'account of hours to crave,
Being your vassal, bound to stay your leisure.
O let me suffer, being at your beck,
Th'imprisoned absence of your liberty,
And patience tame, to sufferance bide each check,
Without accusing you of injury.
Be where you list, your charter is so strong
That you yourself may privilege your time
To what you will; to you it doth belong
Yourself to pardon of self-doing crime.
  I am to wait, though waiting so be hell,
  Not blame your pleasure be it ill or well.

Interesting. WS will often follow one sonnet with either an intensification of the emotion the previous sonnet merely proposed or intimated – or he'll ostentatiously retreat from it. Here it's hard to read. Is he still angry and sarcastic, or is this a kind of psychological retrenching within the original conceit, an attempt to hang on to his sanity through a noisy resignation to his fate? I read more of the latter. ll.1–3 mean something like 'May that god [Cupid, I guess] who made me your slave forbid that I should even *dare* to to think about being able to exert any control over those occasions when it pleases you to see me, or asking you to

58 account for your missing hours.' Oh god: this is *agony* to watch, and such a downer. Quick paraphrase of ll.9–14: 'Be wherever you want – your entitlement is so powerful that you can give your time to what you choose. It's up to you to exonerate yourself of your own crimes. I have to resign myself to this hell of waiting, not blame you for following your whim, whether good or bad.' Why does he resign himself? Because the hell's of his own making. In a sense he knows his behaviour is just as free and autonomous as the YM's. It's a voluntary hell, a hell created, as Cioran would say, *to his own taste.*

l.6 is a brilliantly compact Shakespearian paradox, and I'll borrow KDJ's gloss: 'my prolonged absence from you, a consequence of the freedom of which you avail yourself, which to me is a form of imprisonment'. Got that? It's one of those lines whose untranslated sense is somehow far clearer than its accurate paraphrase.

ll.7–8 *tame* is a verb, I think. 'Let me master my impatience, and take each knock-back on the chin, without accusing you of deliberate hurt.'

59

If there be nothing new, but that which is
Hath been before, how are our brains beguiled,
Which, labouring for invention, bear amiss
The second burthen of a former child?
O that record could with a backward look
Even of five hundred courses of the sun
Show me your image in some antique book,
Since mind at first in character was done,
That I might see what the old world could say
To this composèd wonder of your frame;
Whether we are mended, or whe're better they,
Or whether revolution be the same.
  O sure I am, the wits of former days
  To subjects worse have given admiring praise.

The first of two poems on the subject of time, this sonnet starts off very brightly, but gets worse as it goes on, then ends in the kind of bathetic disaster that would give *War of the Worlds* a run for its money. The first quatrain says 'if there's nothing new under the sun, we're fooling ourselves when we think we write something new: it's like bearing the same child for the second time.' The poem goes on: 'If I could look back five hundred years and find you in some old book, and see what the old world would say about your frankly *amazing* body – then I could judge whether they were better writers, or whether we'd improved on

the description.' Although *Since mind at first in character was*
59 *done* – i.e. when thought was first put into writing – is very neat, I admit. This sonnet is full of the sort of cadence you feel must have influenced Keats. *To this composèd wonder of your frame.*

But O, that couplet. 'Oh, I'm sure these ancient wits have praised subjects worse than you.' Both JK and KDJ contrive to read this unironically, which I find odd. Me, I hear a straightforward Dick Emery litotes, and have stressed it accordingly. Oh you are *awful.* Either way it's a bit rubbish. HV hears one of her 'couplet ties' between l.13 and l.4, a word repeated in the couplet that is often secretly declarative of the sonnet's theme. Here it's *former.* I'm pretty sure WS just forgot he'd already used it. HV also sees a grand dialectic lurking here between 'classical' time – with its recurrent epochal cycles – and the Christian conception of time, where the symmetry is broken for ever by the singular event: namely the Incarnation of Christ, or here (blasphemously) the YM. It's an ingenious and attractive idea, but it's way too generous. This poem is a missed trick and a misfire.

l.11 is a very unusual metrical balls-up; even with the syllable dropped by the syncopic *whe'er* (*where* in the Q, which we think might be an attempt at a contracted *whether*) – it's still a hexameter. You can make it work, just about, by reading the initial *Whether* as an unstressed pyrrhic, making an anacrusis of the first syllable. Don't mention it.

60

Like as the waves make towards the pebbled shore,
So do our minutes hasten to their end,
Each changing place with that which goes before,
In sequent toil all forwards do contend.
Nativity, once in the main of light,
Crawls to maturity; wherewith being crowned,
Crooked eclipses 'gainst his glory fight,
And Time, that gave, doth now his gift confound.
Time doth transfix the flourish set on youth
And delves the parallels in beauty's brow,
Feeds on the rarities of nature's truth,
And nothing stands but for his scythe to mow.
  And yet to times in hope my verse shall stand,
  Praising thy worth, despite his cruel hand.

This is a *magnificent* piece of verse on time's relentlessness, once again echoing a passage from Arthur Golding's *Metamorphoses* (XV, l.178). Cheeky and clever placing, too, on the last minute of the hour, although Spenser had already pulled the same trick in the *Amoretti*. Most of the Sonnets are really Anglo-Italians – or rather English in their music while Italian in their argument. Despite the rhyme-scheme suggesting three strong quatrains, the content and sense often pull in a rather different direction, with the turn on l.9 strongly indicating a division into octave and sestet. But this is an unusually pure-bred English sonnet, with all the quatrains introducing distinct subject matter.

So what do we have? One minute's being overlapped by the next, as waves press towards the shore, all driven forward in their inevitable sequence. The very lines of this poem feel like they're beating away at the great void on the right-hand side of the page, where all the white silence lives – driving against it, receding, driving against it again, enacting their own determined but doomed stay against it. (If anyone ever tells you line-beginnings are as important as line-endings, ignore them. They aren't. The silent pause indicated by the right-hand margin means that whatever comes immediately before it will reverberate in its empty acoustic – the ear will simply hear those words more clearly; and in its composition, the poem will naturally distribute its semantic weight to take advantage of that pattern of end-silences. Enjambment – running the syntax on from one line to the next – is the tool of variation we use to stop it all getting too rhythmically predictable, amongst other things, and works as an accelerator to the end-stopped line's brake.)

Then there's that amazing *Nativity, once in the main of light* . . . 'main' is a wide expanse, but especially as in 'open sea', picking up on the earlier wave-metaphor. No sooner are we radiant in our maturity than we are eclipsed, shadowed; *crooked* means 'malignant' (eclipses were bad omens), but also serves to anticipate the crookedness of old age. Time gaveth, and now it taketh away.

Look at the lines *Time doth transfix the flourish set on youth / And delves the parallels in beauty's brow.* 'Time pierces through the bloom of youth, and digs the trenches in beauty's brow' is something like the standard interpretation, but it's a bit unstable. Since it's contested, I'd like to put in a bid for a slightly

anachronistic misreading of the first line, and hear 'fixes in place 60
the flush of youth', i.e. fixes it in middle-age's ruddiness and rugosity. *And nothing stands but for his scythe to mow*: and nothing that rises to its feet will escape death's scythe. 'Maybe my verses will be read in the future, though, and live on to praise your worth, despite all this.' (*to times in hope* means 'in some future we can dream of', though I want to hear a little fearful hesitation in that 'hope', too.)

l.2 There might be a little French pun in the original – the spelling of *minutes* in the Q is *minuites*, and very close to *minuit*, midnight.

ll.10–12 *mow* / *brow* seems a dialectal full rhyme.

61

Is it thy will, thy image should keep open
My heavy eyelids to the weary night?
Dost thou desire my slumbers should be broken
While shadows like to thee do mock my sight?
Is it thy spirit that thou send'st from thee
So far from home into my deeds to pry,
To find out shames and idle hours in me,
The scope and tenor of thy jealousy?
O no, thy love, though much, is not so great;
It is my love that keeps mine eye awake,
Mine own true love that doth my rest defeat,
To play the watchman ever for thy sake.
  For thee watch I, whilst thou dost wake elsewhere,
  From me far off, with others all too near.

Be patient with this one. The first quatrain is pretty flat: 'Do you *want* to keep me awake all night thinking about you?' is pretty much all it says – but WS needs it to set up a clever opposition. The second quatrain introduces a psychological shift, and accuses the YM of *actively* ruining WS's night. 'Are you sending out your spirit so far from home, just so it can look into my personal business, find out all the shameful and idle things I've been up to? Is *that* how your jealousy operates?' But ochone, ochone: he *knows* it isn't. Oh, we'd *love* the beloved to be as jealous as we are – but we know there's no one keeping us awake but us. 'It's nothing but my own love that defeats my sleep.' (I don't quite know why HV refers to the couplet as 'the sting in the tail', since WS is talking about his own jealous watch from the turn onwards.)

The couplet opens with a phrase that might be momentarily misread, the misreading symbolising the whole sorry delusion: *For thee watch I*, we quickly realise, can't mean 'since you watch me . . .' but 'for your sake I keep watch [jealously, over your image, or what I imagine you doing right now]', or – if we read *watch* in its alternative sense – 'for your sake I stay awake'. Perhaps he intended just such a double-take. If only *wake* would just mean *wake*, but another Elizabethan sense was 'to turn night into day' – i.e. to carouse, and 'far from me, with those others all too near'. Those bastard others, all *too* goddamn near to you . . . What a stomach-churning sexual envy's in that *near*. (Give it a little expressive rise when you read it, but don't ham it up too much.) It's clear that he's thinking 'I know, I know. All the jealousy's on my side. OK, I'm just going to lie here, sweating in the dark, imagining the worst for the next four hours. Hey, it's a hobby.' The *agony* in this poem!

62

Sin of self-love possesseth all mine eye,
And all my soul, and all my every part;
And for this sin there is no remedy,
It is so grounded inward in my heart.
Methinks no face so gracious is as mine,
No shape so true, no truth of such account,
And for myself mine own worth do define,
As I all other in all worths surmount.
But when my glass shows me myself indeed,
Beated and chopped with tanned antiquity,
Mine own self-love quite contrary I read;
Self, so self-loving, were iniquity.
　'Tis thee, myself, that for myself I praise,
　Painting my age with beauty of thy days.

A rather famous sonnet, with some elegant lines – *And for this sin there is no remedy, / It is so grounded inward in my heart* . . . But speaking personally, it's a tough one for a Calvinist to sympathise with. Self-loathing gets us out of bed in the morning, and this self-love stuff doesn't come up much. As read we on, though, it's clear that WS is about to do one of his trademark about-turns, and indeed he does, just where you'd expect it: 'But when I look in the mirror . . . Ah, then it's another story.'

In the couplet, we receive the explanation for his earlier self-delightedness. It shades towards some plausible sense – 'I am so in love that my old, knackered features [WS would have probably been in his early to mid-thirties, after all] have taken on your youthful radiance.' However this claim – that his self-love is just another form his praise of the YM takes, because the two are really one – strikes me as pat, convenient, implausible, and built on a scheme which is logically neat but emotionally specious. Not only do I not believe a word of it, I don't think he does either.

Although HV describes the poet's double-take beautifully, she nonetheless rather takes it all at face value – as do most other commentators, forgetting that poets often just tell folk what they think they want to hear, themselves included. When the conceit seems so thoroughly strained, we're entitled to consider the possibility that the poet is either self-deluded, patently insincere, or a bit of both. A poet need be no more reliable than any other literary narrator; and with so much at stake (in their own minds, at least) on the *reception* of their verses, love poets are the least trustworthy of them all.

(Nonetheless the idea of 'poet as truth-teller' seems culturally unrevisable, along with 'the poem is an act of self-expression'; many of us enjoy playing with this assumption, and subvert the reader's automatic conflation of the poem's *I* with its author through the use of personae, heteronyms, 'displacement', dramatic monologues, and just . . . lying about stuff. Sometimes these performances can have a little too much verisimilitude. I recall one occasion when a furious member of the audience berated Michael Donaghy for his unsympathetic response to his girlfriend's pregnancy termination, described in a poem he'd just read. Mikey failed to convince them of the wholly fictitious contrivance it was; a dangerous game, then.)

If there's *truth* in this poem, though, it lies somewhere in its

62 specific occasion, in the necessity of making this particular response to a particular accusation. Perhaps it was written in *reply* to YM, following his charging WS with self-obsession. This would make WS's confession – whether sincere or not – an attempt at a disarming rhetorical ploy. 'Yes: you're right. I'm completely self-loving. Indeed let me count the ways. But it isn't what you think. It's all about *you*.'

While as Italian as it is English, this sonnet is inconceivable without its couplet, which effectively operates as the punchline.

l.6 *No shape so true*: no body so perfectly proportioned.

l.10 *Beated and chopped*: something like 'weather-beaten and cracked', which together with 'tanned' makes us think of an old piece of leather.

63

Against my love shall be as I am now,
With Time's injurious hand crushed and o'erworn;
When hours have drained his blood and fill'd his brow
With lines and wrinkles; when his youthful morn
Hath travailed on to age's steepy night,
And all those beauties whereof now he's king
Are vanishing, or vanished out of sight,
Stealing away the treasure of his spring;
For such a time do I now fortify
Against confounding age's cruèl knife,
That he shall never cut from memory
My sweet love's beauty, though my lover's life:
  His beauty shall in these black lines be seen,
  And they shall live, and he in them still green.

T*ime* and the damage it wreaks was always going to be the subject of this sonnet, 63 being the grand climacteric year, and all that. (See the notes on Sonnet 49.) If you look at all the poems which are products of the climacteric years 7 and 9 – 49, 63 and 81 – they all have Time as their theme, as does the weird double-grand-climacteric twelve-line Sonnet 126. The twice-49 Sonnet 98 is a sort of double sonnet, weirdly, whose second part has fifteen lines. OK, I'm stalling – I have nothing much to say about this poem, which to my mind seems to have been knocked out for no other reason than our poet requiring a time-themed

63 poem here. There's only one thing likely to produce a dodgier result than a commissioned poem: it's a poem you commission from yourself. You don't even have the cheque to look forward to. Simonides – he of *Go tell the Spartans, passerby / That here, by Spartan law, we lie* (Frank Miller's translation; OK, so I thought *300* was a sublime masterpiece) – invented the poetic commission, you know. Until that time poets hadn't thought to ask for payment for their praise-poems. I'm stalling. Did I say that already? Enough, people. This poem is without interest, and says little WS hasn't said more effectively elsewhere.

l.1 *Against*: in preparation / anticipation of the time . . .

l.5 *steepy*: steep. Go figure. Mind you, in Dundee they say *lighty*. As in 'it's still lighty outside'. Go figure.

l.10 after *age's steepy night,* the isocolonic phrase *age's cruèl knife* is desperate awful.

l.13 *black lines,* i.e. of verse. KDJ says they 'appropriate and redefine the lines and wrinkles of l.4'. Sort of; but not, I'd contend, in a way that actually works. Since there's nothing much else to say here, let me give you a quick domain-theory analysis to explain why this little trick fails to come off. This is an example of a largely undiagnosed trope in poetry, which I had to invent a name for so I could teach it: *isologue,* when you have two elements mapped to one another in the text, but not linked by any syntactic comparison, copula or any other unifying formula – as you do, for example, in your normal *x* is like *y*, or *x* is *y* metaphors and similes. (The term itself is stolen from chemistry.) This means you can't claim one thing is tenor, the other thing is vehicle, even though their relationship is conceptually metaphorical (more correctly, it's inter-domain), as it depends on aspects the two elements share through a common ground. The reader is just

63

supposed to stay alert enough to forge a relationship between them, by comparing the salient connotations or properties they clearly have in common. (Paul Muldoon uses the device frequently, and to brilliant effect: have a look at the mapped but merely juxtaposed elements in a poem like 'Cuba', if you want to see what I mean.) The elements here are *face* and *poetry*; the shared ground of their trope is *lines*, which both have; and the whole thing doesn't work, because the ground is pulling itself apart in semantic antithesis. *Lines* connote *age* on a face, but connote (here) a means of preserving *youth* in a poem. Placed more closely together and you'd have the legitimate figure of paradox, but you can't split a paradox, then bury the halves at opposite ends of the poem; they have to be experienced, otherwise they're felt – as mistakes. Of course no sane reader should know any of this, but that's what's lying behind your feeling of *but hang on . . . something here doesn't quite add up.* Indeed it doesn't. Let's move on.

64

When I have seen by Time's fell hand defaced
The rich proud cost of outworn buried age;
When sometime lofty towers I see down razed,
And brass eternal slave to mortal rage;
When I have seen the hungry ocean gain
Advantage on the kingdom of the shore,
And the firm soil win of the wat'ry main,
Increasing store with loss, and loss with store;
When I have seen such interchange of state,
Or state itself confounded, to decay;
Ruin hath taught me thus to ruminate:
That Time will come and take my love away.
  This thought is as a death which cannot choose
  But weep to have that which it fears to lose.

A fine, straightforward sonnet. WS paints a terrifying picture of a universe in a roiling, time-driven flux, so that nothing can ever be preserved or fixed – not a man or woman, not a monument or building; even 'land' and 'sea' are unstable concepts (and by implication, any meaningful co-ordinate or bearing they might give us). *When I have seen such interchange of state, / Or state itself confounded to decay* is magnificient summary. WS was close enough to Henry VIII's destruction of the monasteries to know that buildings that looked like they'd survive the sun's extinguishing could be razed in days. I dare say anyone who witnessed this would have been prompted to reflect on the uncertainty of all futures – and how, given time enough, *everything* was destined to be lost. In our own time we've seen this with the Bamiyan Buddhas, who gave every impression of seeing out the next millennium – yet were destroyed in a few minutes by religious thugs. (The only ones who were perfectly cool about it, of course, were the Buddhists themselves, who met it with a shrug of non-attachment.)

Which is all very fine and admirable; but what about those attachments *so* powerful, desires *so* strong, they can't be removed? The poem's redolent of that terror you feel when you have a whole day to get through before you can see your beloved; and all you can think about are the number of fatal mishaps and car-accidents that might insert themselves into the waiting hours, the catastrophes that time and fate might put in your way – and the sheer horror of physical law, of space and time, when all you want is to be one thing with another thing. Indeed you do *weep to have that which you fear to lose.*

l.4 Horace: *exegi monumentum aere perennius.* 'I have finished a monument more lasting than bronze.'

l.11 suggests that the word 'ruin' has put WS in mind of 'ruminate' through its sound alone.

65

Since brass, nor stone, nor earth, nor boundless sea,
But sad mortality o'ersways their power,
How with this rage shall beauty hold a plea,
Whose action is no stronger than a flower?
O how shall summer's honey breath hold out
Against the wrackful siege of batt'ring days
When rocks impregnable are not so stout,
Nor gates of steel so strong, but Time decays?
O fearful meditation! Where, alack,
Shall Time's best jewel from Time's chest lie hid?
Or what strong hand can hold his swift foot back?
Or who his spoil of beauty can forbid?
  O none, unless this miracle have might:
  That in black ink my love may still shine bright.

C'mon now – we haven't had this couplet since, oh, Sonnet 63 . . . However the rest of this poem is rather fine, and as usual my preference would be to leave off the couplet and just read it as a twelve-liner, albeit an incredibly bleak one. ll.3–4 contain an elegant legal riff in . . . *hold a plea, / Whose action*, and the second quatrain is stirring stuff: the world's strongest things are only illusorily so, and in the end fare no better than the *honey breath* of summer. And I don't think we get enough of stuff like *O fearful meditation!* these days. But then – that couplet. I preferred *So long as men can breathe or eyes can see, / So long lives this, and this gives life to thee*, because at least it's realistically contingent on a circumstance, i.e. the survival of man. But by the end of this poem, WS has destroyed *everything*. Nothing will *shine bright* in *black ink* if there's no one to read it. 65

Because the couplet is so frequently repeated, it does set you to thinking about the cultural-material circumstances of it all, and the way in which things have changed. If you were to bet on something that would survive the ravages of time these days, would you choose verse? Yes, the transmission of memorable words can be sustained over hundreds of years – but it only takes one amnesiac generation to lose everything. (I suspect it might be mine.) As shaken as I was by the leakiness of the supposedly invulnerable Blue Peter Time Capsule – I can't believe I waited thirty years for *that* – I would probably still go for etching something into palladium and burying it six miles down, or making a billion digital copies and sending them everywhere, like spores, or just firing it toward the Andromeda galaxy, given all man's creation is unlikely to survive *man*, never mind *time's injurious hand*. Or perhaps we'd never *write* such a poem now, given our overweening confidence in our own superior agency?

l.10 *Time's chest*: the coffin, probably.

l.11, if you try and resolve it visually, presents the unfortunate picture of someone being tripped in a race, by someone lying in wait on the road. Lying *flat*. As you do. Or maybe a rugby tackle. It's a mixed metaphor, of course, which WS often pulls off – but not here. *Hand* and *foot* only appear to belong in the same frame, but WS has just flung together two half-dead tropes.

l.12 SB makes an energetic case for retaining the second *or* in the Q's *Or who his spoil or beauty can forbid?*, which everyone

65 else changes to *of.* I don't buy it; no sophistry can get away from the fact that the repeated 'or' is ugly as sin. KDJ suggests *o'er*, which is more plausible. I don't have a clue. I'll stick with *of.*

66

Tired with all these, for restful death I cry:
As to behold desert a beggar born,
And needy nothing trimmed in jollity,
And purest faith unhappily forsworn,
And gilded honour shamefully misplaced,
And maiden virtue rudely strumpeted,
And right perfection wrongfully disgraced,
And strength by limping sway disablèd
And art made tongue-tied by authority,
And folly, doctor-like, controlling skill,
And simple truth miscalled simplicity,
And captive good attending captain ill:
Tired with all these, from these would I be gone,
Save that to die I leave my love alone.

'Folly and strumpets and beggars and limping . . . these are a few of my least favourite things. Get me out of this godless hellhole! You're the only thing keeping me here in this dump.' Here we begin a run of five sonnets, written in what sounds like an very bad mood indeed. This is a strange one, and offers more evidence of WS's hand in the ordering of the manuscript: 66 had a bad rep, being close to 666, the number of the beast; this is a poem about hellish injustice on earth. (What's my evidence for it not being the publisher's arrangement? As I mentioned in the introduction, no publisher or editor involves themselves with

66 *that* level of detail, unless the book has already attained classic status. I've known reputable publishers to print books of poetry by eminent poets that no one in the entire publishing house bar the copy-editor has actually *read all the way through.*) I don't doubt that WS has some rotten individuals in mind here, but the effect of the quality-for-person metonymy (loosely, a something-related-to-a-thing standing in for the thing; here, it's quality-for-person) gives the feel of an older Ricardian allegorical poem. Capitalise the abstract nouns, and bingo.

Compare Hamlet's lament in III. i:

For who would bear the whips and scorns of time,
Th'oppressor's wrong, the proud man's contumely,
The pangs of dispiz'd love, the law's delay,
The insolence of office, and the spurns
That patient merit of th'unworthy takes,
When he himself might his quietus make
With a bare bodkin?

The anaphora of the *Ands* allows WS to stack up the evidence in a way it's hard to refute. It all reads like a very contemporary list, too, which makes it even more depressing. ('And simple truth miscalled simplicity' is the mark of intellectually insecure critics everywhere, for one thing.) Here's a poem where the couplet really works, though. Note the lovely repetition of *tired with all these*, in line 1 and 13, making a parenthesis out of the whole list, which WS dismisses in its entirety when he sets them against one blessing: his beloved. No matter how bad things are, he'll bear them, rather than leave the beloved alone.

l.2 *desert*: 'deservingness', 'a deserving one'.

l.8 We might prefer to read *disabled*, and not wring four

syllables from the word: perhaps WS deliberately crippled the pentameter to echo the sense. It'd be just like him. On the other hand, the rhyme is with 'strumpeted', and *dis-abe-ell-ed* works better.

l.12 is a wonderful line, with the unrelated words *captive* and *captain* yoked together in one clean idea by their linked sounds. A helpful note from SB: 'Captain was a rank commonly appropriated by confidence men pretending to be war veterans.'

67

Ah wherefore with infection should he live,
And with his presence grace impiety,
That sin by him advantage should achieve,
And lace itself with his society?
Why should false painting imitate his cheek,
And steal dead seeming of his living hue?
Why should poor beauty indirectly seek
Roses of shadow, since his rose is true?
Why should he live, now nature bankrupt is,
Beggared of blood to blush through lively veins?
For she hath no exchequer now but his,
And proud of many, lives upon his gains.
  O him she stores, to show what wealth she had
  In days long since, before these last so bad.

... WS seems to have taken advantage of the rather indeterminate subject of *my love* in the final line of Sonnet 66. The last poem took the form of hideous overview, and now, with the distance he's won, he considers the YM's place within the world, referring to him throughout in the third person. This is hardly a rhetorical bombshell, but it's the poem's one interesting feature, so take what pleasure you can from it.

Unlike most commentators, I prefer to read the entire poem within a consistent frame, and think it refers largely to the flash company the YM keeps, of which WS is so jealous. The first quatrain reads 'Why should the YM grace this morally infected rabble with his presence, just so they can milk their association with him?' In l.5, I doubt *false painting* is meant to indicate either painted portraits or the false depictions of WS's rival poets, but primarily just describes the cosmetics favoured by the YM's fancy friends, leaving us an entirely consistent quatrain: 'Why should their tarted-up looks imitate his lovely face, and make dead copies of his *living hue*? Why should you second-rate lookers even *bother* to aspire to your paper flowers, when the real rose walks amongst you?' Which kind of answers its own question, really. What the hell else are they supposed to do?

. . . *nature bankrupt is, / Beggared of blood to blush* . . . is just about the most pointless run of alliteration in the Sonnets, and the sign of a poet clutching at straws. When you have to resort to this sort of thing, it's your imagination that's heading for the receivers; it's time to pack it in, head for the boozer and hit the pool table, where the muse has been standing for the last three hours with a pint in her hand. l.11 says nature has no *exchequer* now (i.e. no source of revenue) but the YM's. l.12's *proud of many* is so obscure that folk have assumed it was a typo. *prov'd of many* is one alternative; JK makes *'prived of many* (i.e. positing *priu'd* in the original), which is a fine suggestion, though his excuse that 'the words look alike in secretary hand' is too speculative. In my secretary hand, *priu'd* could be mistaken for *soup*. It falls before Occam's razor. (HV also corrects to *'prived, without comment.*) *Many* is sometimes corrected to *mon(e)y*, which seems to combine wishful thinking with a perverse desire to make this poem even worse. I dunno. Might the phrase just mean *swollen with many*, i.e. the many whom Nature sustains on the solitary resource of the YM? Again, I think one solution might lie in

67 reading it within a consistent frame. Me, I think maybe it's a half-deliberate mess: *proud of many* is referring to the proud and corrupt company previously referred to, and is a have-your-cake-and-eat-it double-subject sort-of-hendiadys for *proud many*. WS thinks the rules are there for the ignoring, and gleefully stretches all the standard figures to breaking point, in mad approximations of their form. Either way, none of the alternatives seem justified.

68

Thus is his cheek the map of days outworn,
When beauty lived and died as flowers do now,
Before these bastard signs of fair were borne,
Or durst inhabit on a living brow;
Before the golden tresses of the dead,
The right of sepulchres, were shorn away
To live a second life on second head;
Ere beauty's dead fleece made another gay:
In him those holy antique hours are seen,
Without all ornament, itself and true,
Making no summer of another's green,
Robbing no old to dress his beauty new;
  And him as for a map doth nature store,
  To show false art what beauty was of yore.

Ah yes: the 'wig' sonnet. A tirade against wigs, by a baldie. That's always going to get my vote: there's more enterprise in going naked. There's even more enterprise in actually having hair, of course, but there we go. However I sense the author clinging to the coat-tails of his own compliment, a little. He might not have the YM's lovely face and natural flowing locks (though praise of a trichological nature is a bit conspicuous by its absence here: was the YM *also* moving towards slapheadery?) but as we know, WS also went without all ornament and as nature made him: cold and shiny. The poem runs 'And so his face is a map of

68 days gone by, when beautiful people lived and died like flowers – before these illegitimate tokens of beauty were invented, or anyone dared slap them on the living. This was before the golden locks of corpses – which rightly belong in the grave, with the rest of them – were shorn off for the heads of the living, before the beautiful hair of the dead made the living happy. You can see those blessed ancient days in his unadorned beauty, which neither steals someone else's youth, nor robs the old to *dress his beauty new*. Nature preserves him as a record, to show those make-up-artists what *real* beauty actually used to look like.' There's a half-buried theme of profanity and death here, but as much as some commentators would prefer it were otherwise, this is mainly a poem about wigs.

KDJ reckons this poem was likely written *after* the death of Elizabeth, a noted syrup enthusiast, and thus likely to take offence. However in *The Merchant of Venice* (usually dated at around 1594–5) WS has Bassanio say:

. . . Look on beauty,
And you shall see 'tis purchas'd by the weight,
Which therein works a miracle in nature,
Making them lightest that wear most of it:
So are those crisped snaky golden locks
Which make such wanton gambols with the wind
Upon supposed fairness, often known
To be the dowry of a second head,
The skull that bred them in the sepulchre.
Thus ornament is but the guiled shore
To a most dangerous sea . . .

(III. ii.)

– which is at least as Tower-worthy an effort. Writers, in my experience, rarely recycle work so much as rephrase ideas they're particularly delighted with, and do it ten times in the same year. So I reckon we might plausibly date this sonnet mid-90s; though since this isn't a play, and WS can't distance himself from his remarks by putting them in someone else's mouth, it might be some slight evidence of his intention to hold back the poems until Liz had bought the farm.

You will note that the couplet is more or less exactly the same as the previous one.

In much the same way as you could stand up in a church and give a selective hour-long lesson from the good book that would end in your arrest (not to mention a lifetime of nightmares for every child who heard it), you could give a long reading from the Sonnets that would give no hint that it was the great love poem of repute. Similar lies are spun about the true nature of both books, a reliable sign that very few folk have read them all the way through in a while. Yes, there are many great love poems here, poems of great universal relevance. But imagine a pair of literate lovers who hadn't read the Sonnets before; they could open this book at random thirty times, and remain bewildered as to how on *earth* it had acquired its reputation as a lover's vade mecum. I hope someone lets me make a 'Selected Sonnets' one day, though many would still regard that as a profanity. True: we'd lose the narrative, but we'd be able to focus some light on some terribly undervalued poems, and consign some others to the shadows. Much as I also hate wigs, I'd cheerfully send this one into the unanthologised dark.

69

Those parts of thee that the world's eye doth view
Want nothing that the thought of hearts can mend;
All tongues, the voice of souls, give thee that due,
Utt'ring bare truth, even so as foes commend;
Thy outward thus with outward praise is crown'd.
But those same tongues that give thee so thine own
In other accents do this praise confound
By seeing farther than the eye hath shown;
They look into the beauty of thy mind,
And that in guess they measure by thy deeds;
Then, churls, their thoughts (although their eyes were kind)
To thy fair flower add the rank smell of weeds.
  But why thy odour matcheth not thy show,
  The soil is this, that thou dost common grow.

'You smell.' There's a vaguely diverting crux at the end of this, but otherwise it's only of interest because it's refreshingly critical of the YM. It's a tired old effort, though, and I hear all sorts of metre-padding, periphrasis and shoehorned rhymes. (HV keeps herself interested by drawing one of her infamous diagrams, in this case two sets of concentric circles, to represent the way that something converges on some other stuff in contrast to something or other.) The argument runs 'your outward appearance is perfect, all men agree; but those same folk, when they look deeper into your mind and judge you by your actions . . . they change their tune, and *to thy fair flower add the rank smell of weeds* [an awful line, and that strong stress-fall on *the* is an uncharacteristic laziness; you have to make it an emphatic *thee* to keep the metre from collapsing]. So if you don't smell quite as lovely as you look – here's the reason: you have too many friends in low places.' We can probably surmise that the YM has been hanging out with the whores and roaring boys in the alehouse, and that WS is probably less morally outraged than feeling a wee bit left out. I sense a *very* mundane occasion for this verse.

'. . . friends in low places.' At least that's what we *think* the last line means. In the Q, it's *The ſolye is this, that thou doeſt common grow*; *ſolye* is usually emended to *soil*, as it's consistent with the metaphor of weeds and *common* ground, and it was often spelled *soyle* – and the drunk who worked on this part of the Q has the habit of reversing letters. More to the point, *soyle* was in use as a verb meaning 'to resolve, clear up'. Given the Elizabethan penchant for antimeria – the cheerful use of a word in a 'wrong' part of speech – it's not too hard to imagine WS using it as a noun, meaning something like 'the explanation'; this way he can keep his *soil* pun, in the sense of 'basis or ground' (but also perhaps in the half-sense of 'stain'). 'So if you're starting to smell *off* – the explanation is this: you're becoming vulgar' might be too brutal a paraphrase, but it's pretty much what it says. However if that *is* what he intended, the line is destroyed by its own wordplay. As far as stinks goes, this poem isn't in a great position to hurl accusations.

70

That thou art blamed shall not be thy defect,
For slander's mark was ever yet the fair;
The ornament of beauty is suspect,
A crow that flies in heaven's sweetest air.
So thou be good, slander doth but approve
Thy worth the greater, being wooed of time;
For canker vice the sweetest buds doth love,
And thou present'st a pure unstained prime.
Thou hast passed by the ambush of young days
Either not assailed, or victor, being charged;
Yet this thy praise cannot be so thy praise,
To tie up envy, evermore enlarged:
  If some suspect of ill masked not thy show
  Then thou alone kingdoms of hearts shouldst owe.

Dear me: this is a mess in a dress, this one. WS defends the YM against the slanders of the previous poem – possibly guiltily, since he'd joined in the abuse himself by the end. The first two lines are fair enough – 'The fact that folk say bad things about you won't be your discredit: the fair always represent slander's target.' ('Envy shoots at the fairest mark' was proverbial.) l.3 means 'suspicion is the adornment of beauty', by which he really means 'the hallmark of its existence'; but l.4 . . . argh. The metaphor here is that *heaven's air* = beheld beauty, and that the *crow* = the mark of suspicion, which darkens the heaven; but in what way it can be perceived as an *ornament* of heaven is lost on me. I guess you might look up at the crow as it caws, and go *Whatwasthat – Oh! It's a crow. Hey . . . actually – it's a lovely day up there*, but that doesn't help us with *ornament*, unless we give it a perfectly neutral reading of 'something stuck to something else'. A beauty spot, perhaps? The argument and the metaphor are pulling in different directions, and proving contradictory cases. Either suspicion enhances or mars the beauty of the beloved – but it can't do both. The next four lines are fine if dull, essentially 'The more they slander you, the better it proves your worth, in the way a canker-worm loves the sweetest bud; you simply present a delicious perfect target.' The sestet says 'you've survived the temptations of youth, whether by indifference or restraint; yet this praise can't increase your reputation to the extent of stopping the envious from talking, because they'll always be at large [*enlarged*; really. Who'd've guessed]. If your lovely appearance were not masked by at least a *suspicion* of evil, then you should own every heart in the world.' For Will, this is D-minus stuff.

71

No longer mourn for me when I am dead
Than you shall hear the surly sullen bell
Give warning to the world that I am fled
From this vile world with vildest worms to dwell:
Nay, if you read this line, remember not
The hand that writ it, for I love you so,
That I in your sweet thoughts would be forgot,
If thinking on me then should make you woe.
O if, I say, you look upon this verse,
When I perhaps compounded am with clay,
Do not so much as my poor name rehearse,
But let your love even with my life decay;
  Lest the wise world should look into your moan,
  And mock you with me after I am gone.

Once again, the placing of the sonnet is way too clever to have been the work of anyone but the poet. Having completed his three score years and ten, WS now turns his attention to his own funeral. The argument runs: 'After the funeral bells have been silenced – it's all over. Forget about me. I love you too much to have you suffer in your grief. I absolutely insist, d'you hear me, that when I'm worm-food, you let your love die with me, and not mention my name. Like: ever.'

Can we buy a word of this? Yes, we can understand the loving injunction that the rest of the bereaved's life not be taken up with mourning. But *not to grieve*? Speaking personally, I want a three-mile cortège and a New Orleans tailgate band, then everyone in black lace – even the guys – and feeling terrible for five years. Thereafter they may confine their weeping to an hour or two a day, but no less. It's almost superfluous to point out the 'don't think of an elephant' contradiction here; if it's *really* his intention to be forgotten, why even mention it? And worse, why endeavour to make the command so *memorable*? Another sign of its insincerity, surely. *Nay, if you read this line, remember not / The hand that writ it*? . . . *Do not so much as my poor name rehearse, / But let your love even with my life decay*? Oh come on, now.

SB hates this one, and misreads it – or rather reads it far too literally. Referring to ll.6–8, he says '. . . the narcissistic smugness of the speaker's gesture of selflessness is made ridiculously apparent by the logic of the situation he evokes: a survivor rereading a poem about forgetting the deceased speaker must necessarily be reminded of him.' But he's wrong. Or he's right – but only if you choose to read poems as written by trustworthy commentators, in full charge of their faculties, and who can be fairly charged with insincerity or with lying. I'd suggest that we can profitably read more deeply than that, and it's in those readings we learn more about ourselves – which is at least half the point of the exercise. This *is* a heartfelt sonnet. But what's sincere here doesn't lie in the surface sense or apparent meaning, but in the feeling behind the desperate hyperbole. The real tragedy is that you have someone *so* upset that he believes, or *wants* to believe, or wants someone *else* to believe this nonsense. To miss the note of hapless despair that suffuses this poem is to miss the only thing that redeems its patent illogic, so we shouldn't

It all depends on whether you care enough, whether your

sympathies are strongly engaged enough by the human voice of the poet to go to the trouble of giving the poem a psychological as well as a literary reading. Our literary readings, for all their apparent sophistication, are often just too literal. But we don't read poems as machines reading the productions of machines, and naturally posit a vulnerable and fallible human hand behind them. Indeed we do this as instinctively as we meet the eyes of a stranger when they walk into the room; *not* to do so is perverse, and denies a sound human instinct. If we just read the poem, we read half the poem; we should also read the author – with whose lying and dissembling, faltering and fluffing, flailing acts of self-preservation and self-delusion we are as likely to identify with, and be moved by, as anything the poem alone appears to be saying. (I'll bet you can tell by my own zealous overstatement that I used to hold the opposite position – i.e. the New Critical line that one engages with the disembodied text, the poem as some sort of historically disinterested activity – and that's the whole story. I was wrong. There's a continuity between author, text and reader, and a rich reading engages with its whole length.)

The couplet has often been called weak – heaven knows, WS writes some hairy old couplets – but I find this odd, given it's the one part of this poem that's literally true: the forbidden nature of WS and the YM's love would surely lead to *just* such a mocking, were the truth to come out. Indeed the YM might well find himself horribly compromised, were he to make his grief too public. I find it rather moving.

l.4 I'll resist correcting the Elizabethan *vildest* to 'vilest' – it anticipates the 'd' in *dwell* and enhances the music.

❧

72

O, lest the world should task you to recite
What merit lived in me, that you should love
After my death, dear love, forget me quite,
For you in me can nothing worthy prove;
Unless you would devise some virtuous lie,
To do more for me than mine own desert,
And hang more praise upon deceasèd I
Than niggard truth would willingly impart:
O, lest your true love may seem false in this,
That you for love speak well of me untrue,
My name be buried where my body is,
And live no more to shame nor me, nor you.
  For I am shamed by that which I bring forth,
  And so should you, to love things nothing worth.

Oh *enough* already. Who knows what fatal encouragement, or lack of discouragement, had WS persist with this already hard-to-swallow riff for yet another Sonnet: all it does is subtract from the previous one. In short: 'If they ask you to say what virtue I had that made you love me, forget it; you'll just make up some lie to make me look good – and so betray your love for me. Better that my name dies with me, and that no shame attaches to you. Because I'm rubbish. I'm ashamed of everything I write – and so, frankly, should you be.'

Let me be clear: I might be a bit annoyed with the poem, but

the sentiment doesn't strike me as particularly disingenuous.
72 Thinking you suck is often the hallmark of a serious talent, and I am proud to say the poetry list I oversee is stuffed to the gills with men and women tormented by what they think of as their own wretched inadequacy, and their inequality to the demands of the art. This seems to have the effect of making them work harder than just about everyone else, if only to avoid the shame of adding another bad line to the sum of things. (The trouble is that poetry's *medium* is failure. Its project of articulating the near-inarticulable means that just about every line will inevitably have to display some degree of linguistic originality, in the broadest sense of that phrase. But by definition, most original writing is going to risk falling on its face. That's why we don't do it all the time. Words fail poets continually, as their workplace is that remote and half-mapped zone of speech where language itself starts to falter, fail, and pass over in silence that of which it cannot speak. For that reason, it's a perfectly reasonable critical stance to assume that a poem by an author whose strike-rate is unproven is probably bad, until it proves itself good.)

SB notes that this 'hyperbolic modesty' (or meiotic bragging, I guess) was rampant amongst Renaissance writers, and I don't think it was such a bad convention either. The contradiction here, of course, is that I-suck-at-this double bluff only works when the poem is pretty good. Here the bluff's gone triple – three is a crap number for bluffs – and I can see the YM reading this, and thinking to himself . . . *I see your point*. Conceivably we might posit a corrective fourth bluff, where WS has *deliberately* written a bad poem about writing a bad poem to inspire the beloved's pity for his lack of talent, but then again I'm full of the cold and high on Day Nurse. (It's important to remember – OK, for *me* to

remember – that we're judging the poem against the best poems
of *Shakespeare*. Even a relatively lame effort like this still has 72
enough sweetness, enough lyric and rhythmic grace to trump
most of his contemporaries, and by some distance.)

73

That time of year thou mayst in me behold
When yellow leaves, or none, or few, do hang
Upon those boughs which shake against the cold,
Bare ruined choirs where late the sweet birds sang;
In me thou see'st the twilight of such day
As after sunset fadeth in the west,
Which by and by black night doth take away,
Death's second self, that seals up all in rest;
In me thou see'st the glowing of such fire
That on the ashes of his youth doth lie,
As the death-bed, whereon it must expire,
Consumed with that which it was nourished by.
  This thou perceiv'st, which makes thy love more strong,
  To love that well, which thou must leave ere long.

The third of a straight hand of four poems which address ageing, and justly celebrated as one of the most beautiful of the sonnets. It's fuelled by a rather paradoxical, or even questionable premise – a habit he's recently developed. Indeed it borders on straight wishful thinking. 'The more decrepit I look, the more you'll love me, as it reminds you that I'll be gone before you are.' Hmmm . . .

But that second line: Oh! You can't read it without the hairs standing up on your arm. Look at the crazy temporal sequence; do you see how in his development of the tree-image, WS range-finds his own present (his autumn) from either side, first, his leafy summer, then his bare winter? (He might have had his hair in mind, too: WS was a famous baldie – as we all know, a sign of a deep and virile intelligence. However anyone who reads this as the *primary* sense here has lost the plot.) On the other hand, there's a theory that he was also simultaneously running a 'books and writing' metaphor within the metaphor: *yellow leaves*: pages and *choirs*: *quiers*, as it's spelt in the Q – i.e. *quires*, as in a manuscript. If this *is* his intention, I'd rather ignore it, as it's too clever for me to be much moved by it. Readers are perfectly entitled to ignore the clever-clever, the meretricious and the crude wherever they feel they're operating against the primary sense or tone, and are frequently capable of demonstrating much better taste than the poet.

l.4 is even better, describing the empty branches and the absent birds as if they were the ruined, songless chancel (which would have been a familiar enough sight, after Henry VIII's destruction of the abbeys). As to the perfection of the metaphor, listen to Empson's famous unpacking of the line in *Seven Types of Ambiguity*: 'the comparison holds for many reasons; because ruined monastery choirs are places in which to sing, because they involve sitting in a row, because they are made of wood, are carved into knots and so forth, because they used to be surrounded by a sheltering building crystallised out of the likeness of a forest, and coloured with stained glass and painting like flowers and leaves, because they are now abandoned by all but the grey walls coloured like the skies of winter, because the cold and narcissistic charm suggested by choir-boys suits well with Shakespeare's feeling for the object of the Sonnets . . .' It's the sign of a well-formed ground that it keeps generating rhymes between the

sets of the tenor's and vehicle's concerns. Note how Empson
73 takes the trouble to read the metaphor not just in isolation, but within the tonal and emotional ambiance of the whole poem. It's a *brilliant* metaphor, and with those bare boughs he's sketched the entire emotional landscape.

With *Death's second self*, WS is referring to night, though Death's brother has long been Sleep, whom he's also invoking indirectly. (In Greek myth they're the twin brothers Hypnos and Thanatos, and their mother is Nyx, night.) Look at that lovely *seals up*, and its hints of the coffin and grave. Though there's also a pun, now lost on us: 'seel' is to stitch the eyelids shut, as one would a hawk's: remember Macbeth's *Come, seeling night, / Scarf up the tender eye of pitiful day*. In the third quatrain we see a return to WS's fire-metaphor. *Consumed with that which it was nourished by* – life's fire first animates the body and then consumes the body, its fuel. (KDJ says the subject of 'that' is time, but it can be both.)

And then we have that final couplet. Once again you do wonder if the poem – or some better alternative version of it – could have finished at l.12. It would have been an entirely different and incredibly sad poem, true, but we wouldn't have had to suspect WS's wishful thinking here. However I think 'you see all this, and it makes your love stronger, as you know it'll soon be lost' is a misreading. There's another, subtler reading open to us, one I much prefer: 'You see all this; and that must make your love pretty strong, if you can love this decrepit thing as well as you do, especially when you know death will take it from you pretty soon.' If you say it with a little expressive rise – '*This* thou perceiv'st, which makes thy love *more* strong, / To love that *well*, which thou must leave ere long' – you can just about bring out that sense.

(For a little perspective: it's likely that WS wrote this in his
early to mid-thirties. The Elizabethan paper-round was a long 73
one.)

l.10 don't be thrown by the *his*. Elizabethans didn't have *its*. He's still referring to the fire.

❧

74

But be contented when that fell arrest
Without all bail shall carry me away;
My life hath in this line some interest,
Which for memorial still with thee shall stay.
When thou reviewest this, thou dost review
The very part was consecrate to thee:
The earth can have but earth, which is his due;
My spirit is thine, the better part of me;
So then thou hast but lost the dregs of life,
The prey of worms, my body being dead,
The coward conquest of a wretch's knife,
Too base of thee to be rememberèd.
The worth of that is that which it contains,
And that is this, and this with thee remains.

This continues directly from Sonnet 73. Another fine poem, very attractive in its simple sincerity. Perhaps no lines to die for – but in some ways it's even better than the last in the purity of its music and clean cut of its argument. It's immediately comprehensible, too, meaning there's very little to say about it. 'As much as I appreciate you finding it in your heart to love this worn-out husk, don't worry when I die, because you'll inherit the best of me: these lines. They'll remain with you when I'm in the ground.'

l.1 *This fell sergeant Death / is strict in his arrest*: *Hamlet*, V. ii.

l.3 *line*: a line of verse, but with a strong hint of the line of life, i.e. one's life-span as measured and spun out by the Fates. *interest* just means a share, or a right of possession; it had no sense of 'curiosity' in WS's day. WS has a share in the verse, inasmuch as he lives on through it.

l.11 *coward conquest*: cowardly conquest, i.e. his body didn't put up much resistance in the face of the *wretch's knife* – presumably death's scythe, though to call death a 'wretch' is showing him a lot of sympathy. Maybe he's a wretch *because* the body puts up so little opposition. It's a miserable gig, I expect, to be so all-powerful, and always meeting such paltry opposition.

l.12 *Too base of thee to be rememberèd* . . . too base to be remembered by you.

The sestet has a very staccato music; this is down to several runs of monosyllables, with the sound echoing the brisk (and dead) logic of the lines. There's a sweet double sense in l.14, *and this with thee remains* – this verse will *stay with* the YM when WS is dead, and he will endure, *together with* the verse.

75

So are you to my thoughts as food to life,
Or as sweet-season'd showers are to the ground;
And for the peace of you I hold such strife
As 'twixt a miser and his wealth is found:
Now proud as an enjoyer, and anon
Doubting the filching age will steal his treasure;
Now counting best to be with you alone,
Then bettered that the world may see my pleasure;
Sometime all full with feasting on your sight,
And by and by clean starvèd for a look;
Possessing or pursuing no delight
Save what is had, or must from you be took.
  Thus do I pine and surfeit day by day,
  Or gluttoning on all, or all away.

Another rather oddly transparent, plain-English sonnet and immediately comprehensible: I wonder if he wrote this and Sonnet 74 while a little hungover. They're *gingerly* clear, as if he was trying to avoid any loud noises and unnecessary nerve-jangling.

The first two lines are quite misleading, and suggest that there's little here but happy and peaceful equilibrium. However WS soon unpacks the latent tension in the lines, and things take a familiarly tormented turn. That *And* in *And for the peace of you I hold such strife* is cheeky, as it's much more of a *But*. (For this reason the first quatrain is certainly not, as HV puts it, 'a four-line introduction'.) Having nothing much to chew on, SB does his best to pretend to be mystified by this line, but despite his claim that it 'passes all understanding' it's a microcrux, at best. The YM's *peace* is in opposition to WS's *strife*, and the line must surely mean 'and for the sake of your peace [i.e. to keep you placated and sweet, or to keep the idea of you in some kind of equanimous balance] I, on the other hand, am obliged to host a torment' – that torment being double: that of the miser, torn between the enjoyment of his wealth and his paranoia over its loss, and that of the awful cycle of appetite and desire, which passes from hunger, to gluttony, to satiety, to hunger again.

Now counting best to be with you alone, / Then better'd that the world may see my pleasure makes me smile, though. I'm not saying women don't want to share their love with the world too, but there's something very insecure and typically blokeish about the idea that telling the world about it is as important as – or *better* than – the enjoyment of love itself. It's not quite singing it from the rooftops; there's *gloating* in the line, borrowed from the miserly conceit. It all put me in mind of that old and rather psychologically acute joke, where some old geezer and Michelle Pfeiffer find themselves shipwrecked on a desert island, and . . . go look it up yourself.

l.14 *Or . . . or*: either . . . or; *all away* is strange, but clearly must mean 'having nothing'.

76

Why is my verse so barren of new pride,
So far from variation or quick change?
Why with the time do I not glance aside
To new-found methods, and to compounds strange?
Why write I still all one, ever the same,
And keep invention in a noted weed,
That every word doth almost tell my name,
Showing their birth, and where they did proceed?
O know, sweet love, I always write of you,
And you and love are still my argument:
So all my best is dressing old words new,
Spending again what is already spent:
    For as the sun is daily new and old,
    So is my love still telling what is told.

Yet another uncharacteristically plain sonnet; but here, the unadorned style WS has unaccountably found for himself – is he *on* something? – fits his subject well. It might be that, stuck for a theme for Sonnet 76, he began to interrogate the number itself: this will have quickly led him, with no little irony, back to Sonnet 38. Yes: compared with 38's large promises of infinite variety and invention, it *has* all gotten a little repetitive and circular lately, hasn't it? The two poems were certainly written to be deliberately contrasted. The déjà vu we experience is partly down to large thematic elements declared and shared by the both poems, i.e. *verse*, *write*, *argument* and *invention*, but the argumentative cadences of the poems are mirrored too, beginning with two very contrasting questions: where Sonnet 38 had *How can my muse want subject to invent, / While thou dost breathe, that pour'st into my verse . . .?* we now have the grim *Why is my verse so barren of new pride, / So far from variation or quick change?* Of course WS has a smart answer, and for all I know it might be a sincere one. The clear implication here is 'my stylistically monotonous verse is really a reflection of – a tribute *to*, indeed – the unchanging constancy of my love.' Maybe it is. Though maybe his lack of inspiration is also giving him an inkling of his love's slow death.

On the third hand, maybe he's just written far too many poems for this kid – and for all his deep feeling, has nothing left to say; it happens. So much for the *tenth muse.* It's a bit depressing, this one. The last four lines try to draw themselves up to something like an aesthetic nobility, though they're dragged down by the dead weight of WS's growing disillusion, and end up just sounding knackered and bathetic. Even the *sun* the YM is compared to sounds like, well, *The Sun* – making its grim, short journey from fresh newsprint to chip-bag in the course of a day. (Do you recall how *magnificent* this sun-trope used to be, before it was overtaken by its dull, quotidian aspect?)

Note, however, that in the lines *Why write I still all one, ever the same, / And keep invention in a noted weed, / That every word doth almost tell my name, / Showing their birth, and where they did proceed?* we also have a strong defence of his singular style; indeed even though it's cheekily couched as a self-directed criticism, it's a simple vaunt. This attitude is important in the context of the Rival Poet sonnets, which begin very soon, at Sonnet 78.

76 (As we'll see, Sonnet 77 – as with 81 – has been shoehorned in as a 'time-themed climacteric poem' and stands apart from the current sequence.) KDJ notes that *new-found methods* and *compounds strange* may be a nod or a sideswipe at Drayton, and his more experimental sonneteering in the *Idea* – with its 'wilde, madding, jocund, & irreguler' style, as its own author put it. However, as WS knew, nothing dates quite like the wilde, madding, jocund, & irreguler. Reading the *Idea* – *'Tis nine years now since first I lost my wit; / Bear with me then, though troubled be my brain*, etc. – I feel like my kids feel when they watch the first series of *Monty Python*, bewildered at what it was their father once found so thigh-slappingly hilarious.

l.6 *a noted weed*: a distinctive garb, i.e. an immediately identifiable style.

❧

77

Thy glass will show thee how thy beauties wear,
Thy dial how thy precious minutes waste.
The vacant leaves thy mind's imprint will bear,
And of this book, this learning mayst thou taste:
The wrinkles which thy glass will truly show
Of mouthèd graves will give thee memory;
Thou by thy dial's shady stealth mayst know
Time's thievish progress to eternity;
Look what thy memory cannot contain,
Commit to these waste blanks, and thou shalt find
Those children nursed, delivered from thy brain,
To take a new acquaintance of thy mind.
  These offices, so oft as thou wilt look,
  Shall profit thee and much enrich thy book.

Sonnet 77 seems something of an interruption in the development of WS's thought, which is steadily turning towards the business of his poetic rivals. This is another meditation on decrepitude: the YM is invited to consider various objects as kinds of memento mori, in which he might see his own death foretold. The mirror shows how his *beauties wear,* and how his wrinkles will remind him of the grave; the pocket-clock how, by his *dial's shady stealth*, his life ebbs away. That stealthy stealing shadow on the YM's pocket-watch is a gorgeous little unit metaphor, and is, of course, supposed to put us in mind of a sundial.

77 However the *vacant leaves* of his notebook offer him some solace. (*This book,* it becomes quickly apparent, is not the Sonnets – but the YM's notebook, which WS intends that he fill with his own writing.) True, by morbid association, they might also remind him that a dead brain holds no thoughts, or at least that time often corrupts the memory, and steals its better ideas – but the book also offers some solace. 'Look, write *down* these thoughts that you'll later forget – and when you read them in future years, you'll find those brainchildren will have grown to maturity [he doesn't say by what they're *nursed* in the meantime, however], and they'll be like new friends to you.' It's avuncular advice, too; WS is clearly speaking with the authority of experience here.

Pooler and many other commentators have blithely proposed that this poem accompanied a gift of a book, a blank notebook, a mirror, a pocket-watch, or indeed some contraption that incorporated them all. This cool new clockbookmirror would, presumably, make you the envy of punctual literary narcissists everywhere. Nah – possibly there was a gift of a notebook involved, but even if we knew that for a fact it would add or subtract nothing from the poem. Skip ahead, though, to Sonnet 122 for a delicious and ironic reversal, where the *YM* seems to have made a gift of a notebook to WS – who claims that he has no *need* of such a remembrancer, since his memory is so perfect. (For which read: he lost it.)

KDJ indicates WS's employment of the staggeringly obscure (but allegedly hackneyed) figure of 'correlatio', which might well exist, for all I know – but I would've just called it 'enumeratio', where you list the effects or consequences of the subjects previously declared; perhaps she means some more didactic figure that links several examples in a formulaic way. You'll recall Raleigh's 'To His Son' as a great example of this sort of thing: *Three things there be that prosper up apace / And flourish whilst they grow asunder far . . . And they be these – the wood, the weed, the wag. / The wood is that which makes the gallows tree; / The weed is that which strings the hangman's bag; The wag, my pretty knave, betokeneth thee . . .*

I still think there's a strong chance that the theme was proposed solely by the sonnets' numerical position: 77, being 7 x 11, makes it a big climacteric multiple (and it's exactly half of the final sequence), and Sonnets 49, 63, 81, 126 and 154 improvise variations on much the same death-and-time riff. This might also further suggest that this run of poems was *not* composed in strict sequence, since 'Oh – damn – we're at 77. Better do another mortification-of-the-flesh number. There . . . Now where was I?' seems improbable. Far more likely, I'd have thought, that the climacteric poems were shoehorned in later – perhaps even closer to the date of publication, when WS was arranging the final sequence. On the other hand, Dowden makes the ingenious suggestion that this *does* indeed form part of the Rival Poet sequence, if we read its injunction as essentially 'OK! It's true. I suck. I'm out of ideas. Here's a notebook – fill up the damn thing yourself, then.' (I paraphrase.)

l.10 the Q has *blacks*, but SB's idea that it was a misread nunnation mark is surely correct, given that there are precedents for this kind of error elsewhere.

ll.13–14 offer, SB alleges, 'another example of Shakespeare's efficient use of syntactic imprecision'. I think he overcomplicates things. *Offices* surely must refer to the three Zen mortification exercises that WS has just described: the YM's contemplation of his own ageing, his own dying, and his own amnesia – the last, within the pages of the blank book, with its concomitant death-inspired invitation to fill it all up, and have his pen glean his teeming brain while there's still time. So the lines say little more than 'These things I've proposed – so often as you can bring yourself to face them – will profit you, and [via the wisdom so gained] enrich your book.' That *much* in l.14 seems awfully superfluous, though, if we assume the notebook is for no other purpose. However I suppose if this sonnet *had* been flown in late, it might support KDJ's position that the *book* might be an ms. of the Sonnets, to whose *waste blanks* the YM was being invited to add his own thoughts and commentary. (When I was seventeen I used to think that was what all these *waste blanks* at the backs of poetry books were *for*, being sweetly ignorant of the 64-page extent. *Please* tell me it wasn't just me.) This would certainly make sense of the *much*, as there'd already be something in the book to be enriched. I fear, though, that it's just padding the metre.

78

So oft have I invoked thee for my Muse,
And found such fair assistance in my verse
As every alien pen hath got my use,
And under thee their poësy disperse.
Thine eyes, that taught the dumb on high to sing,
And heavy ignorance aloft to fly,
Have added feathers to the learned's wing
And given grace a double majesty.
Yet be most proud of that which I compile,
Whose influence is thine, and born of thee:
In others' works thou dost but mend the style,
And arts with thy sweet graces gracèd be;
    But thou art all my art, and dost advance
    As high as learning my rude ignorance.

The word's out: 'I've invoked you so often [and by implication, so successfully] that now every halfwit who owns a pencil is doing the same.'

The poet-as-avian stuff in the second quatrain is prepared for and later echoed by some pretty play on *pen* and *style*, if you keep in mind their origins in the Latin *penna*, feather, and *stilus*, a writing implement. ('Mend the pen' was to sharpen a quill, giving us a nice pun in l.11.) However ll.5–8 give the unfortunate impression of a large, bald, mute and flightless bird, possibly the turkey this poem resembles. That's is the danger of running consecutive metaphors where the vehicles are way too similar to each another, and too easily conflated in the same conceptual domain.

O that the muse had picked up the phone that day; for the YM to *be most proud of that which I compile* would be a struggle, on this evidence. The sestet is better, at least. While the YM's inspiration merely *mends the style* of those others, he constitutes *all my art*, and so his influence is vastly the more powerful here, elevating the untutored WS to the ranks of the most learned. Presumably WS's loud declaration of his noble savagery worked before, which is why he keeps repeating the ploy, though I really don't know how cute the 'stupid' card is at the best of times.

Though he's still plural, one feels the Rival Poet start to make his presence felt here, though you might have detected him vaguely in Sonnet 76, lurking on the other side of its preparatory defences. (As we've just seen, Sonnet 77 was taken up with other business.)

l.4 *poësy* has three syllables, i.e. *po-eh-zee*. Forgive my ugly diaeresis.

l.5 if we assume the YM here to be William Herbert, KDJ suggests that this line might allude to one Captain Tobias Hume, who dedicated something called *The First Part of Ayres* to Mr WH, all the while protesting his lack of eloquence. I'm not sure. I do wonder if it might be a more general swipe at the massed ranks of the YM's paeaneers, given that 'dumb' also carried the connotation 'stupid' from early in its history.

l.14 *advance* also had the sense 'move upwards'.

79

Whilst I alone did call upon thy aid,
My verse alone had all thy gentle grace;
But now my gracious numbers are decayed,
And my sick Muse doth give an other place.
I grant, sweet love, thy lovely argument
Deserves the travail of a worthier pen;
Yet what of thee thy poet doth invent
He robs thee of, and pays it thee again.
He lends thee virtue, and he stole that word
From thy behaviour; beauty doth he give,
And found it in thy cheek; he can afford
No praise to thee, but what in thee doth live.
  Then thank him not for that which he doth say,
  Since what he owes thee, thou thyself dost pay.

A bleak, plain and forlorn little poem. He's on time-share, or hot-musing, and it's the RP's turn. I find the first quatrain dreadfully moving, not so much for what it says, as the downcast resignation of its half-mumbled, half-whispered, undecorated speech. 'Now you've given room to another, *my gracious numbers are decayed.* [Listen to that lovely chiastic /ɛə/ə/- /ə/ɛə/ assonance, physically performing the antithesis of *gracious* and *decayed.*] I grant you, you're worth a better writer than me. Yet all *he's* doing is stealing from you, and giving it back to you again.'

Between ll.8–14 he just says the same thing over and over again

into his doublet; I can see WS walking the streets, muttering to
79 himself. By implication, then: 'That's not what *I* do when I praise you. I *add* something.' Immortality, for one thing. It has terrific dramatic verisimilitude, this little speech, and it's so natural and heartfelt you get the impression it barely knows it's a sonnet: in its unthinking conflation of form and content, it's like listening to Bach improvise a fugue. Don't let this brief commentary suggest there's nothing to this poem; sometimes the poem says it all.

ll.7–8 look at that pretty reversal of *of thee* / *thee of*, occupying the identical position in each line.

80

O how I faint when I of you do write,
Knowing a better spirit doth use your name,
And in the praise thereof spends all his might,
To make me tongue-tied speaking of your fame.
But since your worth, wide as the ocean is,
The humble as the proudest sail doth bear,
My saucy bark, inferior far to his,
On your broad main doth wilfully appear.
Your shallowest help will hold me up afloat,
Whilst he upon your soundless deep doth ride;
Or, being wracked, I am a worthless boat,
He of tall building, and of goodly pride:
  Then if he thrive and I be cast away,
  The worst was this: my love was my decay.

Let it *go*, man. This develops the truly awful metaphor of the YM as an ocean upon which WS's *saucy bark* and the RP's proud-sailed galleon ply their poet-y trade. By *Your shallowest help will hold me up afloat, / Whilst he upon your soundless deep doth ride* WS means, I assume, 'The very smallest favour, the merest half-smile of approval, is enough to float *my* wee boat; but his overblown-if-magnificent vessel can only ride on your great patronage.' Maybe with a hint of 'He can only write about your great virtues, whereas I can write an exquisite hymn of praise to that spot on your nose.'

80 So it's preferable, all in all, to be a *saucy bark.* But no: 'if I'm wrecked, it's because I'm a worthless little boat, whereas he is stately and magnificent [and so presumably *not* wrecked]. If that happens . . . there's no worse thought than this: my love turned out to be my very ruin.'

At this point, one turns desperately to SB for some innuendo to lighten this wretched conceit, which is creaking like a rivet on the *Titanic.* Come on, Steve, don't let me down. 'This sonnet contains many words used elsewhere in sexual senses . . . none of them is fully activated here.' Damn and blast. GRL disagrees, however: '"Perhaps he is a proud galleon sailing on the sea of your generosity", it seems to say, "but he has a big mouth, a big arse, and for all I know, a big dick".' Oh, would that it did, but it doesn't. Next . . .

l.2 collapse *spirit* to a monosyllable: *spirt.* Impossible for Scots, who should adopt a US accent for 0.1 seconds.

81

Or I shall live your epitaph to make,
Or you survive when I in earth am rotten;
From hence your memory death cannot take,
Although in me each part will be forgotten.
Your name from hence immortal life shall have,
Though I, once gone, to all the world must die;
The earth can yield me but a common grave,
When you entombed in men's eyes shall lie.
Your monument shall be my gentle verse,
Which eyes not yet created shall o'er-read;
And tongues to be, your being shall rehearse,
When all the breathers of this world are dead.
  You still shall live, such virtue hath my pen,
  Where breath most breathes, even in the mouths of men.

I don't know – you wait forty sonnets for a half-decent climacteric, and then they all come at once. Why just about everyone has failed to identify Sonnet 81 as one such poem beats me – it strikes me as screamingly obvious, for a couple of reasons: firstly, 81 is the square of 9, and 9 and 7 are the two big climacteric numbers. (11's case is unproven; Sonnet 121 displays no awareness of its being in a significant position, and so probably isn't. I suspect that 77 and 99 were counted only because they repeated the numbers.) There's no *way* an arithmomaniac like WS isn't going to make play with *that*; and secondly, as with Sonnet 77, WS has

81 clearly broken his train of thought. Despite the fact this poem is often included in the RP sequence, it really has nothing to do with it; although its familiar subject – the immortality of WS's poetry vs. the all-too-mortal poet – could be read as standing here as a kind of lofty taunt to the RP, but more by luck than design, I feel. (At Sonnet 82, WS clearly picks up his little green thread again.)

Like the other climacteric sonnets, WS's temporal meditations lead him to anticipate some future condition. The poem unpacks the simple idea 'Whichever of us survives the other, fear not: you're safe, sweetie. Your eternal *monument shall be my gentle verse*.' The first quatrain stays just the right side of hackneyed: all the riskiest and most interesting registers run very close to the worst and most banal. Just as a line that risks sentimentality can be deeply moving, so these so-nearly-trite lines come off as forcefully direct and plain-speaking. The *common grave* WS refers to isn't literally so – even then, he must have had an inkling he'd find the honoured resting-place he finally did (in the chancel of Holy Trinity Church in Stratford); he simply means that Death will swallow us all. The bald truth of it, in the end, is literally breathtaking: *all the breathers* of his world *are* dead. Yet here we are, as he predicted, *the tongues to be your being*; contemplating not the YM, perhaps, but certainly the love he inspired, its nature and its source. *Breath*, by the end, is something closer to the idea of *psyche*, the spirit, the animating genius that is most alive in the mouths of living men.

In one way, it's just the by-now-familiar absurdity, of course: the *eyes not yet created*, i.e. ours, are o'er-reading his *gentle verse* because of WS's talent, not the YM's virtues. Unless, unless . . . Unless what WS says is simply true: that we're somehow prevented from seeing that great poetry really *is* the work of several hands; that poetry of genius requires a commensurate genius of love to draw it forth, and the distinction between poet and muse is, in the end, trivial, and formed by our own habitually egocentred perspectives; that without the sperm and ovum of lover and beloved – no poem. Is this the last irony? That the absurd, pseudo-humble self-deluded lie we've been railing at throughout the Sonnets, yet forced, again and again, to face, consider, and reconsider – is actually guiding us towards a deep truth: that certain kinds of talent are nothing without a reciprocal condition in the world, a form of mirrored suffering, whether in the form of person or circumstance, to draw the current of that art forth, as anode to cathode? Leaving us less with 'we're nothing without each other', than 'without each other we don't actually exist'?

ll.1–2 *Or . . . Or*: Whether . . . or

l.1 note that the line is ambiguous, and can mean both that WS writes (make, as in *makar*) the YM's epitaph, and *is* his living epitaph.

l.4 *in me each part*: all of me.

82

I grant thou wert not married to my Muse,
And therefore mayst without attaint o'erlook
The dedicated words which writers use
Of their fair subject, blessing every book.
Thou art as fair in knowledge as in hue,
Finding thy worth a limit past my praise,
And therefore art enforced to seek anew
Some fresher stamp of the time-bettering days.
And do so, love; yet when they have devised,
What strained touches rhetoric can lend,
Thou, truly fair, wert truly sympathized
In true plain words, by thy true-telling friend;
  And their gross painting might be better us'd
  Where cheeks need blood; in thee it is abus'd.

Where were we. Ah yes: those rivals. This is a great wee poem, a fine defence of plain speaking. Yes; it's a bit rich coming from this guy, but WS *has* weirdly simplified his style of late. I wonder if this was less in contrastive response to easily fingered rivals such as Chapman, than to the increasingly dandyish and experimental efforts of Davies, Drayton and his other drinking buddies. Either way, any poet finding themselves in the same situation, take note: you won't find it better expressed. The first line declares a wry and almost sarcastic tone, but WS keeps it in check to argue his case brilliantly well: 'OK – it's not as if you were *married* to my poetry; so you can, without the slightest disgrace, read what those other poets say in the works they've dedicated to you – you, *their fair subject, blessing every book.* You're as smart as you are lovely, though, and know damn well that your worth is something I'm incapable of praising sufficiently – so you've little choice but to venture out again, and seek out [sarcasm alert] some better, fresher representative of the literary advancements of the day. By all means, go ahead and do that, Love; yet, when these poets have devised whatever strained devices rhetoric can afford them, [think on this:] being truly beautiful, you were truly represented by the *true plain words* of your truth-telling pal. The exaggerated depictions of those other poets would be better applied to folk who *need* some colour in their cheeks. In your case, this kind of tart's make-up is shockingly misapplied.'

Brilliant. Yes – they're really only any good for *lying*, the other lot, using their perverse and cheap, novel skills of exaggeration where they're most needed, making the pale and ugly look presentable. With you, though, they perfume the rose. It might be inadequate, but my truthful reportage is the nearest you'll get to a *true* hymn of praise.

l.8 *fresher stamp*: something like 'newer representative creation', but we're also invited, via a short chain of close connotation directed by the poem's specific domain, 'stuff about poets and writing', to read it as 'writer'. This happens via another Shakespearian metalepsis, but this time it's almost a *triple* metonym: *stamp*: imprint: thing which results from an imprint: book: one who makes a book: writer. Essentially, a strongly constructed specific domain (or what I prefer to call a 'thematic domain' in poetry – basically 'what the poem's about', which is

82 just as thorny a subject as you might think) – provides a sort of prepared semantic watercourse, meaning the author doesn't have to do much to direct the sense down this or that path, since the channels are already cut. I think of it as analogous to the practice of 'pre-creasing' in origami, so tough-to-fold models fall into their shape more easily. In more technical language, I'd refer to it as a 'supercharged semic field'. It's a bit complicated, and to do with the poem being charged both with the author's intent, the reader's expectation, and the fact that the poem stores more and *more* of that charge, like a battery, in the dynamic process of its reading and rereading – but here's another way to think of it: if prose is a web, then a poem is a web with a great big spider at the centre, tensed and primed to react to the slightest vibration. In short, the mad game of the poem leaves us with something that has agency and intention in a way prose cannot. It has *designs* on you.

If I can talk about metonymy for a moment: remember – this is why, in a conversation between two train-inspectors, they're allowed to refer to you as 'Peterborough' within the specific domain of train-travel, as in (points to you) 'Peterborough's missed his last connection and is going to need a taxi'. The arbitrary rules of the train-domain (contained in the vague set composed by the ideas of tickets, destinations, stations, seating plans, bookings, fares, etc.) construct the frame that permits the metonymy, and allows 'the woman who's going to Peterborough' to be shortened to 'Peterborough' and save him the breath. The inspector might have called you 'the super-saver' or '13A', if those aspects of 'train-you' had been particularly relevant at the time. Where am I going with this? Well, poems work in exactly the same way, and form their own little mad train, or hospital, or church, or dog-show, or bedroom – a little planet spun from the

crazy-yet-consistent rules and logic that they insist are *the case*, 82
within the imaginative space they construct.

No one, however, has exploited the possibilities of the thematic domain quite like WS, who will often sever words from their native part of speech and even primary denotation, and allow them to float free and orient themselves according to the weird magnetic force-field of the poem alone. It's why it's often a rather pointless approach, as SB does, to pursue all possible ambiguities to the nth degree: it's really missing the point. WS doesn't split the referent so much as totally destabilise the signs of the word. He changes its valencies and suggestive possibilities, and permits the reader a more fuzzy interpretation; this, in turn, allows the word to make its contribution to the overall meaning as much through a kind of 'semic ambience' as through any paraphrasable sense. This, incidentally, would only be possible through the conscientious over-construction and *overdetermination* of the individual poem's thematic domain through WS's almost echolalic repetitions and parallel effects, which keep us constantly focused on the subject at hand: these HV misreads as something far more formulaic. It isn't such a simple game, however. WS does this to lay down the new rules that permit him new play, and allow him to undermine the relationship between signifier and signified; and it's his exploitation of the imaginative possibilities presented by this destabilised language that has won him his reputation as our most virtuosic and original performer. WS generates so much heat and movement, he turns the language from solid to liquid. The beauty is that we needn't know of *any* of this for it to work – but it's what lies behind our reaction of 'Wow – *crazy*.'

83

I never saw that you did painting need,
And therefore to your fair no painting set;
I found, or thought I found, you did exceed
The barren tender of a poet's debt;
And therefore have I slept in your report,
That you yourself, being extant, well might show
How far a modern quill doth come too short,
Speaking of worth, what worth in you doth grow.
This silence for my sin you did impute,
Which shall be most my glory being dumb;
For I impair not beauty being mute,
When others would give life, and bring a tomb.
   There lives more life in one of your fair eyes
   Than both your poets can in praise devise.

This sonnet follows on from the last. It's a slightly tum-te-tum effort, an effect produced by its sense-rhythm kowtowing to the i.p. in a rather un-Shakespearian way. Rhythmically, at least, it sounds more like a poem by one of his contemporaries. It does, though, contain a simple and honest explanation for the lack of elaborate physical description in the Sonnets: 'I never thought you *needed* painting, and therefore I didn't paint your beauty.' *Paint*, I think, in both the senses of 'depict' and 'tart up'. But I think it's *true*: the beauty of the beloved should transcend description. I don't know about you, but when I read *lavish* physical descriptions of the poet's alleged love-object, I suspect the poet of not being in love at all, and guilty of artificially working themselves into a lather. They sound inauthentic because love – in its infatuated stage, at least – so often replaces the face of the beloved with either an angelic countenance or a mirror, and there's very little to say about either of them. The first is beyond all human superlatives, and the second is either filled with some transformed version of your own face – or else it's terrifyingly empty.

In l.3, I love that parenthesis (*or thought I found*), which anticipates l.9 – where the poet is rebuked for his silence. (Though it's hard, admittedly, to imagine the YM tapping his watch and screaming 'So where's me bloody sonnet?' We can probably assume the rebuke was milder than WS makes out.) 'Yes, I've been sleeping on the job, figuring that as long as you were alive, all you'd do is show how far short my pen falls in describing your worth. You decided my silence was a fault: but hell, I'm proud of it. This way I don't do any damage to beauty. Those others – who *think* they give life to you in their verses – are just bringing a tomb. There's more life in just one of your eyes than all your poets could summon by their praises.' (That *both* in *both your poets* can mean more than two, but there's clearly also a rhetorical contrast intended between *one* and *both*.) A rather strange and contrived compliment in the couplet – full rhyme in English has the habit of producing strange contrivances – but it's a pretty good sestet. Or it would have been, if the metre hadn't been rocking us to sleep.

84

Who is it that says most, which can say more
Than this rich praise that you alone, are you –
In whose confine immurèd is the store
Which should example where your equal grew?
Lean penury within that pen doth dwell
That to his subject lends not some small glory;
But he that writes of you, if he can tell
That you are you, so dignifies his story.
Let him but copy what in you is writ,
Not making worse what nature made so clear,
And such a counterpart shall fame his wit,
Making his style admirèd every where.
  You to your beauteous blessings add a curse,
  Being fond on praise, which makes your praises worse.

Another superblydirected blast at the ranked nincompoops of the RPs for their naïve and misguided attempts to gild the lily. Not like *our* man. We've been here already, of course, but I don't think it's been so eloquently put. This poem would function as a grand all-purpose praise-poem, a lovely thing for a lover to hear read out to them, even today; it simply says *you're beyond compare.* Well, it would do if it weren't for the last two lines, which make it too personal and specific. The poem ends with a barb. Despite being *described* as perfect, the YM isn't; he still suffers from the sin of vanity. WS criticises his addiction to praise, and more or less charges the YM with having *invited* this torrent of lousy poems. (Which again might suggest that the YM is someone in the position of *commanding* praise; perhaps someone whose patronage can be bought in this way.) A bit of a shame, as it diminishes the poem's general applicability – but doesn't diminish the poem, of course. It just reminds us WS was writing these poems for himself, and for his man.

The first four lines are confusingly punctuated in the Q, and there's a great deal of scholarly speculation as to their exact meaning. Though I think the sense is plain enough: 'Which poet says the most? Which of them can say more than this rich praise: that you alone are you, [continuing the idea] in whose own confines alone we find the close-guarded store, the image or archetype that would constitute the only other thing that could possibly exemplify you, with which you could be compared?' (i.e. 'you can only be compared to yourself, or to your own essence'.) Unless I'm *really* missing something. I've punctuated the poem to bring out that sense.

The sonnet continues: 'Any writer who doesn't have the ability to lend his subject a little glory is on a road to the poorhouse; but if someone writes of *you* – all they have to do is report plainly that you are yourself: that alone will dignify his work. Let him just copy your original, and not make worse [by his own unnecessary additions] what nature's inscribed in you, and made perfectly clear; such a simple copy will make his style a famous one.'

Then the twist: 'But to the blessings of your own beauty – you add a curse: you *love* all the praise [the secondary meaning of *fond* implies he might be slightly *daft* with it] – and the encouragement you give these writers leads them to write even worse

84 poems than they did before.' For me, the most effective English sonnets employ a kind of double volta, and graft to the Italian a second turn at the couplet, taking advantage of the national talent for the parting shot.

85

My tongue-tied Muse in manners holds her still,
While comments of your praise richly compiled,
Reserve thy character with golden quill,
And precious phrase by all the Muses filed.
I think good thoughts, whilst others write good words,
And like unlettered clerk still cry ‘Amen’
To every hymn that able spirit affords
In polished form of well-refinèd pen.
Hearing you praised, I say ‘’tis so, ’tis true,’
And to the most of praise add something more;
But that is in my thought, whose love to you,
(Though words come hindmost) holds his rank before.
  Then others for the breath of words respect,
  Me for my dumb thoughts, speaking in effect.

Another patently disingenuous poem, if not necessarily an *insincere* one; we’re obligued to articulate a distinction here. At least everything’s right there in the window, from the very first line. *My tongue-tied Muse in manners holds her still* . . . Tongued-tied? Silent? The poem’s eloquent existence contradicts that flatly, and therein lies the most productive tension in the poem – not in the content of the poem itself, which is a little bit dull. ‘While I stay silent, the golden praise mounts up; all I add to it is a silent “*Amen*”. But judge my superior love by my silent deeds.’ That pretty much covers it. But one subtext runs: ‘and here’s *my* best

85 effort – and it isn't nearly good enough, is it?' As a gesture, this lies somewhere between an over-modest propitiation of the Muse, and fishing for a big fat compliment.

However note that word *manners*; WS is already beginning to introduce the idea that *his* conduct might be the superior. There's also a not-very-convincing deference offered to the better productions of his rivals. (Perhaps not *the* RP.) 'Oh yes – their praise of you is terribly precious and aureate and inspired, and all that – to which I can only contribute my illiterate "amens". But at the end of the day, it's all just *words* with you guys.*'* Only in the final couplet does WS allow his sly criticism of the hollowness of their praise to become more plain: theirs is an inferior devotion. Fine, appreciate them for their *breath of words,* by all means; but my love is superior, perhaps *beyond* words, and speaks in two ways: in my deep thoughts of you, and in the actions (*effect*) they provoke.

Look at . . . *with golden quill, / And precious phrase . . . In polished form of well-refined pen*, etc.: personally I find the practice of omitting articles to fit the metre, then passing it all off as tasty poetic diction just as annoying in Elizabethan as I do in contemporary poetry; but it might not bug you quite so much. (HV glosses *precious phrase* as 'inkhorn style', but 'precious' didn't have the connotation of 'affected' for at least another fifty years.)

l.3 The jury's out on this one, and its sense depends on what emendation of the potentially dodgy Q you accept. In the original, we have *Reserve their character with golden quill*; if we correct this to *Reserve your character with golden quill* (or *thy character*, which I far prefer, as its diphthong assonates with *character*, and is most likely what WS wrote), it means 'retain your appearance with a lovely style of writing'. It wouldn't be the first time one of the compositors mistook *thy* for *their*, so there's justification for the change. If we just leave it, and accept *Reserve their character with golden quill*, the antecedent to *their* is *comments of your praise* in l.2, so it must mean something like 'hoard away their comments in un-devaluable golden writing'. I think we should go with the correction, as it's far more natural (its unnaturalness being precisely the reason, incidentally, that SB thinks we should stick with the original.) I give up. You choose.

l.6 *And like unlettered clerk still cry 'Amen'*: the parish clerk would lead the congregation in their responses.

l.7 *hymn*: a pun, surely, on 'him'.

86

Was it the proud full sail of his great verse,
Bound for the prize of all-too-precious you,
That did my ripe thoughts in my brain inhearse,
Making their tomb the womb wherein they grew?
Was it his spirit, by spirits taught to write
Above a mortal pitch, that struck me dead?
No, neither he, nor his compeers by night
Giving him aid, my verse astonishèd.
He, nor that affable familiar ghost
Which nightly gulls him with intelligence,
As victors of my silence cannot boast;
I was not sick of any fear from thence.
  But when your countenance filled up his line,
  Then lacked I matter; that enfeebled mine.

Oh, I love this one. It's alarmingly accurate in its description of how the poet's mind works. To paraphrase: 'Was it my rival's brilliant poem – the one he wrote to you, my beloved – that made my own poem a stillborn? Was it the immortal company he keeps by night that raised his game to a similarly immortal height? Was it *that* shut me up? No. Neither my rival, nor . . . some other bloke [I'll get to him] can claim that. But when *your* approval, dearest, filled up his line [as the wind a sail] – then I was fatally weakened. Bang went my subject matter.' The RP is troubling WS not because he is a great poet. WS *knows* he is as good, or better. What's troubling WS is that universal law which states that a poet cannot share a muse. (Another universal law: they often have to. Too many poets, too few muses.)

From Auden's essay on the Sonnets:

> *It is also nonsensical, no matter how accurate your results may be, to waste time trying to identify characters. It is an idiot's job, pointless and uninteresting. It is just gossip, and gossip, though it can be exceedingly interesting when the parties are alive, is not at all interesting when they're dead.*

Oh, I don't know. It's certainly pointless, now the protagonists are long gone and unable to confirm a damn thing one way or the other, but it's not uninteresting. My five-minute attention span will be the judge of that, thank you. Anyway here's my contribution to idiotic speculation. As far as I can tell it is entirely original, i.e. most likely wrong, but hear me out.

Now: there have been many candidates for the post, but I reckon the best guess at the identity of the RP is still George Chapman, of 'Chapman's Homer' fame. Why? Because Shakespeare will have been jealous of his success, and – with his little Latin and less Greek – of his classical learning: he translated the *Iliad*, bragging that he had been inspired by the ghost of Homer himself – 'by spirits taught to write'. Most compellingly, though, Chapman dedicated poems to WS's patron Southampton, Henry Wriothesley, still our prime contender for the YM's identity. But who is this *affable familiar ghost*? It's presented a huge problem to critics; but it's clearly cryptic, and cryptic usually indicates some definitive answer. Anyway, I think it's . . . Kit Marlowe. Picture this: Chapman, indulging his talent for ventriloquising the dead, invokes the ghost of Marlowe to help him complete

86 Marlowe's unfinished poem *Hero and Leander*. This must have stuck in WS's craw. Marlowe and WS were great pals, literary rivals, drinking buddies, and possible collaborators (early WS plays show signs of Marlowe's input and vice versa, though it's all rather unproven). As identically matched, world-beating talents and almost exact coevals, the two men identified deeply with one another. 'Familiar' is the key word here. (*Affable* is just heartbreakingly affectionate.) Not only was Marlowe a ghost – one meaning of the word *familiar* – he was also 'familiar' in the simple senses of close, often encountered, recently dead and (in the Middle English sense) 'on a family footing'. Going into my Vendleresque kabbalistic mode, he's even lurking in the very consonants of the word.

Marlowe, we think, worked as a secret agent or 'intelligencer' in the proto-secret service Francis Walsingham established for Elizabeth I, and in all likelihood conducted espionage abroad. Surely this would have come out over a pint of ale or five? Nothing, I'd suggest, would have delighted WS more than the thought of the ghost of Marlowe *gulling* the proud Chapman with false *intelligence*, and it will have offered him some comfort in his fight for the muse of Southampton. Not only that, Marlowe's presence in the poem reinforces the theory of the RP being Chapman, i.e. the evidence is now mutually supportive. (Convenient, I admit.) I rest my case.

l.3 *inhearse*: to coffin up. A brilliant rhyme, no?

ll.5–7 have caused some confusion (unless we just assume it's Chapman, in which case there's none), but to most poets the sense will be plain enough, regardless of the RP's identity. As poet you improve under the tutelage of the Dead Greats.

l.11 *cannot:* sounds wrong (the sense asks for *can*) but the

Elizabethans used double negatives for emphasis.

l.10 *gulls*: deceives.

l.13 *countenance* is a pun, meaning both 'face' and 'patronage'. SB also hears 'cunt' buried there, but I think it's just him.

Incidentally, Marlowe is occasionally fingered as the true author of the Sonnets (yawn). One of the pieces of 'evidence' sometimes cited is an acrostic – actually more of a cryptogram – buried in the text, which allegedly reads 'KIT MARLOWE WROTE THIS'. Even by the unbelievably convoluted means employed, it actually just says 'KIT MARLOWE WROTE THI' – and more or less identical methods can be used to derive the phrase 'PARIS HILTON WROTE THIS', and indeed 'LLIW DELLIK I'. See Sonnet 114 for my own contribution to this hugely scientific enterprise. Moving on . . .

87

Farewell! thou art too dear for my possessing,
And like enough thou know'st thy estimate;
The charter of thy worth gives thee releasing;
My bonds in thee are all determinate.
For how do I hold thee but by thy granting,
And for that riches where is my deserving?
The cause of this fair gift in me is wanting,
And so my patent back again is swerving.
Thy self thou gavest, thy own worth then not knowing,
Or me to whom thou gav'st it else mistaking;
So thy great gift, upon misprision growing,
Comes home again, on better judgement making.
  Thus have I had thee as a dream doth flatter:
  In sleep a king; but waking no such matter.

This is the first of several sonnets in which WS *really* loses the plot, and scapegoats himself for absolutely everything he can think of, short of starting the Spanish war. Remember, we can give the poem three kinds of directly engaged readings: we can read what the poem tells us, what the poem tells us about us, and what the poem tells us about the author. And this is a fascinating poem, in all three ways.

Our man has had enough. I can't think of a poem that better captures the sadness, as well as the emotional (and, goddammit, rhetorical) complexity of the I'm-not-good-enough-for-you routine; a routine oft performed, but rarely as *sincerely* as it is here. With the misplaced optimism of the truly infatuated, though, WS will be holding out hopes of the situation improving. Given that, we may read this as a gambit, a gamble – a bit of nicely judged overkill, which he hopes will be corrected with a *look, Will: no, no – it's not like that.* The initial *Farewell!* does have a rather Burnsian self-conscious flounce about it. He's overacting, and possibly overreacting; this is a very elaborate and stagy leave-taking. (It all rather put me in mind of a *New Yorker* cartoon, inverting the famous line from *Jerry Maguire*. A woman is standing, suitcase in hand, in the open door to an apartment; the guy is on the sofa, watching TV. The caption reads 'You had me at goodbye.')

But how much snarl did WS *know* he was putting into the poem? *Thou art too dear for my possessing* sounds awfully close to 'you're frankly more trouble than your worth'. Similarly, the *And like enough* in *And like enough thou know'st thy estimate* has a hell of a sarcastic bite to it. The YM really does sound like his character has taken a nose-dive: he was far more appealing when himself he just gavest, his own worth then not knowing. What kind of love falters when you decide that your boyfriend just isn't *good* enough for you? *So thy great gift . . . Comes home again* is telling: 'I'm returning the gift of yourself to you' certainly seems to imply, again, that the YM is a narcissist. The language is all financial and legal, as it often is when WS's passions are running high. Sometimes I sense he uses the rigour, logic and Latinity of this jargon to keep those passions in check, but there's probably a more mundane reason: it's something else that excites him. (WS's mad investment skilz apart, money is just *very* important to writers. If you overhear two writers talking, there's a 50 per cent

87 chance it'll be about money. This isn't because writers are greedy, it's because writing isn't a living.)

The final couplet is an exquisite metaphor, and supremely sad. The barely noticeable transformation of *king* to *waking* enacts it beautifully in the reader's ear. I'm putting a colon and a semicolon in there, and hamming it up even more. So sue me.

Throughout we have feminine rhyme (bar lines 2 and 4, which are nonetheless polysyllabic). Each line ends on a kind of mini-bathos, and that's a whole bunch of weak-stress endings; their cumulative effect is one of passive resignation, of weakness before the inevitable loss. 'Feminine numbers' was already current for trochaic endings – Samuel Daniel was using the phrase in 1603 – so we're perhaps justified in suspecting that the feminine rhyme may be a metatextual pointer to, well, other things too. (Look at its use in the only other feminine-rhymed poem, Sonnet 20, where he quite clearly intended it to reinforce the 'feminine' theme.) Put this together with a pun on 'had' in *Thus have I had thee*, and the innuendo buried in the repeated *-ing* participle endings: 'ingle' or 'ningle' was a catamite. Oh, I don't know.

l.11 You can also read this line as saying that 'the gift of you has *grown* while in my admittedly mistaken possession; I've contributed to your present worth'. Of which he'll see nothing. As Kanye West rapped so memorably, *We want pre-nup!*

88

When thou shalt be dispos'd to set me light
And place my merit in the eye of scorn,
Upon thy side, against myself, I'll fight,
And prove thee virtuous, though thou art forsworn:
With mine own weakness being best acquainted,
Upon thy part I can set down a story
Of faults concealed, wherein I am attainted,
That thou, in losing me, shalt win much glory;
And I by this will be a gainer too,
For bending all my loving thoughts on thee,
The injuries that to myself I do
Doing thee vantage, double-vantage me.
  Such is my love, to thee I so belong,
  That for thy right, myself will bear all wrong.

This looks like nothing, and indeed it isn't much; but the argument reveals the speaker as mentally unbalanced, if you ask me. It's *utterly* bizarre. 'When you feel disposed to put me down, and make me the object of scorn – I'll take *your* side in matters, and argue against myself; that way I'll prove you're virtuous, even though you're lying about me.' OK: we're used to this *beat me, whip me, spank me / just make it right again* (Tim Buckley, ar.1971) routine by now, and indeed it's become almost normal. But note that *though thou art forsworn*: i.e. 'I might be siding with you against myself, but the substance of your accusations is false.'

88 Then he goes on: 'I know my own weaknesses better than anyone, though, and I can tell the tale of my own [by implication, my *real*] hidden faults, by which I'm [*really*] disgraced – so that in the act of getting rid of me, you'll be positively admired.'

You *what*? Aha . . . so the YM is accusing you of the *wrong* sins, and you're going to make sure that you're hauled up for the correct ones: sins far worse than the ones the YM knows about, by the sounds of it, seeing as the end result is going to be the YM's glorification for bringing such an unscrupulous cad to light, and twanging him into the Thames. What *have* you been up to? Dear me. (Am I alone – I hate starting sentences like that – am I alone in hearing a *confession* snuck in this tired old routine? You can imagine the conversation the poem is bound to prompt. 'Erm: thanks for saying and all, but these . . . *faults concealed*, old chap: something you need to get off your chest?')

Then we get a variation on the old 'Me–You, so whatever helps you is going to help me too' line; *double-vantage*, because not only is WS the beneficiary of the YM's glory, he's even *more* damn attractive and lovable and meritorious following his glorification, or something, so WS is a *double*-winner. Let's avoid the infinite regress of WS's winning adding *more* reflected glory to the YM, which in turn would add . . . etc. And thank god it didn't occur to him, or we'd be here all year. So the last few lines go something like 'And I'll be a winner too, because in turning all my loving thoughts towards you – whatever injuries I do to myself might help you, but will help me doubly: my love is such, I belong to you so completely, that for your *right* I will take every *wrong* upon myself.'

To which the logical objection (one WS seems at least vestigially aware of elsewhere) is that if WS *is* the YM, the YM is hardly likely to be *vantaged* by association with the infinite guilt WS is desperate to bring down on his own head. *Au contraire.* Essentially, this plan only works if you buy the conceit that there are two WSs: a higher WS with whom the YM is conflated, and a whipping-boy husk of a WS he can stand and hurl stones at. Dear lord what a lot of nonsense.

89

Say that thou didst forsake me for some fault,
And I will comment upon that offence;
Speak of my lameness, and I straight will halt,
Against thy reasons making no defence.
Thou canst not, love, disgrace me half so ill,
To set a form upon desirèd change,
As I'll myself disgrace, knowing thy will;
I will acquaintance strangle, and look strange;
Be absent from thy walks and in my tongue,
Thy sweet belovèd name no more shall dwell,
Lest I, too much profane, should do it wrong,
And haply of our old acquaintance tell.
   For thee, against my self I'll vow debate,
   For I must ne'er love him whom thou dost hate.

Apparently that didn't go far enough. Not only will WS assume every fault he or anyone else can think of, he won't settle for anything less than total banishment. Actually *that's* not far enough either: by the end he's knocking lumps out of himself, like Ed Norton in *Fight Club*. 'Say you left me for some fault – and I'll expand on it; say I'm lame, and I'll limp; you can't disgrace me half as much as I'll disgrace myself, as soon as I find out what you want. I'll make out I don't even know you, play the stranger, and make sure you don't run into me; I won't even bring your name up, so it isn't tarnished by your old association with me. For your sake I'll fight against myself – I mustn't love someone you hate.' 89

This is embarrassing. I mean we should be *embarrassed* for him. In the course of this exercise in raving self-abasement he's won a certain rhetorical power, but talk about overkill. It puts me in mind of a great (and no doubt now-suppressed) poem of Derek Mahon's, an improvisation on the theme of Matthew 5: 29–30 which begins 'Lord, mine eye offended / So I plucked it out' – only 'the offence continued', and not until the speaker has destroyed his skin, organs, bones, every trace of himself in the memory of others, all humanity, all life, the entire planet, all the heavenly bodies . . . does he declare himself 'fit for human society'. This has something of the same headlong senselessness, with the one difference that Mahon's intention was clearly ironic. Here we're supposed to *believe* it. Or at least *someone* is: there can be little reason for carrying on like this unless your plan is get some attention. Reading this poem as a flailing bid for sympathy is certainly the kindest way to excuse it.

1.6 *To set a form upon desirèd change* has inserted itself between two fluent, continuous and comprehensible lines – because he needed a line. It contributes nothing but bamboozlement. My best stab is something like 'by laying out the manner in which you'd want me to change', although that seems to suggest that the YM's criticisms are part of a more general, positive programme of Will-improving, as opposed to Will-dissing, and that might be wishful thinking. Actually – that's an argument *for* that interpretation, isn't it, knowing our deluded poet as we do. Either way, this line is a testament to the destructive power of padding. If you have nothing to add, and then you *do* add, the result is always subtraction.

90

Then hate me when thou wilt, if ever, now,
Now, while the world is bent my deeds to cross,
Join with the spite of fortune, make me bow,
And do not drop in for an after-loss.
Ah, do not, when my heart hath 'scaped this sorrow,
Come in the rearward of a conquered woe;
Give not a windy night a rainy morrow,
To linger out a purposed overthrow.
If thou wilt leave me, do not leave me last,
When other petty griefs have done their spite;
But in the onset come, so shall I taste
At first the very worst of fortune's might;
  And other strains of woe, which now seem woe,
  Compared with loss of thee, will not seem so.

A simple, strong and absolutely heartfelt poem, which says the same thing over and over again: 'things are bad *enough* right now; so if you're going to hate me, if you're intending to dump me – please do it now, while I'm suffering with all the other stuff. Better to face all the bad weather in one hellish night, than drag it out into the next day. In fact – if you're going to do it, do it *before* all my other misfortunes hit the beach, and then all those other woes will seem a walk in the park [sorry] by comparison.' It's a poem of quite *desperate* self-preservation. There's nothing more agonising in love than an uninterpretable silence, in not knowing where you stand with someone; even the *worst* news is more bearable than none at all. HV hears the poem as a plea – a ploy, a play – for pity: 'could anyone . . . bear to add to the strains of woe so enumerated?' It's certainly possible to read it that way. But I don't, personally: I find his condition . . . recognisable. I think he actually means it, and there's nothing disingenuous here. The man's pain is intolerable.

What deeds of WS's the world is bent to cross, we can't say, of course; writing being the career it is, it's possibly something like a recent theatrical flop, but who knows. Eight lines of the poem have *-ow* or *-oh* endings, and the overall effect is of an O-shaped wail. Ochone, ochone.

l.4 the line is clear enough in sense – 'don't hit me with a late blow' – but still very weird. l.6 embroiders a military metaphor, so perhaps l.4 is another one, but it seems unlikely. *Do not drop in* definitely doesn't mean 'don't pop round to the house for a cup of tea', and an *after-loss* – even though SB thinks it's a nonce-word – sounds awfully like a bit of sports jargon to me, so perhaps the entire line is. Though *what* sport, heaven alone knows. 'Yup – I was up a triple-beezer until he dropped in the jack for an after-loss in the third rubber.' I have no idea. After considering several alternatives, SB offers this: 'a more inviting possibility is the croquet-like variety of pocket billiards', which cracked me up, for some reason.

(I've just realised how few *laughs* there are in SB. And HV. And CB. And KDJ. JK at least has a go, occasionally. I mean you'd think this was . . . organic chemistry, or something. *Inorganic* chemistry. Serious literary criticism, fair enough; but *overly* serious literary criticism does literature a wee bit of a disservice, because it fails to honour the spirit of play in which the work was

conceived. Can't we lighten up? When did we become so cir-
90 cumspect? It's all just . . . monkeys speaking to each other, not a deep interrogation of the nature of physical law. But it's another symptom of the extent to which the scientific research model has infected the Humanities, which have succumbed to terminal physics envy. Though it's nothing that can't be solved by making everyone read Randall Jarrell for a month. Or – if they really think that serious research and chortling are incompatible – Joseph Shipley's dictionary of Indo-European roots, *The Origins of English Words*. The truly perverse thing is that science writing discovered this decades ago, and is full of the kind of wry, free, outrageously speculative and ludic stuff that was supposed to be *our* birthright.)

❧

91

Some glory in their birth, some in their skill,
Some in their wealth, some in their body's force,
Some in their garments though new-fangled ill,
Some in their hawks and hounds, some in their horse,
And every humour hath his adjunct pleasure,
Wherein it finds a joy above the rest;
But these particulars are not my measure;
All these I better in one general best.
Thy love is better than high birth to me,
Richer than wealth, prouder than garments' cost,
Of more delight than hawks and horses be;
And having thee, of all men's pride I boast –
  Wretched in this alone, that thou mayst take
  All this away, and me most wretched make.

'Others might glory in their wealth and possessions, their skill and rank – but I have your love, which betters them all. My only worry's that you might take it all away.' Not a classic, and somewhat dashed off – but a simple, effective and rather stylish poem, build around two or three tried-and-tested rhetorical figures: the anaphora of the repeated initial word *some*, the epiphonema of ll.10–11, where he gives a little summary of everything so far; then the overall shape of the *some do this, some do that; but . . .* scheme, a pleasant little tension-builder, perennially popular in all forms of British song. (Think of *The British*

Grenadiers.) Despite the bright pace of the poem, he somehow
91 finds enough time on the ball to have a pop at contemporary fashion-victims (*new-fangled ill* can mean either badly made, or fashionably bad).

The couplet is rather rugged and unsatisfactory. The repetition of *wretched* doesn't really work, and almost sounds like a word he'd forgotten he'd already used. I'm sure it was deliberate, of course: I think his double intention was (a) an antanaclasis, using *wretched* in the sense of merely 'unhappy' in l.13, but something like 'destitute' in l.14, having been bereft; and (b) to expect the reader to follow the theme of comparison: 'Oh, all that wealth and rank and skill and stuff, that's *good*; but I *better* them, in the *general best* of my love'. So that by the time we get to the final line, we stress *most* quite emphatically – his point being less the condition of wretchedness than the degree. His *best* is contrasted with another superlative – the *most* wretched of them all, a position to which he'll accede if his beloved abandons him. So we're left with 'my general best might indeed be better than all those particular bests . . . but I know I'm putting all my eggs in one basket. And it's not even me holding the basket.'

l.4 *horse*, like 'sheep', could be plural.

l.5 *humour*: temperament. You knew that.

92

But do thy worst to steal thyself away;
For term of life thou art assured mine,
And life no longer than thy love will stay,
For it depends upon that love of thine.
Then need I not to fear the worst of wrongs,
When in the least of them my life hath end;
I see a better state to me belongs
Than that which on thy humour doth depend.
Thou canst not vex me with inconstant mind,
Since that my life on thy revolt doth lie.
O what a happy title do I find,
Happy to have thy love, happy to die!
  But what's so blessed-fair that fears no blot?
  Thou mayst be false, and yet I know it not.

Bit of a rollercoaster, this one: an instinctive piece of self-protective logic, which – when WS sees its flaws – rises to a kind of hysterical protective charm, then turns into plain old hysteria, and then ends in tormented doubt. Following on from the previous poem, WS, realising that he's placed all his *riches* in his faith in the YM's love – at once sees the foolishness of such a move. This poem attempts to lend it some coherence, through the now-familiar strategy of finding a sensible argument to fit its senseless emotional form.

ll.1–2 say 'Do your worst, because I have you for the duration of my life [*term of life* is also legalese, and refers, achingly, to marriage rights].' Admittedly that's not saying much, because – as we see in ll.3–4 – 'I'll die if you *do* stop loving me.' But still, it's *some* comfort. ll.5–6 expand rather superfluously on the idea: 'Then I don't have to fear the *worst of wrongs*, since at the *least* [I assume WS means the first, earliest hint of the YM's withdrawal] my life will end.'

However, the next two lines are the sound of someone thinking aloud, and evidence – to me at least – of the extempore nature of this sonnet. The thought immediately follows that comfort does *not* lie in his knowledge that his increasingly short life being one with his love – c'mon, it's casuistic nonsense, and he knows it – but in the fact he'd be better off dead. Bring it on. Peace of the grave. Sounds great. This is *truly* exasperated stuff: 'I'd be better off dead, come to think of it, than being slave to the vagaries of your goddamn moods. You cannot torment me [much longer] with your fickleness, as your next change of heart will kill me outright.' This last is declared as a superstitious charm against that pain, a defiant promise. Tonally, *O what a happy title do I find, / Happy to have thy love, happy to die!* is poised somewhere between sarcasm and lunacy. The poem ends 'But what's so perfectly blissful that it fears nothing? You might still be false even now, and I wouldn't know it.'

What I like about this poem is the fact that it shows WS's mind changing in relation to his problem; indeed he's using poetry as a means of *exploring* that problem. Too often poems tell you what poets have thought. Most of those poems are bad, as poets think the same rubbish as everyone else. My preference is strongly for poems that show you poets *thinking*, as they're much more exciting. Here, the poet is using the formal resistance of the poem as a means of hammering a bad, received, or lazy idea into a good one. The first kind of poem usually means the poet has decided what to write in advance; the second shows you the poet's excitement in *not* knowing what they're writing about, exactly – only their commitment to use the weird procedure of poetic composition to lever out the truth from their own minds. In other words, the true poem leaves you with documentary evidence of the epiphany that took place *while* the poet was writing, not a record of something that happened before pen was set to paper. This way the reader can re-enact the poet's own journey. (Wordsworth might have experienced 'emotion recollected in tranquillity' when he was writing the boring bits of the *Prelude*, but otherwise I think something very different was going on.)

This poem shows more prevarication and uncertainty than most, and feels far more of an improvisation. I sense little revision (at least of the poem's content, if not its form), and little attempt at any real coherence, beyond the concatenation of its thoughts. Either way, WS's faith in the YM's constancy is deeply shaken. ll.11–12 are evidence of real psychological torment. HV rightly points out that if this poem is really addressed to the YM, the poem is a form of emotional blackmail; but I think this particular suicide note has been stuck to his own fridge.

93

So shall I live, supposing thou art true,
Like a deceived husband; so love's face
May still seem love to me, though altered new,
Thy looks with me, thy heart in other place;
For there can live no hatred in thine eye,
Therefore in that I cannot know thy change.
In many's looks, the false heart's history
Is writ in moods, and frowns and wrinkles strange;
But heaven in thy creation did decree
That in thy face sweet love should ever dwell;
Whate'er thy thoughts or thy heart's workings be,
Thy looks should nothing thence but sweetness tell.
  How like Eve's apple doth thy beauty grow,
  If thy sweet virtue answer not thy show.

I'm very fond of this often overlooked sonnet; it's a gloriously straightforward, open and rather graceful poem on the rather grubby subject of tormented jealousy, and the way the jealous obsesses over something they *know* to be unknowable: what does the face betray of the heaheyrt? WS's prime concern in many of his plays is the difference between appearance and reality – especially the face a man or woman presents to the world, and how much or how little it betrays of their *heart's workings*. Here, he frets over the YM's suspected perfidy, something raised explicitly in the previous sonnet. Again, WS can't resist paying a

compliment in the middle of the accusation: *But heaven in thy creation did decree / That in thy face sweet love should ever dwell* 93
. . . a face able to *tell* nothing but *sweetness*, regardless of whatever's *really* on your mind. (Frustrated by having much less than usual to get his teeth into, SB embarks on a little tour de force of overinterpretation here.)

l.1 *supposing thou art true* is very sad. It's choicely phrased here, and *supposing* can mean both 'firmly positing', and 'cautiously assuming' or even 'imagining'.

l.14 *If thy sweet virtue answer not thy show*: if your virtue isn't reflected in your appearance.

94

They that have power to hurt, and will do none,
That do not do the thing they most do show,
Who, moving others, are themselves as stone,
Unmoved, cold, and to temptation slow:
They rightly do inherit heaven's graces,
And husband nature's riches from expense;
They are the lords and owners of their faces,
Others, but stewards of their excellence.
The summer's flower is to the summer sweet,
Though to itself, it only live and die;
But if that flower with base infection meet,
The basest weed outbraves his dignity:
  For sweetest things turn sourest by their deeds;
  Lilies that fester smell far worse than weeds.

A fine, sophisticated poem so full of psychological insight it's worth making a quick précis. 'There are some who, in their great beauty, have the power to hurt – but they don't; they inspire sexual temptation in others, but won't succumb themselves. Those paragons of self-control are worthy of all our praise, and indeed inherit god's grace. But just as we find the summer flower sweet (even if its own sweetness is a matter of indifference to the flower itself), if it succumbs to disease or rot – well: even a weed is more fragrant. Nothing stinks like a festering lily.' And so, we can infer, nothing stinks quite like a beauty gone to bad, to rotten behaviour: all the more reason to praise those who stay fresh. (Me – I *like* being able to infer, and it's a relief that the argument took WS fourteen lines to develop. Otherwise I suspect we'd have had two lines of subtitles-for-the-thick again.)

Of course it's more likely that WS is just worried about *himself* getting hurt, and in one sense the poem seems written for its author alone. Imagine that: the YM has steadfastly refused sexual contact, but WS has turned this steadfastness into a compliment he can pay the youth – *and*, ingeniously, a way of consoling himself that if he *had* jumped him, things would actually be very much worse. (I suppose there's a more 'wholesome' reading where the subject is really the YM's bachelorhood, and the provocation his beauty presents to the laydeez, etc., but I don't buy it.) Nonetheless a residual annoyance persists in his description of these paragons of continence – *are themselves as stone, / Unmoved, cold . . .* which is oddly unflattering language to use of someone you're allegedly praising. However if we map *though to itself it hardly live or die* to the YM, WS credits him with an almost Buddha-like serenity and detachment. This purity makes the YM even more vulnerable to infection, of course, but through the flower-conceit, WS has devised a way of allowing the YM to 'sin passively' while attaching no blame.

ll.13–14 don't quite fit. *Sweetest things turn sourest by their deeds*, maybe – but a lily will fester just by sitting in a vase. This is a flaw in the conceit, but it's a trivial one, and we should bleep over it. The last line occurs in the anonymous play *Edward III*, indicating that WS either had a hand in it – or had it handy. Anon rarely sues.

Incidentally, the Aleister Crowley of English Verse – J. H. Prynne, whose single-mindedness I've come to admire more and

more of late – has written a book-length exegesis of this sonnet,
94 subjecting its every part to unbelievable lengths of forensic Boothification, and in doing so, out-scholarising every Shakespeare scholar in history. Its controlled explosion – vaporisation, really – of the form of the academic commentary feels very much like an eat-my-smoke riposte to the criticism of having published nothing very much in the many decades of his donship. And as far as it goes, it's a very funny one. If, y'know, largely unreadable. It is prefaced by this exquisite epigraph: *But it is in the maner of some to* languish about wordes*, and in seeking deeply after nothing, to loose not onely their time, travell, and thankes, but their wits also* (John King, 1594). Its title, *They that haue the powre to hurt*, is of course wholly unironic. Oh he's a card, that lad.

95

How sweet and lovely dost thou make the shame
Which, like a canker in the fragrant rose
Doth spot the beauty of thy budding name:
O! in what sweets dost thou thy sins enclose!
That tongue that tells the story of thy days,
Making lascivious comments on thy sport,
Cannot dispraise; but in a kind of praise,
Naming thy name blesses an ill report.
O! what a mansion have those vices got
Which for their habitation chose out thee,
Where beauty's veil doth cover every blot
And all things turns to fair that eyes can see!
  Take heed, dear heart, of this large privilege;
  The hardest knife ill-used doth lose his edge.

This isn't a great poem, but it has its interests. The first three lines are oddly self-contradictory, as if WS hasn't quite decided how he's going to play his hand here. 'How sweet you make it look, that sin that spoils your reputation, just as a canker-worm sullies a fragrant rose.' (*canker* is used here in the general sense of 'blight', I think.) Huh? Make your mind up: either the YM's shame is staining him or it isn't; either the rose is sullied by its blight, or we overlook the blight because of the rose's beauty – or to state it even more strongly, its beauty transforms the blemish and makes it beautiful too. Choose *one*, though. The OED records the first use of 'beauty spot' fifty years later, but l.3 does make you wonder if they were around earlier. Certainly the paradoxical idea of a blemish presented as an *adornment* of beauty (its function, I read here, was to 'heighten by contrast the charm of some neighbouring feature') ties together the poem's various incompatible ideas pretty neatly. ll.4–8 also decline to nail the sense: 'The [collective] voice that talks about you might comment on your exploits [*lascivious* is somewhere between a modifier of *comments* and a transferred epithet from *sport*, i.e. sexual pleasure, again keeping the meaning and judgement imprecise] can't dispraise, exactly . . . but in a *kind* of praise, the very fact your name is attached to all this seems to give sin itself a good name.' You see what I mean? The poem is turning into an exercise in sustained shilly-shally and mealy-mouthery.

O! what a mansion have those vices got / Which for their habitation chose out thee are fine lines, and conveniently sidestep the opinion he's not having much success in articulating anyway. Then he finally nails his colours to the mast. ll.11–12 tell us about the nature of this mansion: '. . . where the veil of beauty covers every fault, and all that's *visible* appears beautiful.' So the fault is now hiding *below* the beauty, maybe showing through its diaphanous layers enough to be visible, but misidentified as another lovely feature; again, WS ties it all up by alluding to the difference between outward appearance and inner reality. I think that's as much as we can do to help this crippled wee thing along.

The couplet is the most interesting thing here. Having essentially finished the poem, such as it is, at l.13 WS is obliged to make something up – and as so often in these situations, it's all rather revealing. (It reminds me of those old vinyl fade-outs, where you'd whack up the volume to hear the musicians letting their professional guard drop – chatting, swearing, mucking about or screwing up.) Essentially it amounts to 'Take heed, m'dear: the most hard-edged knife will blunt if you use it on the wrong things.' It sounds proverbial, but it probably wasn't; this is WS's very own little phallic saw, whipped out and sharpened for the occasion. It's a clever rhetorical double-bluff: it *sounds* like it should have a broader application, but within the thematic domain of the poem, we have little choice but to map the vehicle of its statement to a sexual tenor, especially when we've been prompted by the innuendo in *hard* and *used*. Yes, it sounds like there's a generic sense of 'don't misuse your gifts'; but *knife* maps to 'penis' a lot easier than *beauty* here. Ugh. Forgive my squeamishness, but the old 'penis as bludgeon' trope hasn't done it for me in a long while.

96

Some say thy fault is youth, some wantonness;
Some say thy grace is youth and gentle sport;
Both grace and faults are lov'd of more and less;
Thou mak'st faults graces that to thee resort.
As on the finger of a thronèd queen
The basest jewel will be well esteemed,
So are those errors that in thee are seen
To truths translated, and for true things deemed.
How many lambs might the stern wolf betray
If like a lamb he could his looks translate?
How many gazers mightst thou lead away
If thou wouldst use the strength of all thy state?
  But do not so; I love thee in such sort,
  As thou being mine, mine is thy good report.

This poem slyly and wryly repeats the couplet from Sonnet 36. (It was sixty poems ago. Is his hour up?) The words may be the same, but the sense has crucially shifted. In the earlier poem, he meant 'don't acknowledge me in public: you'll sully *your* good name – and since you and I are one, I've as much to lose'; but here he's saying something closer to 'but since we're one – please don't sully either your own or *my* name with your faults and errors'.

The plot of the sonnet is interesting. In the octave, it's the usual flattery-by-dodgy-logic. 'You're so beautiful, graceful and all-round goddamn amazing that even your *faults* are enhancements – think of the way a cheap ring on the finger of a queen is transformed by her regality.' ll.7–8 are a little less certain, though: *So are those errors that in thee are seen / To truths translated, and for true things deem'd.* This seems to leave open the possibility that there's been some *mistake* in this rather generous and lenient transformation of fault into truth. The sestet enlarges this suspicion, and compliments the YM rather ambiguously on his restraint in not using his wiles of concealment, his ability to bury and transform fault through his personal charm. For several sonnets now, we've had the growing sense of WS mentally preparing himself for the end; he's trying to *stop* identifying quite so strongly with this individual. As the Latin poet Cassidius famously remarked, *fractum factum difficilis est.*

l.3 *are lov'd of more and less*: are loved by the great and small, the high- and low-born.

97

How like a winter hath my absence been
From thee, the pleasure of the fleeting year!
What freezings have I felt, what dark days seen,
What old December's bareness everywhere!
And yet this time removed was summer's time,
The teeming autumn big with rich increase
Bearing the wanton burden of the prime,
Like widowed wombs after their lords' decease:
Yet this abundant issue seemed to me
But hope of orphans, and unfathered fruit;
For summer and his pleasures wait on thee,
And, thou away, the very birds are mute;
Or if they sing 'tis with so dull a cheer
That leaves look pale, dreading the winter's near.

Me and Coleridge like this one, but no one else, as far as I can make out. I wish that was paying me a compliment, but Coleridge had bloody awful taste. I should confess I enjoy reading this poem all wrong, or at the very least I overinterpret wildly. I'll explain later. The long and the short of it: 'My separation from you has been like a cold, hard winter; but isn't it ironic that it's taken place in summertime, a time full of *increase* and rich harvest.' (Autumn was then included in the period of summer. In Scotland we conflate them unconsciously, as a pyschological survival strategy.)

I love the way the miserable tone of the metaphor *Like widowed wombs after their lords' decease* – when he's supposed to be trying to keep the description relatively neutral – cheekily anticipates the even *more* miserable metaphor in *Yet this abundant issue seemed to me / But hope of orphans, and unfathered fruit . . .* He's got no logical right to that *Yet* whatsoever. It's an *and.* And why does summer's mellow fruitfulness leave him literally cold? *For summer and his pleasures wait on thee.* For all their *appearance* of being here, summer and his entourage are spiritually only to be found where the beloved is. *And thou away, the very birds are mute.* Or if they *do* sing, it's a song so forlorn that the very *leaves* turn pale in fear, thinking winter must be just round the corner again.

What's not to like? It's a great wee poem. And it's not too sad, really: summer will come again. Maybe in winter. OK, here's my questionable interpretation, and it comes from reading the poem in a biographical frame, for which the poem itself gives no real prompt. I always imagine WS has left for London for the season, and that's been responsible for his absence. (Remember London was a much smaller place than it is now, and you'd notice a lot more natural evidence of summer than just an eye-watering rise in BO on the tube.) I hear a strong sense of *increase* from his pen, not just nature; and *the wanton burden of the prime, / Like widowed wombs after their lords' decease* might be his feelings towards the successful gestation and delivery of brilliant work – whose inspiration was seeded earlier in the year through the YM's inspiration (where we might choose to read the springtime of *prime* as 'the period of greatest perfection' – SB). Yet it's as if those dramatic glories are *unfathered fruit*, because their muse is now so distant. It's just me, isn't it.

97 There's not much to talk about in the 90s, so for a laugh – as in *muahaha* – let's look closely at that *wanton burden,* and make some attempt to describe the weird brain-sensations such a phrase provokes. As well as making a phrase you might choose to read as 'frolicsome little bundle of joy', *wanton* is also an adjective clearly stolen from *prime*, where it more sensibly belongs; *prime* meaning, in its uppermost sense here, 'the season of spring'. WS uses the phrase 'wanton spring' elsewhere, and SB glosses *wanton* in its *prime*-connection as 'amorously sportive', which seems on the money. He also identifies the figure here as something called 'hypallage', a figure where the natural position of two words are switched, but with a resulting change in the sense; it's a kind of hyperbaton with added disaster, really. I'm a bit dubious about this, not least because hypallage has always been so wretchedly defined, and I think it muddies things.

Now: WS will frequently stick a modifier next to a noun which is not the one it appropriately qualifies. The word it *does* qualify is sometimes totally absent, sometimes it isn't. Either way, the adjective is now also working in a metaphorical sense, a point just as important as noting that it got there through a syntactic sleight-of-hand. This shenanigans is known as the 'transferred epithet'. There are two basic kinds of transferred epithet. One is a weak metaphor formed from the drifted modifier of a literal and text-present subject, as *prime* is here. Yes, you can correctly identify it as some form of hyperbaton, some kind of mangling of the natural word-order; however this is a grammatical description. The result is a metaphor, since two conceptual domains blend in a single unit, *wanton burden.* The origin and much of the sense of *wanton* is immediately given by *prime*, though crucially not *all* of the sense: *burden* will contribute its own valencies to that new sense too (hence our 'frolicsome bundle'; the brain's first attempt to process information is nearly always literal). 97

The qualifier *wanton* is not a central connotation of *prime*, however, so *prime* can't be derived from it – i.e. it has to be text-present if we're going to form it clearly in our minds. In other words, *wanton burden* alone wouldn't mean that much, and we need *prime* hanging around in the wings somewhere. However in the second kind of transferred epithet, the origin can be derived: *a tall-sailed cloud* invokes the text-absent 'ship', by naming an unequivocally close and direct relational term. (In this case, the synecdoche *sail*.) This gives us a strong metaphor, with the vehicle text-absent.

The first kind of transferred epithet, our *wanton burden*, feels more 'wrong' than the second – hypallage is a deviant old figure – not just because of our sense of grammatical glitch: it's because *prime* is also multitasking here. It's both part of the literal sense of the sentence, *and* it's the source of the vehicle-quality *wanton* in the metaphor *wanton burden.* (So the transferral means that the brain now has to process the sense as not just *the wanton burden of the prime*, but both *the burden of the wanton prime*, and – through the copula opened up by the process of transferral itself and its blurring of domains – *the burden in some sense is/is like the wanton prime*.) We're used to metaphor in normal speech – but we're not used to having things double as *both* literal substantives and non-literal vehicles. Somewhere in the temporal lobes a wee light goes on, and softly groans the word *zeugma*, another multitasking effect ('He took his car-keys and his leave') which is probably crawling round the same confused neural circuit. It's the syntactic equivalent of the Möbius strip.

(To be completist: *his waning face was like a moon* would be a

contrived example of a transferred epithet from a non-literal sub-
97 stantive, i.e. the vehicle of a metaphor; this move just about works. *His white face was like a moon* names an attribute native to both vehicle and tenor, and thus working in an unproblematic ground; so the epithet *white* is not transferred, exactly, but does have dual nationality. *A fast cloud*, on the other hand, where the writer's intention is to convey *a cloud like a fast ship*, would be an example of a failed transferred epithet from a text-absent vehicle, since, unlike *tall-sailed*, the relation *fast* is secondary to the concept of *ship*, already relatively native to *cloud*, and would require *ship* to be text-present for it to make anything like the desired sense, leaving us with another example of attribute-sharing. *A salted cloud*, in its strangeness, clearly *advertises* the fact that there's probably a text-absent vehicle indicated, and that we have a metaphor here; but the reader is left scrabbling much too hard to have *salted* serve as a ground between two concepts when (a) we have no way of linking the word directly to *cloud* except by the most unnatural means and (b) it does not have enough indexical strength to point firmly to the text-absent vehicle. I don't know what it is either. Let's say . . . 'peanut'.)

Anyway, for anyone still listening: many errors in metaphor-construction come from miscalculations over the relational strength between attributes and their subjects, the muddling of secondary connotations and native aspects, and their subsequent under- or over-representation in the text. Poets have to be especially keen students of collocation in the language and of connotation in the mind. They must be hypersensitive to the delicate consensus on which the most effective communication rests – and this is why it's hard to write good poetry in a language you did not learn as a child. More often than not, a poem's best effects

are created just where that consensus *is* most delicate: in that per-
centile of idiomatic speech a native speaker learns last. This is 97
also the reason it can never be 'faithfully' translated, since while a language's *words* might have rough synonyms in another tongue, its vast network of idiomatic collocation is wholly unique – and that's before we even get to the poet, whose work on that idiomatic part of the language often takes a subversive form.

98

From you have I been absent in the spring,
When proud pied April, dress'd in all his trim,
Hath put a spirit of youth in everything,
That heavy Saturn laughed and leapt with him.
Yet nor the lays of birds, nor the sweet smell
Of different flowers in odour and in hue
Could make me any summer's story tell,
Or from their proud lap pluck them where they grew;
Nor did I wonder at the lily's white,
Nor praise the deep vermilion in the rose;
They were but sweet, but figures of delight,
Drawn after you, you pattern of all those.
  Yet seemed it winter still, and you away,
  As with your shadow I with these did play.

I wish these Elizabethans would get their seasons sorted out. *This time removed was summer's time*, a moment ago; but he's *been absent in the spring* too, apparently. Whatever. There's much sexual symbolism just below the surface here, in *proud*, *lap*, *pluck*, *lily*, *rose*, but its contribution is more ambient than coherent. (I wish I could claim that *the lays of birds* was also an innuendo, but alas no.) Why Saturn is leaping in spring I have no idea, other than the fact he's been pressed into service because he's old and sluggish and heavy and grim. What a sluggish and heavy and grim old line. Anyway, none of this leaping and singing is infecting our man: those pretty flowers are sweet, yes, but mere *figures of delight, / Drawn after you* i.e. mere empty forms sketched in your likeness, not real things. (SB finds some connection between *your shadow* and *Drawn after you,* which seems far-fetched.) Anyhoo . . . it's just like winter. Again. This is pretty dull stuff.

The last line, however, strikes me as unconsciously revealing, although I'm desperate to be struck by something, and a half-brick would come as a relief right now. Perhaps he's as bored as we are with this sonnet, and in his inattention has committed something close to a Freudian. Think about it: l.14 means something like 'I played with these flowers as if I was playing with your image.' Firstly, it seems to contradictorily confess to a *little* more fun – albeit of a desultory kind – than he's claimed he's been having; secondly, *play* can have overtones of 'naughty frolics', especially if we allow it to be infected by the preceding innuendo, and read some sexual content into the flowers themselves. (*Lily* and *rose* were courtly conventions for ladies' complexions; but *rose* also meant what 'cherry' means now.) So he may be 'fessing up to a bit of sullen, spare-time heterosexual defloration (or local equivalent) here, as a displacement activity, seeing the YM in the faces of his unfortunate surrogates.

l.2 *proud pied* is often hyphenated, though I don't know why. As KDJ points out, 'April is personified, as is conventional, as a gaudily dressed young man'. So *proud* really just modifies the stock phrase *pied April.*

99

The forward violet thus did I chide:
'Sweet thief, whence didst thou steal thy sweet that smells,
If not from my love's breath? The purple pride
Which on thy soft cheek for complexion dwells
In my love's veins thou hast too grossly dyed.'
The lily I condemnèd for thy hand,
And buds of marjoram had stol'n thy hair;
The roses fearfully on thorns did stand,
One blushing shame, another white despair;
A third, nor red nor white, had stol'n of both,
And to his robb'ry had annexed thy breath;
But, for his theft, in pride of all his growth,
A vengeful canker eat him up to death.
  More flowers I noted, yet I none could see,
  But sweet, or colour it had stol'n from thee.

This seems to follow on so smoothly from the previous sonnet, some editors have ended the last with a colon in an effort to improve it. Given how dodgy it was, running it on to the menu from my local Chinese takeaway is going to improve it, frankly, but there's no colon: this is an odd little thing in its own right. Not a great sonnet, but a sweet one; WS sees his love in all the pwetty flowers. Tame stuff, but WS is expert in wringing something halfway original from the stalest tropes, which he treats not as something to be avoided, but a challenge to his ingenuity. Here he gives it a little piquancy by accusing the flowers of having borrowed or stolen from his love's beauty. WS himself stole almost the entire thing from Henry Constable's *Diana*, and you do wonder if the plagiarism may have proposed the theme.

The sonnet is also unique in that it isn't one, and has fifteen lines. The first 'quatrain' is five lines long. We can only keep guessing as to what WS intended, since none of those guesses have yet been positively confirmed in our close reading of the text. The most popular theory is that it's simply unfinished. Nah . . . it may not be great, but it's finished. Maybe the first line was from an early draft, which was accidentally printed. True: the sonnet could plausibly start on l.2, and we'd have quickly figured out it was a flower of some sort. But such sly, conceal-your-hand withholding of the subject, while epidemic these days, isn't very Elizabethan, and the other flowers in the poem are quickly named. Or did he just slap in the first line *after* he'd written the second, noticing that he hadn't named its subject? Or was he signalling the theft of the poem with a deliberate imperfection? (It's a common enough conceit, however.) Or is it a 'dating' sonnet? Is he just telling the readers of the future that the year is 1599? It might well just be that – WS is forever making paratextual play with the Sonnets' numbering. Or is it metatextual? Perhaps he's *enacting* the surplus, the excess of the flowers here – *More flowers I noted* – so many that I need another line? Or is he trying to alert us to the presence of something hidden or encrypted here – as someone held captive might write an apparently innocent letter with a deliberate mistake, obvious only to the recipient?

There are so many crazy theories, I might as well contribute one more. Perhaps he *didn't notice*? Dudley D. Watkins, who

drew half of the UK's comics either side of WW2, was famous for
99 his astonishing draughtsmanship. In Scotland he was best-known for drawing two cartoons in our Kailyard *Pravda*, the *Sunday Post*: *Oor Wullie* and *The Broons*. *The Broons* strips would usually end with a long panel featuring the whole extended family chasing a parrot round the room, hunting for Granpa's false teeth, sitting down to a vast dinner, or playing football in the glen. (I'm getting there.) In one memorable strip, the character of Horace the swot appeared in the same frame *twice*: Watkins worked from left to right, and had just forgotten he'd already drawn him. Great facility can commit great big errors of the kind a lesser, slower, more careful talent would be incapable of making. WS was also rewriting someone else's work, which would have speeded up the process even more than usual. So he may just have miscounted. Yes, it's unlikely, I know. My money would be on the '1599' explanation. Whatever it was, it was a bad idea, as its quindecadicity has become the most interesting thing about this poem.

ll.14–15 are very flat, and bad enough to be by Barnabe Barnes. *But* is the word that gets on KDJ's nerves; but it's that *more* in l.14 that does for me.

100

Where art thou, Muse, that thou forget'st so long,
To speak of that which gives thee all thy might?
Spend'st thou thy fury on some worthless song,
Dark'ning thy power to lend base subjects light?
Return forgetful Muse, and straight redeem,
In gentle numbers, time so idly spent;
Sing to the ear that doth thy lays esteem,
And gives thy pen both skill and argument.
Rise, resty Muse, my love's sweet face survey,
If Time have any wrinkle graven there;
If any, be a satire to decay,
And make time's spoils despisèd everywhere.
   Give my love fame, faster than Time wastes life,
   So thou prevent'st his scythe and crooked knife.

A rather fine sonnet, frequently missed. This is from the poems-about-being-unable-to-write-poems genre, an understandably popular one with the stuck, the dry and the all-washed-up. Don't the first two quatrains make a wonderful self-contained prayer for the blocked writer? I particularly like the novelty of hearing someone so plain annoyed, so *openly* accusatory of the muse, to whom we're conventionally very respectful and deferential. (On the other hand, I hear just a hint of WS's reflexive misogyny here. *Resty* is used of horses, and is one up from 'lazy cow'.) Of course the criticism is really self-directed,

or at least it's an elaborate way of deflecting self-criticism: why
100 *has* he been neglecting the YM? I mean no one bar Robert Graves and the certifiably insane *really* believes in the existence of the muse. (Although perhaps poets certainly do *during* the act of composition, which can be a condition close to madness anyway. See below.) Why did WS's inspiration fail? Was it that *wrinkle graven*, that horrific first symptom of the YM's fall from his angelic status?

The poem says: 'Where have you been, muse, and why have you been neglecting the very subject that gives you your power, namely my YM? Don't you know what side your bread's buttered?' ll.3–4 are often read as meaning that WS *himself* has been spending his fury on some lesser subjects – his plays, perhaps – but I'm not so sure. For one thing, the question would be a bit redundant, and purely rhetorical, given he'd presumably *know*. I think the implication here is that the muse is freelance, and has been off helping *other* poets tart up their worthless songs, their base subjects. I think we can also infer a fair gap of time between Sonnets 99 and 100 – not least because he's started to write well again.

The couplet is pretty hairy, though, and we've been here many times before: we might have read these lines eighty sonnets ago. Many of these couplets, obsessively repeating the same wishes, desires, injunctions – might be more generously read as something like the burden of a song, differently phrased each time; here, it's our old familiar assault on *Time*. Me, I skip it.

l.3 *furor poeticus*, as I mentioned earlier, was a common term for poetic inspiration (derived ultimately from Plato, in the *Ion*). Which I only bring up again as an excuse to quote this lovely speech from Socrates:

> *And as the Corybantian revellers when they dance are not in their right mind, so the lyric poets are not in their right mind when they are composing their beautiful strains: but when falling under the power of music and metre they are inspired and possessed; like Bacchic maidens who draw milk and honey from the rivers when they are under the influence of Dionysus; but not when they are in their right mind. And the soul of the lyric poet does the same, as they themselves say; for they tell us that they bring songs from honeyed fountains, culling them out of the gardens and dells of the Muses; they, like the bees, winging their way from flower to flower. And this is true. For the poet is a light and winged and holy thing, and there is no invention in him until he has been inspired and is out of his senses, and the mind is no longer in him: when he has not attained to this state, he is powerless and is unable to utter his oracles.* (Plato, *Ion*, Jowett's translation)

We forget this at our peril – especially when we make the mistake of reading WS as anything *like* a reliable narrator.

l.9 *resty*: sluggish, indolent. Despite my queasiness over its use here, it's a great word we should reintroduce, as we have no good adjective from 'rest' any more. (Though it would probably lead to even more confusion. I won't out the boss who once wished us all 'a merry Christmas and a restive New Year'.)

l.11 *If any* elides the 'and' – i.e. 'and if you find any wrinkles'...

l.13 is an awful line, and scans like a drunken clog-dance. There's no way round this. One option is to insert a comma after *fame*, which mitigates the reversal of the metre at *faster* (inversions are easier for the voice to accommodate at the start of a

phrase), but it slows the line down – i.e. it enacts a sense at odds
100 with the one conveyed. So it's not very satisfactory, nor indeed very grammatical, but I've done it anyway. Note, too, that any time a poem is couched in the imperative mood, you're going to have a whole bunch of overstressed vowels: the musical register of the poem is going to be pitched up a third or so from normal delivery.

101

O truant Muse what shall be thy amends
For thy neglect of truth in beauty dyed?
Both truth and beauty on my love depends;
So dost thou too, and therein dignified.
Make answer, Muse: wilt thou not haply say,
'Truth needs no colour, with his colour fixed,
Beauty no pencil, beauty's truth to lay,
But best is best, if never intermixed'?
Because he needs no praise, wilt thou be dumb?
Excuse not silence so, for't lies in thee
To make him much outlive a gilded tomb
And to be praised of ages yet to be.
  Then do thy office, Muse: I teach thee how
  To make him seem, long hence, as he shows now.

High joshing with the muse again – I mean now he's just getting *fresh* – but it's all done quite beautifully, and with no little grace. 'Where on earth *are* you, muse? ['Right here, as you well know,' she's winking back, of course.] But maybe if you *were* here you'd just say – "Look, Will: what's to add to perfection?" So are you just going to be *dumb,* since my beloved *needs no praise*?' ['Seems you've answered your own question.'] And then WS finds a better reason for the Muse to get off her resty backside: 'Look, you can't excuse your silence that way – because something *else* lies in your power, something greater: you can

help me make a poem that *so* honours him, he'll outlive the tomb
101 [the *gilded tomb* we may also read as both a metaphor and metonymy for "the works of men" that time will sweep away] and be praised by *ages yet to be.* Then do your job, Muse: I'll teach you how to make him look in the far future just as he does now.'

'I teach *thee how*'? Whoah boy. Maybe WS shouldn't be getting *quite* so familiar. On the other hand, he may now be aware that these poems are plainly good, and they've allegedly been written without her divine assistance – so maybe he's within his rights to feel a bit pleased with himself. (The Q has a comma after the *how*, which complicates the interpretation, but doesn't make it less hubristic.) At the end of the day I think it's just old-fashioned, flirtatious *cheek* he's setting up here. This poem isn't doing much other than having some fun; but more broadly, I suspect it's also serving to bury WS's earlier accusations against the YM, and restore him to his former sweetness and light. Compare this pretty thing with some of the toxic Dark Lady junk toward the end of the sequence, and it's hard to believe it's the same poet.

102

My love is strengthened, though more weak in seeming;
I love not less, though less the show appear.
That love is merchandized, whose rich esteeming
The owner's tongue doth publish everywhere.
Our love was new, and then but in the spring,
When I was wont to greet it with my lays
As Philomel in summer's front doth sing,
And stops her pipe in growth of riper days.
Not that the summer is less pleasant now
Than when her mournful hymns did hush the night;
But that wild music burthens every bough,
And sweets grown common lose their dear delight.
  Therefore, like her, I sometime hold my tongue,
  Because I would not dull you with my song.

T*hat love is merchandized, whose rich esteeming / The owner's tongue doth publish everywhere.* Oh yes – overpublication is a terrible thing in a poet, and only arouses suspicion. It looks like it's coming way too easily, meaning either it's not costing you enough, or you're insincere, or you're probably repeating yourself. (And it's all too easy to do: readers like to read their poetry as if it were something rare and precious. A poet can saturate his or her market just by publishing every three years.) WS's excuses for his own recent silence imply a deeper criticism of his peers; that *rich esteeming* is really a celebration not of love, but of their

102 own voices. Broadcast it too widely and too frequently, and your 'love' is a mere commodity.

WS's excuse for his inattentiveness rests, rather conveniently, on one of his perennial obsessions. Yep – the fracture between appearance and reality. '*My* love might be less widely broadcast, but that just hides its depth.' Do you buy this? The reality is more likely to be that his love has moved from its early, lyric, oxytocin-sluiced, walking-on-air phase into something more prosaic, inspiration-thin and humdrum.

However he symbolises his idea beautifully in the metaphor of the nightingale, who sings in early summer, but stops *not* because there's anything wrong with the weather – on the contrary; but now that every bloody songbird who can hold half a tune is warbling the YM's praises, the nightingale doesn't *want* her song drowned and cheapened by the rabble. She would rather button it, than be one voice amongst many. The last two lines say 'like her, I hold my tongue: because I don't want to bore you [one early sense of *dull*], or take the shine off you with my song.' You will have noticed that those lines are utterly redundant. Yet again, I'd rather read this with finger over the couplet, as it does nothing more than explain and explain away WS's lovely metaphor. It's a 12-liner. One has the sense that the Elizabethan poets didn't really trust their readers yet.

l.8 *And stops her pipe in growth of riper days* – most folk emend the Q's *his* to *her*, since the nightingale is here in her mythic female form, Philomela. Although the Elizabethans had no 'its', i.e. there's a good argument for leaving it as *his* – WS uses 'her' as an 'its' substitute elsewhere. But to change it makes very little difference to the music, and removes a contemporary

glitch in the sense, so I'll follow suit. (To be honest, I think he
screwed up, and had conflated himself with the nightingale so 102
thoroughly, he momentarily muddled the genders.)

103

Alack, what poverty my Muse brings forth,
That having such a scope to show her pride,
The argument all bare is of more worth
Than when it hath my added praise beside.
O blame me not, if I no more can write!
Look in your glass, and there appears a face
That overgoes my blunt invention quite,
Dulling my lines, and doing me disgrace.
Were it not sinful then, striving to mend,
To mar the subject that before was well?
For to no other pass my verses tend
Than of your graces and your gifts to tell;
And more, much more, than in my verse can sit,
Your own glass shows you when you look in it.

OK, the joke's wearing thin, now. Either write a sonnet or shut up, but please – no more sonnets about not being able to, or having nothing much to say, because soon you'll be believed. *Damn* soon, on the strength of this: it's bad enough to meet the first line without raising the slightest objection. We can see what the governing figure of these last few Sonnets has been, though – it's 'aporia', i.e. 'talking about the inability to talk about' or 'feigned doubt about how to proceed'. (Don't confuse it – if you're the sort of person given to this sort of confusion – with *aporia* in the philosophical sense, or Derrida's 'wayless' impasse.) There's probably some really cool Lacanian stuff about parallax and observation and absence and ego we could do with the triangle of WS, the YM and the YM's mirrored image here, but it's midnight, and I'm not convinced this poem is worth it. Although . . . I'd make one observation: women tend to get their social bearings from two co-ordinates, and men from one. A woman will walk into a room and see two people in conversation and ask 'what is she/he to him/her', and triangulate her own position from the answer; whereas a guy will roll in on his knuckles and ask 'what is she/he to *me*'. So the triad here, created via the subterfuge of doubling the Other in the glass, may be symptomatic of a more feminised and socially sensitive turn of mind than we would normally expect from a bloke. The Sonnets are haunted not just by the question 'what are you to me', but 'what are you to *you*, and where do I fit in to this'. Almost no men of my acquaintance are sufficiently interested in other people to get as far as this thought, and indeed rarely get as far as 'what am I to *me*'. I know I don't. The poem still sucks.

l.1 *Alack* is probably a pun on 'a lack'.

l.3 *The argument* is either just 'a bare summary', or a metonym for something like 'subject matter', i.e. the YM.

l.4 *beside*: as well.

l.7 *over-goes*: goes beyond, transcends.

ll.9–10 essentially mean 'if I added anything I'll only make it worse'.

l.11 *pass*: event.

❧

104

To me, fair friend, you never can be old;
For as you were when first your eye I eyed,
Such seems your beauty still. Three winters cold
Have from the forests shook three summers' pride;
Three beauteous springs to yellow autumn turned
In process of the seasons have I seen;
Three April perfumes in three hot Junes burned,
Since first I saw you fresh, which yet are green.
Ah, yet doth beauty like a dial-hand,
Steal from his figure, and no pace perceived;
So your sweet hue, which methinks still doth stand,
Hath motion, and mine eye may be deceived;
  For fear of which, hear this, thou age unbred:
  Ere you were born was beauty's summer dead.

Here's a good one. The octave doesn't appear to say much, really: 'you still look as young as the day I met you three years ago' is about it. It's light and simple enough for song-lyric, if you can forgive that unfortunate *eye I eyed*, which might put you in mind of Carmen Miranda. SB identifies pun, polyptoton and epizeuxis in this phrase, which is more-or-less accurate, but showing off. Elsewhere his description of the effect as a 'self-conscious rhetorical gimcrack' seems more on the money. HV points out that Olivier, reading the poem to Katherine Hepburn in *Love Among the Ruins* reveals them as 'the stammering of a lovestruck boy' – which, while not ideal, is still a better look than fruit on your head. Read the words with a ghost-comma after *eye*, if you want to avoid getting a laugh.

The poem is much cleverer than it first appears, though. Look how the three time-spans are constructed to *feel* successively shorter: winter–summer; spring–autumn; April–June (because of their weaker contrast, the second item feels briefer than the first), so we have a sense of beauty's erosion coming ever closer, especially when we've read the poem more than once, and we're up to speed with its theme. The pace quickens horribly, emphasised by the careering and brutal *unbred/born/dead* woven through the couplet.

The sestet is utterly gorgeous. *Ah, yet doth beauty like a dial-hand, / Steal from his figure, and no pace perceived; / So your sweet hue, which methinks still doth stand, / Hath motion, and mine eye may be deceived; / For fear of which, hear this, thou age unbred: / Ere you were born was beauty's summer dead.* I just wanted to say it again. To paraphrase miserably: 'Ah! But beauty steals away from its outward appearance continually, like a clock-hand. In the same way, perhaps your beauty – which seems to me to stand still – is changing too, and my eyes are deceived. In case that's true – hear this, you unborn generations: the greatest example of beauty was already dead before you were born.' Oh, I hear it, Will, sitting here in Starbucks in Dundee in 2010, a member of that *age unbred*; I believe you, and I feel appropriately bereft.

It's hard to know how seriously one can take this as a 'dating sonnet', though some have tried. WS seems very clear on those *three winters*, but the idea of three years as an idealised love-span was a well-established poetic convention. Ronsard and Daniels employed the three-year rule, though Daniels later upped *Delia*

104 to a more plausible five years in the reprint; KDJ reminds us that Tennyson imposes the same three-year timeline on (the equally homoerotic, in its own way) *In Memoriam*, though we know it took him seventeen years to write it.

JK helpfully points out that Horace may have set the precedent in *Epodes* XI, 5–6: *hic tertius December ex quo destiti / Inachia furere, silvis honorem decutit*: 'The third December, since I ceased to lust after Inachia, is now shaking the glory from the forests.' (JK seems to have borrowed the observation from SB, who credits Leishman, who credits Wilkinson, who might credit his mum, for all I know.)

Others have attempted more ambitious sums, multiplying all the threes, taking away the number you first thought of, etc.; but without a good start-date, forget it. For my money . . . those three years probably *are* accurate. I get the impression that WS wasn't thrall to those stylised conventions anyway. Besides, it's not as if we sense the progress of those three years anywhere else in the sequence. I reckon he'd merely reflected on the fact that – goodness me – it'd been three years since he succumbed, and its coincidence with the triennial topos was just a happy one. 'Heavens . . . Time flies. There's a poem in that.' I think there's at least half a chance it's a decade further on from the procreation sonnets, though, and addressed to a second YM – WS having moved on from HW to WH, from Henry to the younger William. How's *that* for idle speculation.

105

Let not my love be called idolatry,
Nor my beloved as an idol show,
Since all alike my songs and praises be,
To one, of one, still such, and ever so.
Kind is my love today, tomorrow kind,
Still constant in a wondrous excellence;
Therefore my verse, to constancy confined,
One thing expressing, leaves out difference.
Fair, kind and true, is all my argument,
Fair, kind and true, varying to other words;
And in this change is my invention spent,
Three themes in one, which wondrous scope affords.
  Fair, kind, and true have often lived alone,
  Which three, till now, never kept seat in one.

There's not much in this, but then WS didn't intend there to be. Sensible criticism should surely consist in discovering a poem's own ambitions, and measuring its success or failure against *them*, not those of the poem you'd prefer to be reading. (Not that 'unambitious' isn't a fair criticism to hurl at a body of work; just not at an individual poem. It might not want to be ambitious. Some folk complain when a poet turns in a piece of light verse, but they forget that it also serves to make the heavy verse look even heavier.) As lame as many commentators find this sonnet, it does what it says on the tin, and with great wit. It's

105 repetitive, sure – but in many ways it's a poem *about* repetition; or rather it's about the apparently meagre subject matter of his poetry, and the way that, in spite of its invitation to say the same thing again and again, he rings the changes, *varying to other words*.

(The question is where you draw the line between enacting the subject in the poem's form, and invoking your subject by inducing its effects. For example: it may be OK for a poem about repetition to be repetitive; but is it right for a poem about boredom to be boring? The distressing subtlety here is that effects produced in the reader purely through the formal – as opposed to the contentual – elements of the text are really metatextual, and perilously close to those postmodern and reflexive techniques that make the reader aware of the text-as-text. The reader then has to break the spell of the poem so they can step outside, and gain the distance needed to acknowledge the relationship between the effect so produced, and the poem's sense – because they're two different things. 'Aha! You're frustrating me because this is a poem *about* frustration. Cool! I think.' It's pretty much the same argument we see when poets say 'I broke the line in an awkward place to enact the awkwardness I was describing'. Mostly, the reader just goes '*that* was awkward'. The trouble is that after noting your genius, they then have to get back into the poem again, which can be as hard finding your way back into an enjoyable dream after the dog has woken you up. Personally, I think such an approach trivialises its subject. It sheds no light. Better to write a *moving* poem about frustration, as a frustrating poem about frustration would only 'honour its subject' in the most facile and meaningless way – and won't be read twice. No one thinks 'I'm in the mood to read something *frustrating* this evening.' This makes it a self-conscious and not an innocent, emotionally engaged exercise.

Sure, it can be fun; but it's very mild, secondary kind of fun at the expense of a whole lot *more* fun.)

Getting back to the poem, the charge of idolatry that detains him might seem poorly refuted. He *clearly* idolises the YM. But 'idolatry' is used in a much more specific sense here. SB sheds light on WS's use of 'idolatry', and then subtracts it again. While I was still able to follow him, I learned that 'idolatry' – despite its traditional connection with polytheism – was used in Shakespeare's England as an accusation hurled at Catholics for their worship of saints, of Mary, and of relics, in addition to the Christian god. So we might infer that WS had been charged with treating the YM 'like a saint' (perhaps with a buried accusation of closet leftfootery) – only to deliver the even more scandalous refutation '*A saint*? Never! I'm no idolater. On the contrary, my YM is the *one true god.*' Oh, I'd like to think so.

He claims the YM is godlike through invoking a trinity of virtues: beauty, kindness and faithfulness. Individually, these might not be that much to write home about, but a unique condition obtains: never before have those three qualities resided in one individual. This trinitarian riff is, of course, supposed to put you in mind of our beardy imaginary friend: the poem is completely blasphemous. I love this guy. (It also sends me back to the dedication page, with the encrypted nods I hear towards an unholy Trinity.) As George Wyndham first pointed out, these are 'nothing else than the three primal categories of philosophy – the Good, the Beautiful and the True' – giving us, in other words, a bold Neoplatonic programme to set against the Christian, as well as a merely blasphemous one. Now if you want *really* pointless repetition, you may wish to peruse the Athanasian Creed, which was the kind of thing WS was seeking to echo here. Here's an excerpt from the considerably longer whole:

105 *. . . As also there are not three uncreated; nor three infinites, but one uncreated; and one infinite. So likewise the Father is Almighty; the Son Almighty; and the Holy Ghost Almighty. And yet they are not three Almighties; but one Almighty. So the Father is God; the Son is God; and the Holy Ghost is God. And yet they are not three Gods; but one God. So likewise the Father is Lord; the Son Lord; and the Holy Ghost Lord. And yet not three Lords; but one Lord. . . . There are three Gods, or three Lords. The Father is made of none; neither created, nor begotten. The Son is of the Father alone; not made, nor created; but begotten. The Holy Ghost is of the Father and of the Son; neither made, nor created, nor begotten; but proceeding. So there is one Father, not three Fathers; one Son, not three Sons; one Holy Ghost, not three Holy Ghosts. And in this Trinity none is before, or after another; none is greater, or less than another. But the whole three Persons are coeternal, and coequal . . .*

Argh! Make it stop . . .

ll.3–4 *Since all alike my songs and praises be / To one, of one, still such, and ever so* – certainly seems to torpedo my half-baked 'Two Young Men' theory, but when did you ever trust a poet.

❧

106

When in the chronicle of wasted time
I see descriptions of the fairest wights,
And beauty making beautiful old rhyme,
In praise of ladies dead, and lovely knights,
Then, in the blazon of sweet beauty's best,
Of hand, of foot, of lip, of eye, of brow,
I see their antique pen would have expressed
Even such a beauty as you master now:
So all their praises are but prophecies
Of this our time, all you prefiguring;
And for they looked but with divining eyes
They had not skill enough your worth to sing;
    For we, which now behold these present days
    Have eyes to wonder, but lack tongues to praise.

Very sweet; tight as a nut, this one. It's a very simple and affecting idea: 'All those descriptions of beauty I come across in old books – if the authors hadn't had the gift of prophecy, they would have failed . . . because it was *you* they were seeing. Just as well, really – because those of us who have to deal with your beauty in the living present are overwhelmed by it, and we lack the tongues to praise it.' Yes, it's another aporial 'I can't write a poem – so here's a poem about it' poem. It's so lightly lyric in its music and unknotted syntax it *looks* more like a tetrameter than the pentameter it is, and the language is so chirpy and happy you

106 could mistake the whole thing for Herrick, from the corner of your eye.

Now if it'd been *my* sonnet . . . I'd have had the present beholders tongue-tied or dumbstruck by the radiance of the YM; *lack the tongues to praise* is open to a number of interpretations (even though I reckon 'dumbstruck by radiance' is the right one; it requires reading *lack tongues* as 'lack such tongues as would be able to adequately describe your beauty', not just 'lack skilful tongues'). It's also pretty blasphemous, in its quiet way. Prophets proclaim the coming of the Saviour, not the divine incarnation of WS's boyfriend.

l.1 *wasted* is an odd word here – I think the sense is more 'time consumed' than 'pointlessly spent'.

l.2 *wights* means 'persons', an appropriately archaic word. As is the heraldic term 'blazon', but here it's used in the more familiar sense of 'a poetic litany of good attributes'.

l.12 there's some controversy over the word *skill*, emended from the dubious 'still' in the Q. There's an argument for 'still' being correct, if you read it as 'as yet', but it's a weak one. A better suggestion (T. G. Tucker's) is that it could be the late medieval spelling of 'style', which works perfectly well. And picks up on the 'stylus' of the pen in l.7. I like 'style'. Hell, I'll change it. Hang on – in Sonnet 32, WS spells style 'stile'. I know the Elizabethans weren't big on consistency, but I'd better change it back. Damn.

l.13 *For we, which*: since we who.

107

Not mine own fears, nor the prophetic soul
Of the wide world, dreaming on things to come,
Can yet the lease of my true love control,
Supposed as forfeit to a confined doom.
The mortal moon hath her eclipse endured,
And the sad augurs mock their own presage;
Uncertainties now crown themselves assured,
And peace proclaims olives of endless age.
Now with the drops of this most balmy time
My love looks fresh, and death to me subscribes,
Since 'pite of him I'll live in this poor rhyme,
While he insults o'er dull and speechless tribes;
    And thou in this shalt find thy monument,
    When tyrants' crests and tombs of brass are spent.

One of the most famously bewildering or bewilderingly famous of the sonnets; its obscurity has given it undeserved prominence. It's certainly generated a lot of commentary – among contemporary critics, SB spends six pages on it, and JK a whopping eight, most of it much more entertaining than the poem itself, which is a pretty average effort. ll.5–6 are fine, resonant lines, I guess, but in sound alone. The main interest lies in the business of trying to work out the literal events to which the poem clearly refers, but our distance from them means the game has become pretty difficult. However, there's something to be won: if

107 we *could* nail this poem to some historical event, it would allow us to date the sonnets rather accurately, or at least this one; so you can understand the excitement.

Amazingly, none of this mad speculation seems to concern HV *whatsoever*; either she's unaware of the controversy or (more likely) has no interest in it. She seems happy to have it make only a shadowy metaphorical sense that remains wholly unresolved. I have some admiration for this approach – if less for her identification of a score of buried puns and correspondences, all of which would have come as a complete surprise to the author – but I think we're then left with no poem at all, not even a dull one. However I think we can rule out one theory, which is that the poem *isn't* encoded, and *doesn't* allude to topical events. The hook is too heavily baited, and the poem is too prophetic in tone, too full of Nostradamus-like specific-yet-deeply-obscure detail. The principal signifier here *is*, in fact, the poem's gleefully displayed obscurity: WS wants us to *know* there's something being riddled.

So what does it all mean? Well, I do think it's possible to apply your man's razor here, and if we opt for the theories that match most closely the more-or-less literal interpretation of the lines which we're always *entitled* to make, at least we've kept our dignity, even if we end up wide of the mark. Of the available hypotheses, far and away the most sensible seems to be that the moon refers to that pale-faced celestial, Elizabeth I. Not only was it common to flatter Elizabeth with comparisons to Diana, virgin goddess of the hunt and the *moon*, she's *mortal* and *eclipsed*; this sounds a lot like 'dead' and 'unthroned' to me. (I also hear a little satisfaction in that *mortal.* WS's relative on his mother's side, Edward Arden, had been tortured and put to death by Elizabeth, accused of a non-existent Papist assassination plot. I doubt he forgot.) If we accept this as a reference to her death, we can date the poem at 1603 – which conveniently corroborates the theory that the YM was Henry Wriothesley: the gorgeous Earl was indeed *confined* in the Tower that year, after a public scrap with Lord Grey of Wilton (*Supposed as forfeit to a confined doom* sounds like a desperate lover's forgivable exaggeration). He was swiftly released on James's succession to the throne. With *incertainties now crown themselves assured* we can now make an almost literal inference: James's accession went off in an unusually peaceful and straightforward fashion – this, despite the predictions of doom and gloom from those inept *augurs*, now laughing at their own lousy forecasts. Civil war had been a distinct possibility, as Elizabeth had no heir, and there were umpteen contenders for the throne; however James's succession went remarkably smoothly. As for *peace proclaims olives of endless age* – James did exactly that, avoiding not only civil war but finally making peace with Spain. This wasn't until 1604, though, and it seems likely (to me at least) that this poem was probably written more in joy at his friend's release than anything else. I dunno. I'll put a tenner on spring 1603, since Southampton was released pretty swiftly after the coronation.

Finally, and most compellingly, *Now with the drops of this most balmy time* is a very lightly encoded line, and definitely seems to refer to a coronation. Balm was dribbled in the ceremony, and WS makes mention of this elsewhere. (This, from *2 Henry IV*, IV. v: *Then get thee gone, and dig my grave thyself, / And bid the merry bells ring to thine ear / That thou art crowned, not that I am dead. / Let all the tears that should bedew my hearse / Be drops of balm to sanctify thy head . . .*)

107 *Death to me subscribes* I hear as joyous, all-powerful, it's-all-gone-to-my-head-and-I'm-superhuman stuff: nothing could have delighted him more than his lover's release. *I'll live in this poor rhyme . . .* '*I'll* live on'? We're used to seeing only the *YM* gain his immortality through WS's verse. It seems a bit harsh on the poor *dull and speechless tribes*, however: WS is a lousy winner. We might generously say that *speechless tribes* had been proposed by the difficult rhyme-word 'subscribes', but when the first rhyming line shows a syntactic inversion (hyperbaton) and the second doesn't, the chances are the second was written first. Either way, the rhyme has guided him into hyperbole.

And then, inevitably, we get the usual cut-and-paste couplet of . . . and you shall survive in this verse, when all the other monumental works of man have blah, blah, etc.

You can understand a political dissident writing in such a cryptic manner, but all's right with the world – so why didn't WS just write something more explicit? Why all the secrecy, when there's no apparent risk? This might not have been the case ten years earlier, with both sides of WS's part-Catholic family under the scrutiny of the Elizabethan police state, but if this is 1603, all's looking up. Maybe it's force of habit. There's nothing like watching one of your own in-laws hanged, drawn and quartered to propose a lifetime of excessive caution. But I think the answer is simply that it would have been tonally at odds with the rest of the sonnets, in two ways: firstly, an explicit discussion of these events would have detracted too much from the Sonnets' theme, his love for the YM; couching it all in such vague, heraldic, allegorised terms allows the subject of his love to be seamlessly woven in. Secondly, to point out the deeply obvious – topical references would have nailed these poems to a date. All along, WS's project has been to create something timeless, something everlasting, something *always* contemporary; so he's bound to be worried about anything that, in both senses, 'dates' the work.

Most Elizabethan poetry defaults to the same rather self-conscious *sub specie aeternitatis* POV inherited from the classical model. It was wee a bit limiting, surely; to fix something in time needn't age it. On the contrary, the colour and flavour of contemporary detail can be trapped in the amber of the poem, and rendered precious for ever. (*. . . and the moon rattles the lost stones / among the rocks and the strict bones / of the drowned, and I put out the light / On Mailer's* Armies of the Night. – Derek Mahon, 'Beyond Howth Head'.)

Either way, we find any emotionally engaged reading of the poem completely bulldozed by the amount of intrigue it has generated, so in one sense we might account the poem a failure; but it's too interesting, in just about every other sense.

108

What's in the brain that ink may character
Which hath not figured to thee my true spirit?
What's new to speak, what new to register,
That may express my love, or thy dear merit?
Nothing, sweet boy; but yet, like prayers divine,
I must each day say o'er the very same;
Counting no old thing old; thou mine, I thine,
Even as when first I hallowed thy fair name.
So that eternal love, in love's fresh case,
Weighs not the dust and injury of age,
Nor gives to necessary wrinkles place
But makes antiquity for aye his page,
  Finding the first conceit of love there bred,
  Where time and outward form would show it dead.

This is a moving sonnet, wonderfully knackered in tone, but rousing itself in the sestet to declare his love, a love too deep to be diminished by mere changes in the beloved's outward form. It's also a convincingly sincere defence of all that repetition in the Sonnets I've been moaning about, too, and makes me inclined to forgive him everything. The octave says 'What is there to say of my love, or of your virtue, that I haven't said already? Nothing. But like a prayer, I'll keep saying those worn-out things every day. We're as bound to each other now as that day when *first I hallowed thy fair name.*' (Again, note the blasphemous reference to the Lord's Prayer.)

I love that *So that eternal love in love's fresh case*; *case* as in situation, as in 'I got a bad case of loving you' (sort of) – and *case* as in 'casing', suggesting that the precious essence of eternal love is protected by a self-renewing outer shell. 'Eternal love doesn't pay attention to the outward signs of ageing, but makes age itself, time itself, for ever his young servant; and finds, *Where time and outward form would show it dead*, love's first conception.' Although *eternal love . . . Finding the first conceit of love* is a bit of a stretch, subject and predicate are just about widely separated enough for us to wing it.

Sidney's *Astrophel and Stella*, which had been kicking around since the early 1580s, consists of 108 sonnets – a number imitated by a number of other sonneteers; though its significance is obscure, so whether they did this out of admiration or something more numerologically significant is hard to say. Many commentators see WS's acknowledgement of having reached the big 1–0–8 in this poem, using its implied closure to look back over his work so far, and take stock. It's plausible, I suppose – but you could also contrive such an argument for 109, or indeed a dozen other sonnets. However KDJ argues brilliantly for 108 also being a significant organising number in Shakespeare's own sequence. I'm neither convinced nor unconvinced, but it's very interesting: the first section is 1–17, where WS tells the YM to go forth and multiply, until he's blue in the face and possibly elsewhere; then we have the central series of 108 sonnets, from 18 (where WS first explicitly declares his love) to 125; then we have our only bit of creative accountancy – sonnet 126, the mysterious twelve-liner, which is partly (I think) a postmodern lark, so can be legitimately discounted; then finally, the closing sequence of the 28 Dark

108 Lady sonnets, 127–54. KDJ plausibly suggests that 28 might reflect the lunar month and menstrual cycle; this would be no surprise, in a sequence so disturbingly obsessed with the uncleanliness of women's bodies. Actually I *do* find all that pretty convincing.

l.2 *true* in the senses both of 'loyal' and 'real'.

l.3 the Q has *now to register*, but it's probably *new*.

l.8 I've said before, HV's theory of 'key words' repeated deliberately in each quatrain is a dud. In this poem, she hears the word 'love'. So do I, but not that way. As well as occurring twice in the second quatrain, it's also buried in 'hallowed', apparently: *hal-lowe-d*. No it isn't. 'Hallowed' is already a hard-won effect, brilliantly picking up on the metaphor of WS's poetic repetitions as a form of prayer, and alluding to the most famous prayer of all (as well as quietly elevating the YM, again, to the status of godhead). It's deeply unlikely that it's also ticking the 'key word' box here. It's quite beyond the ability of any human mind to construct such a three-dimensional felicity, and honour so many compositional rules simultaneously – even this mind. WS has more important games to play.

l.11 *necessary*: HV reminds us of the Renaissance meaning of necessary as 'fated'.

l.12 JK thinks *antiquity* adheres to the beloved, but I'm not so sure. I think WS is talking about love in general, that lovely intercessor that makes both *thou mine* and *I thine*, and that *antiquity* is equally general, almost a synonym for 'age' or 'time'. *Page* as in page-boy, but also the blank page of the poet, where first he set pen to paper in praise of love, when his tropes were fresh and his conceits unhoary. HV thinks it's *just* page as in 'paper', and cites the recent 'chronicle of wasted time' poem, Sonnet 106, with its talk both of poetry and a *literal* antiquity. I think WS certainly expects the proximity of that poem to draw out just this sense – but apart from the paradox being irresistibly sweet, the pun on *page* was already popular, following Thomas Nashe's deployment of it in his picaresque *The Unfortunate Traveller*. Back then, puns held a lot more entertainment value than they do now; they had to. A good new pun did the rounds like a viral video.

109

O never say that I was false of heart,
Though absence seemed my flame to qualify;
As easy might I from my self depart
As from my soul which in thy breast doth lie:
That is my home of love; if I have ranged,
Like him that travels I return again,
Just to the time, not with the time exchanged,
So that myself bring water for my stain.
Never believe, though in my nature reigned
All frailties that besiege all kinds of blood,
That it could so preposterously be stained,
To leave for nothing all thy sum of good:
    For nothing this wide universe I call,
    Save thou, my rose; in it thou art my all.

A great little prepared excuse, this one, even if its logic bears little inspection and its moral integrity even less. As a rhetorical exercise it's effective, though, and I suppose it might have some contemporary application. It depends entirely on your lover's susceptibility to this sort of stuff, and the strength of their bullshit detector. If there's an ounce of juice in the battery, though, it'll go off like a fleet of ambulances. Maybe the best approach with this sonnet is just to translate it from bullshit into English:

109

O never say that I was false of heart,

– Please don't call me a cheating piece of garbage

Though absence seemed my flame to qualify;

– just because my total avoidance of you recently may somehow have given you the idea that I'm not as nuts about you as I used to be

As easy might I from my self depart

– Listen: I'd find it as easy to divorce myself

As from my soul which in thy breast doth lie:

– as I would split up from my soul – no, I know that sounds like a tautology, but if you bear in mind that my soul lives in *you* . . . whaddya mean 'get it out of me now'

That is my home of love; if I have ranged,
Like him that travels, I return again,

– Anyway what I was saying was – *you* are my home, even if your impression is that, as you say, I treat you more like a twenty-buck motel, and if I *have* been shagging around lately, well: like him that travels – like *me* that travels, I guess, I dunno why I said that – I'll always return

Just to the time, not with the time exchanged,

– right bang on time, the same goddamn handsome sexy bastard I was when I left

So that myself bring water for my stain.

109

– so you see: me coming back makes up for the crime of me going away! Don't you think? Please don't throw that

Never believe, though in my nature reigned
All frailties that besiege all kinds of blood,

– Look: don't think for a second – even though my being suffers from the same onslaught of temptation as would every other handsome sexy bastard in the same position

That it could so preposterously be stained,

– that my being could be so absurdly morally corrupt

To leave for nothing all thy sum of good:

– as to leave you, my prince, for one of those cheap tarts or cheaper sailors

For nothing this wide universe I call,

– For I call this wide universe 'nothing' – and no, I 'couldn't just say that, then' – *you* try making a full rhyme in this half-arsed Friesian excuse for a language without recourse to hyperbaton

Save thou, my rose; in it thou art my all.

– except for you, my common appellation of affection: you are everything. Everything is you. I don't know. The Stylistics. OK I'll get my coat.

There we go: I think we're up to speed.

110

Alas, 'tis true, I have gone here and there,
And made my self a motley to the view,
Gored mine own thoughts, sold cheap what is most dear,
Made old offences of affections new.
Most true it is that I have looked on truth
Askance and strangely; but by all above,
These blenches gave my heart another youth,
And worse essays proved thee my best of love.
Now all is done, have what shall have no end;
Mine appetite I never more will grind
On newer proof, to try an older friend,
A god in love, to whom I am confined:
  Then give me welcome, next my heaven the best,
  Even to thy pure and most most loving breast.

Much the same story as Sonnet 109, but with a sense of the author holding up his hands in more sincere apology. And he seems a little more honest with himself, too. 'It's true – I've gone here and there, and made myself look a fool.' (*motley* was worn by court fools, of course.)

In l.3, *Gored* is probably intended as a pun on *gore* as in 'defiled with filth or blood' and 'divided into wedges of cloth' (OED defines the noun: 'any wedge-shaped or triangular piece of cloth forming part of a garment'), the latter running with the idea of *motley*. l.4 means 'used new friends to commits my old sins'.

110 However with this sudden lurch into plain speaking he's only managed to alight on a defence even more rebarbative than ever, and this passage rivals Burns for self-absorbed insensitivity: *Most true it is that I have looked on truth / Askance and strangely; but by all above, / These blenches gave my heart another youth, / And worse essays proved thee my best of love.* 'Yes, I've looked on this fidelity stuff very strangely. But by heaven, those strange ways I regarded love [*blenches*: looks or glances] have made my heart young again, and my lousy experiments have served to show me that I love you best.' Yes: the irony is that our miserable infidelities *can* serve to make us more appreciative of the beloved. Nothing like a little lousy away-game contrast to throw their virtues into high relief. The thing is, they're not *nearly* so chuffed to hear all this as you might think. This is the strategic error of a 17-year- old.

'But I've finished with that now: know our love will never end.' l.10 is nice: he's raising the dead metaphor 'whetting the appetite'. Here, the knives of desire are *ground*; a far sexier verb, to boot.

HV hears the couplet as 'saccharine'; however there's one way of reading it that leaves a very bitter aftertaste. Look at that *pure and most most loving breast.* WS needn't just be saying that the YM's breast is bestest. *Most most* is pretty lousy filler; so bad, in fact, that it seems to alert us to the presence of an alternative sense. SB hears this as 'most loving breast which love the *most*', i.e. the many. To my ear, this presses *loving* into service as an awkward zeugma. But might WS not mean 'the most out of *all* your most loving breasts', a sly way of saying not only 'I know you have several in service; we both know you're every bit as bad as me', but even worse, 'and I know you pull this *most loving*

routine with everyone *else* you're sleeping with too'? Oh I think
he just might, you know. 110

111

O, for my sake do you with Fortune chide,
The guilty goddess of my harmful deeds,
That did not better for my life provide
Than public means, which public manners breeds;
Thence comes it that my name receives a brand,
And almost thence my nature is subdued
To what it works in, like the dyer's hand;
Pity me, then, and wish I were renewed,
Whilst, like a willing patient, I will drink
Potions of eisell 'gainst my strong infection;
No bitterness that I will bitter think,
Nor double penance, to correct correction.
  Pity me then, dear friend, and I assure ye,
  Ev'n that your pity is enough to cure me.

Pretty average effort, really, although the lines *And almost thence my nature is subdued / To what it works in, like the dyer's hand* are wonderfully aphoristic, and make a virtuosically musical noise that rolls its vowels all over the mouth, while anagramming nasals, dentals, sibilants and not much else. (*The Dyer's Hand* is a book of essays by Auden.) The lines seem to refer to the 'stain' that WS receives from his work in theatre, of which more in a moment; but it's hard not to also see him up to his elbows in ink, and just as tainted by the poet's dark art as the actor's sleazy one. The argument seems to have shifted, and he's now addressing the taint that his day-job *brings* him, rather than any stain he has brought more directly on himself; passing the buck, in other words, to Dame Fortune.

Quick paraphrase: 'Oh, you're cursing my luck – the luck which is behind my bad deeds – and the fact that it didn't provide me with more of a living than to have to work with the public, which has infected my behaviour. It's given me a bad name – and just as a dyer is stained by his work, so it's polluted my nature. So take pity; I hope I can get back my old unstained self. I'll drink bitter medicine, I'll do double penance. Pity me, and your pity will cure me.'

Far and away the most interesting thing about this poem is its direct reference to WS's day-to-day, and you do have the sense of the curtain parting for a moment, revealing the real messy life behind the performance of the Sonnets. As I mentioned, it's hard not to read *public means which public manners breeds*, and the *brand* – the stigma it consequently gives – as a reference to the theatre: amongst the Puritans, the theatre enjoyed a reputation as something which brought shame, disgrace, and a stain to the character generally. G. R. Ledger directs us to this splendid tirade from the Puritan pamphleteer, Philip Stubbes:

> *Do they not maintain bawdry, insinuate foolery, and renew the remembrance of heathen idolatry? Do they not induce whoredom and uncleanness? Nay are they not rather plain devourers of maidenly virginity and chastity? For proof whereof but mark the flocking and running to Theaters and Curtains, daily and hourly, night and day, time and tide, to see plays and interludes, where such wanton gestures, such bawdy speeches, such laughing and fleering, such kissing and*

111 *bussing, such clipping and culling, such winking and glancing of wanton eyes, and the like is used, as is wonderful to behold. Then these goodly pageants being ended, every mate sorts to his mate, every one brings another homeward of their way very friendly, and in their secret conclaves (covertly) they play the sodomites, or worse. And these be the fruits of plays and interludes, for the most part.* (The Anatomie of Abuses, 1583)

The miracle is that English theatre managed to survive in the face of this fundamentalist lunacy, given it only takes a generation to destroy everything. Scottish theatre was annihilated by it, and met its nemesis in the form of Ayatollah John Knox, who stepped smartly into the hole created by the decampment of the Scottish court to England with the accession of James. He promptly turned the vacuum to suck, and the theatres went dark for 150 years. (In Calvinism, the *imagination itself* is fundamentally sinful, a nice refinement.)

l.10 *eisell*: vinegar. Used for stain-removal, as well as a medicine. As Geoffrey Hill points out, *infection* is likely an etymological pun, as it derives from *inficere* – 'to dip in, stain, taint, impregnate, spoil' (OED).

l.14 has *Euen* in the Q, but we have to elide the second syllable to make the metre.

112

Your love and pity doth th'impression fill,
Which vulgar scandal stamped upon my brow;
For what care I who calls me well or ill
So you o'er-green my bad, my good allow?
You are my all-the-world, and I must strive
To know my shames and praises from your tongue;
None else to me, nor I to none alive,
That my steeled sense or changes right or wrong.
In so profound abysm I throw all care
Of others' voices, that my adder's sense
To critic and to flatterer stopped are.
Mark how with my neglect I do dispense:
  You are so strongly in my purpose bred,
  That all the world besides me thinks y'are dead.

Yikes. SB explores the various textual knots and cruces here at some length, and very instructively, but let's see if we can find a more direct route through the poem, and take it line by line. OK. Suit up, scrub up, and on with the gloves. This is going to get messy. At least five lines here present real interpretative problems. Scalpel . . .

Your love and pity doth th'impression fill,
Which vulgar scandal stamped upon my brow;

– 'Your love and pity have smoothed out the dent which

common scandal has put in my brow', i.e. it has made up for the
112 damage done to my public face, my reputation. *Scandal* is probably also used in the older sense of a 'stumbling block' (it seems to have its origins in a root-word meaning 'snare or trap'). However this gives the unhappy picture of WS tripping, smacking his head on the aforementioned block, and having the dent smoothed out with the polyfilla of the YM's pity, which strikes me as at least as funny as tragic, so I'd rather not dwell on it. *Stamped* as in 'printed like a book' seems a weaker and on even less consistent metaphor, and not worth pursuing, whether it was intended or not.

For what care I who calls me well or ill,
So you o'er-green my bad, my good allow?

– 'Because what do I care about who calls me good or bad, as long as you gloss over the bad things about me, and praise the good things?' Hmm. More suction, nurse. We could treat *o'er-green* (*ore-greene* in the Q) as a crux, as some have insisted on doing, suggesting all sorts of mad alternatives – but the OED's gloss seems hard to improve upon (though it loses some authority by providing this line as its sole example): 'To cover with green, clothe with verdure; hence fig., to cover so as to conceal a defect, embellish.'

You are my all-the-world, and I must strive
To know my shames and praises from your tongue;

– 'You're all the world to me, and [so] I must try to figure out the good and bad about myself from what you say.' Hey, this is a breeze. Suture . . .

112

None else to me, nor I to none alive,
That my steeled sense or changes right or wrong.

– . . . Whaddya mean his pressure's dropping? Argh! It's burst – clamp! Clamp! 'Purblind and obscure', the 18th-century commentator George Steevens called these lines. However I don't think they're quite as impenetrable as they first appear. We can get somewhere by reading them as a continuation of the previous two lines, and a development of its thought. l.7, when you look closely, is pretty straightforward. 'It's as if no one else matters to me and I don't matter to anyone else alive' seems reasonable, given the YM has already been named as the *all-the-world*. The second line is a bigger problem, and indeed makes no damn sense at all. It's that first *or* really. Steevens glosses the two lines as 'You are the only person who has the power to change my stubborn resolution [*steeled sense*] *either* to what is right or what is wrong', which is sensible. KDJ follows T.G. Tucker and changes the text to the ingenious *o'er-changes* (*overchange* meaning 'to transmute') – which also happily echoes *o'er-green.* That would alter the sense to 'so that my strengthened [by you] senses transmute both right and wrong'. The trouble is the Q doesn't say *right and wrong*, but *right or wrong.* One amateur suggestion of my own might be that first *or* might be a misprinted *nor*, meaning *neither*, giving us the opposite sense from *o'er-change*, one I prefer: 'so that my strengthened [by you] senses transmute *neither* right or wrong' – i.e. are unaffected by the advice of the *other voices* WS then goes on to describe. This would probably mean that the standard emendation of a stop for the comma after *wrong* needn't be correct, and would be better changed to colon. This sense also seems to sit better with his argument, but depends on

112 the correlative conjunctions *neither . . . nor* being represented by *nor . . . or*; though *nor . . . nor* was a common Elizabethan construction. Either way, I think he's stabilising. Phew.

In so profound abysm I throw all care
Of others' voices, that my adder's sense
To critic and to flatterer stopped are.

– 'I throw my anxieties over the opinions of others into such a deep pit [i.e. I have such a deep contempt for what others say] that my deaf senses are cut off from both criticism and flattery.' ['as deaf as an adder' was proverbial; I guess the epithet *adder's/deaf* is transferred here, since he means 'sense *made* deaf by my ignoring others'] There we go. Stitch him up, junior, I'm heading for the bar.

Mark how with my neglect I do dispense:
You are so strongly in my purpose bred,
That all the world besides methinks y'are dead.

– What? He's *haemorrhaging*? From his *ears*? Calm down. I think it's just jam. l.12 must be something like 'Mark how, with my neglect of those other voices, I disregard' (i.e. disregard all 'the world'; one obsolete sense of *dispense* in the OED). l.13 must mean something like '[I have the strong sense that] you have been brought into being for my own concerns'. Now we can simplify matters considerably if we just *ignore* all the controversy at l.14. Several commentators assume the text is erroneous, and correct to something like *That all the world, besides, methinks, are dead*, i.e. 'everyone in the world seems dead to me, except you'. But what's wrong with the line as it appeared in the Q? If we read it as 'everyone apart from me thinks you are dead', it just seems an outrageously hyperbolic way of saying that 'I am *so* alive to you, I have constituted you as my personal world to such an extent, that relatively speaking, you appear to everyone else as dead.' What's wrong with that? What's not consistent with the argument? I *like* it. It's just over the top. That's poetry for ye. Nurse: wet wipe, we're done here.

But is the poem any good? I think so, and not least because it's such an extreme expression of his love. The YM has to be dead to the world, every other voice in the cosmos has to fall into the abyss, just to satisfy WS's desire to possess wholly and be wholly possessed. It's over-the-top enough to be ironic or even humorous, but I think it's likely just deranged. Just below the poem's surface, though, is a psychotic jealousy that leaves no room for anyone else at all; frankly, it would've made me feel just a tad claustrophobic, in the sense of 'frightened for my life'. I can imagine the YM reading this in WS's presence, smiling and nodding, and thinking to himself 'Great! A bunny-boiler. How the *hell* am I going to get out of *this* one.'

113

Since I left you, mine eye is in my mind,
And that which governs me to go about
Doth part his function, and is partly blind;
Seems seeing, but effectually is out:
For it no form delivers to the heart
Of bird, of flower, or shape which it doth latch;
Of his quick objects hath the mind no part,
Nor his own vision holds what it doth catch:
For if it see the rud'st or gentlest sight,
The most sweet favour or deformed'st creature,
The mountain or the sea, the day, or night,
The crow, or dove, it shapes them to your feature.
  Incapable of more, replete with you,
  My most true mind thus maketh mine untrue.

Very pleasant little number, this, and a relief after the contortions of Sonnet 112. I hear it as something like a Jimmy Webb B-side, a little cheesy but with something undeniably classy about it; Glen Campbell would've made a very decent job of this, in his 'The Moon's a Harsh Mistress' mode. In a nutshell: 'Since I left you I've been looking inward [*mine eye is in my mind*, i.e. I'm preoccupied], and my eyes only half-function; I can see, a bit, but I can't identify the form of anything, the birds or flowers. Whatever I see – rough or gentle, lovely or deformed, day or night, crow or dove – my eyes contrive to shape into your image.

Incapable of anything else, and full with your image, my faithful mind makes me see everything false.' A convincing description of the permanently twilit world of the febrile, besotted soul, where all the forms of the world are vague and shadowy, and every other human appears as a ghost – and if anything *does* happen to impinge on your conscious awareness, it's only because it reminds you of the beloved, in however weird or random a way.

... *Doth part his function, and is partly blind; / Seems seeing, but effectually is out: / For it no form delivers to the heart / Of bird, of flower, or shape which it doth latch* ... are beautiful lines, whose ghostly fricative and affricate music allows the breath to flow through them, like a spring breeze through a lace curtain.

The last line is generally treated as a crux. I don't see it that way, but let's look at some alternative readings first: one method of removing the alleged confusion is to read *mine* as *my*, when *untrue* then stands revealed as a noun, leaving us with 'then my most faithful mind is the cause of my untruth', i.e. his unreliable or false perception of the world. SB hates this, as *untrue* is never used as a substantive in this way; and despite KDJ's support for it, this reading strikes me as dodgy as hell. Other efforts have shoehorned in 'eye' or 'eyes', reading *mine* as an unusual spelling of the already highly suspect contraction *m'eyne*, perhaps taking too much encouragement from the innovative spirit WS apparently displays with *y'are* in the previous poem. This is great for the sense, but strains and snaps all credibility. However the wily SB defends this as WS's intention by essentially decrying its *failure*, seeing it as symptomatic of the poem's more general failed experiment. He says that 'in a poem that begins with such a line as line 1 is, the syntactic outrage of *m'eyne* ["mine" in Q] – the final violent unification of *mine*, *I*, *eye*, *eyne*, and *mind*, a

capsulation of everything the poem has logically distinguished in
113 the course of reporting a fanciful collapse in distinction of function – is all but inevitable'. Which is pretty convincing. (SB is much too hard on the poem as a whole, and divines a kind of linguistic ambition I just don't think the poem has. It's a bonny little thing, and not much more.)

I disagree, though, and I think it's really simple. WS just thinks that 'eye' is understood. By boldly advertising the symmetry of the first and last lines, WS is requesting that we keep l.1 in our heads, so we recall 'eye' as the noun still modified by the possessive adjective in l.14: *Since I left you, mine eye is in my mind . . . My most true mind thus maketh mine* [eye] *untrue.* This is easy enough to do, as *mine eye* is the grammatical subject of the whole poem, except for the last two lines. No crux.

l.6 . . . *which it doth lack* in the Q, but as there's no precedent for such a bad rhyme, everyone treats it as a misreading of *lach*, and emends to *latch*, in the sense of 'apprehend'.

l.7 *his quick objects*: the live things that the eye beholds. Crying out to be the title of a classy police procedural.

114

Or whether doth my mind, being crowned with you,
Drink up the monarch's plague, this flattery?
Or whether shall I say mine eye saith true,
And that your love taught it this alchemy,
To make of monsters and things indigest
Such cherubins as your sweet self resemble,
Creating every bad a perfect best,
As fast as objects to his beams assemble?
O 'tis the first, 'tis flatt'ry in my seeing,
And my great mind most kingly drinks it up:
Mine eye well knows what with his gust is 'greeing,
And to his palate doth prepare the cup.
  If it be poisoned, 'tis the lesser sin
  That mine eye loves it and doth first begin.

Somewhat redundant continuation of Sonnet 113, with a couple of fine lines and a warmed-over 'king' conceit, which the poem attends to in a rather half-hearted manner: love 'crowns' WS's mind; love plagues him with *flattery*, like a king; he arranges the world to his kingly taste; his eyes are employed as an official taster to the mind's king, etc. But half-heartedness means just that: WS's heart really isn't in it. Partly because the question the poem is predicated on – 'which has sinned against me more, my mind or eye?' – isn't emotionally *real*. 'Is my mind reliable, or has it succumbed to the flattery of your love? Or does

114 my eye see true, *taught* by your love the magic power to transform the monstrous to the angelic? No: it's the first. My eye knows what I like, and that's just what it's serving up me. It can be excused, I guess, inasmuch as *it* likes these things too – and however poisonous these falsehoods are, at least it has the decency to taste them first.'

ll.2–3 I would like to point out that the sequence of letters . . . *y / Or whether shall I say mine* can be rearranged to spell *Henry Wriothesley has mail.* Coincidence? I think not.

l.5 *indigest*: (a) undigested, crude; (b) shapeless.

l.8 is far and away the best of them, essentially meaning 'as fast as objects fall into his sight', but also implying that the eyebeams actively assemble a perfect reality from an external chaos or inferior reality. The line temporarily elevates the poem to a level of metaphysical elegance the poem just can't sustain, being, in SB's harsh-but-accurate words, a 'self-consciously cute, basically frivolous exercise in intellectual ingenuity'.

l.11 'my eye knows well what agrees with the appetite of my mind'; *gust* and *'greeing* make a very nasty alliteration.

115

Those lines that I before have writ do lie,
Even those that said I could not love you dearer:
Yet then my judgment knew no reason why
My most full flame should afterwards burn clearer.
But reckoning Time, whose millioned accidents
Creep in 'twixt vows, and change decrees of kings,
Tan sacred beauty, blunt the sharp'st intents,
Divert strong minds to th'course of altering things;
Alas! why, fearing of Time's tyranny,
Might I not then say, 'Now I love you best,'
When I was certain o'er uncertainty,
Crowning the present, doubting of the rest?
    Love is a babe; then might I not say so,
    To give full growth to that which still doth grow?

This poem worries away at the following thoughts: 'How can a love that I have perceived as burning at full intensity *increase*? Since I now observe that it *has* increased – does that mean that the perfection I once witnessed was *not* perfect?' And lurking darkly behind all this (a) 'Might this mean that your current full luminosity is *itself* inferior to some future intensification of feeling I might experience?' as well as the more logically maddening (b) 'Isn't something that increases an ideal *condition* of perfect love anyway?' But let's be clear – only someone completely crazed by love could be detained by this nonsense; for nonsense it is. Its only intellectual justification lies in WS's Platonic essentialism, which we see clearly expressed in something like Sonnet 116. But the daftness of the paradox stands as testament to the intensity of the feeling; and the poem is quite beautiful. No one reads this one either.

It's a contradiction, incidentally, that John Donne pursues in 'Loves Growthe' –

I scarce believe my love to be so pure
As I had thought it was,
Because it doth endure
Vicissitude, and season, as the grass;
Methinks I lied all winter, when I swore
My love was infinite, if spring make it more.

– although I prefer WS's handling of it to Donne's contrivance. As fine as Donne's poem is, WS's (as usual) seems less manufactured, less antiseptic in its symmetries, and more humanly convincing. Methinks these two poems are also too much of a coincidence, though it's not inconceivable that they arrived at the theme independently, given its natural appeal to the Elizabethan turn of mind.

Anyway, to the poem. WS sees that, because his love has grown, his earlier claims to his love's perfection must have been false; he defends this earlier claim, however, because it was made while he was cowering before an uncertain future; what else could he have said, when he was so thrall to the present moment? The last two lines give a specious but nonetheless brilliant resolution to the paradox, which we'll get to shortly.

The first quatrain says something like 'The poems that I wrote before *lie*: those very poems where I said I could not love you more than I already did. But back then I had no reason to think that the flame of my passion, already full, could burn any brighter.' The second quatrain is fairly clear in its sense, but its grammar is really tough to unravel. I think the key lies in reading the entire poem as consistent in tense, describing WS's attitude in the past, specifically at the time of *Those lines that I before have writ.* I reckon the speaker is probably the subject of *reckoning*, and that this subject is belatedly declared in the *I* of l.10. That leaves *But reckoning Time* meaning *But [back then when I was] reckoning Time.* (Though there's certainly a way to read it as qualifying *Time*: *reckoning Time* meaning 'Time which reckons', i.e. ticks, counts, adds up – is hardly a stretch, especially alongside the neologistic verb *millioned*, which to my ear sounds like an active multiplication on Time's part.) The passage on Time is a long dependent clause, which says 'Time, whose infinitely multiplied accidents creep between lovers' promises, change kings' decrees, age beauty, dull the sharpest intentions, divert the strongest wills to the course of changing circumstances . . .'

Now, that ellipsis is placed there advisedly, because I think WS might have used one if he could've (the Q has a colon, but impoverished Elizabethan punctuation had to multitask like crazy). This is not, to my knowledge, how anyone else reads this passage; but all commentators scratch their heads at this point – the grammar of ll.5–12 seems unresolvable – and this solution strikes me as no worse than many. It also has the merit of being perfectly grammatical. We simply read the construction of these lines as an aposiopesis (a figure where the speaker breaks off in mid-sentence), with the interruption in the grammar occurring at the turn, between ll.8 and 9. At the end of l.8 we hear WS drift off in the mid-flow of his long parenthetical description of time . . .

115 and then remember his subject, the reckoning *I* of the past; this he prepares for by way of l.9, where *fearing of Time's tyranny* works as a recapitulation, to get us up to speed again on where the sentence was heading. The finally understood sense would then be:

But [back then when I was] reckoning Time, whose millioned accidents
Creep in 'twixt vows, and change decrees of kings,
Tan sacred beauty, blunt the sharp'st intents,
Divert strong minds to th'course of altering things . . .
Alas! why [back then, when I was reckoning Time], fearing of time's tyranny,
Might I not then say, 'Now I love you best,'
When I was certain o'er uncertainty,
Crowning the present, doubting of the rest?

It dramatises the speech, certainly, and this solution may be too hammy for some. Works for me, though.

The third quatrain is knotty too: ll.9–10 aren't so bad – 'Alas! Fearing time's tyranny as I did, wasn't it reasonable at that time for me to say "My love for you could never be greater than it is now". . .' – but ll.11–12 are a different matter. Gaily skipping over the textual controversies, I think they probably mean something like '. . . when I'd triumphed over uncertainty by means of *my* certainty, holding the present moment to be prime, the best it possibly could be – and doubtful that the future could bring better?' That's my best shot. I don't really understand the more generally accepted reading that *doubting* should mean 'fearful' here; it doesn't seem consistent with the argument. WS has already said that he'd been broadly fearful of the future. The couplet, too, is a bit ambiguous, especially that *then*, but I'm sure he must mean something like 'Love itself is eternally a baby [i.e. Cupid], so wouldn't it have been quite *right* for me to have claimed my love for you was fully grown, even though it keeps on growing still?' If that's right, it's a brilliant way of squaring the paradox. Love might grow, but in the present moment it can't ever be perceived as doing so – because love is always new-born.

KDJ's Arden predecessor, C. K. Pooler, asks of l.2 'Can this refer to lost sonnets?' To which we must boldly answer 'Nope.'

116

Let me not to the marriage of true minds
Admit impediments; love is not love
Which alters when it alteration finds,
Or bends with the remover to remove.
O no, it is an ever-fixèd mark,
That looks on tempests and is never shaken;
It is the star to every wandering bark,
Whose worth's unknown, although his height be taken.
Love's not Time's fool, though rosy lips and cheeks
Within his bending sickle's compass come;
Love alters not with his brief hours and weeks,
But bears it out ev'n to the edge of doom.
  If this be error and upon me proved,
  I never writ, nor no man ever loved.

One of the most famous of all the sonnets, and even Coleridge thought this one was special. It's generally true of popular poems that they can be open to a number of interpretations (nearly all perennially popular poems are also great, apart from the 10 per cent that are awful). Although I doubt this was WS's intention, that's certainly how it's panned out here. Generations of anthologists, lovers and marrying couples have all given it a cheerfully one-sided reading, all rather conveniently forgetting the circumstances that gave rise to it.

ll.1–2 are certainly supposed to put us in mind of the marriage service – *if any man can show any just cause, why they may not lawfully be joined together, let him now speak.* And indeed this poem is still frequently heard at weddings. Which is pretty funny. Firstly, this is not a union of the flesh but of *minds*; and secondly, and somewhat more to the point, of two men. This is its tragic frisson, of course – WS's church would never sanction *this* marriage. (SB thinks that the *O no* in l.5 'presents a logically incidental example of a suitable prefatory exclamation introducing an impediment volunteered by a parishioner', but if that had been the plan, the ejaculation would've been *Yes!* No?)

The kind of love described here exists on another plane from the two lives it unites. It doesn't change when it finds change in the beloved, or even when the beloved leaves – which does pose a question: *what* is it loving, exactly? Is this love so pure it's intransitive, and doesn't need to take an object? Not really: it's predicated, again, on the existence of a *substance* – in this case, of the YM; a pure essence of him, of which his outward space-time manifestation is a mere shadow. This love, as a uniter of essences, requires no body-in-time at all.

The poem is sandwiched between two others which address WS's own wandering, but this poem stands apart from their temporal and earthly concerns. Though the truth is that we'll *always* find ourselves falling short of such an ideal love, and quite unable to honour it, even if we believe it exists. Such ideals are a way of prolonging the romance, I suppose; but in the end they don't make us feel so good about ourselves. It probably won't surprise you to hear that I think this is just because they're founded on wholly dodgy philosophies. There *are* no essences. There's stuff; there's us chickens; there's the dreams us chickens have (and mistake for reality) – but that's the whole story.

116 *It is the star to every wandering bark* is a justly famous line. One reason it's so effective is the strong assonance between *bark* and *star*, which draws the two words together, making the contrast between the star's fixity and the boat's wandering even more sharp. The next line is a brilliant development of the metaphor: a star's height (as in 'its measurable height in a sextant') can be known, but its distant celestial 'worth' can't be. This is something *so* above it all, *so* beyond the reach of temporal dimension, physical law, and death itself – that, like God, we cannot know its value. *Wandering* is an interesting word; yes, it's used contrastively, but we're supposed to also map it onto either the lover or the beloved, whose 'wandering' – inconstancy, perhaps – is kept under control by holding to the steady star of perfect love. It's important to know that *mark* in l.5 is a 'seamark', a sailor's beacon or landmark or lighthouse, a light that will literally out-stare tempests, and remain unextinguished.

SB is a pig for this sonnet, and essentially writes two commentaries on it. In the second he develops – quite brilliantly – the idea that while the poem is initially impressive, a second reading seems to reveal it as so much bombast; but a *third*, as a construction of much greater and subtler sophistication than either of the previous readings could have uncovered. In other words, he asserts the importance of *rereading* in the true understanding of a great poem. As usual he finds much (bi)sexual innuendo: Q2 'is always ready to turn into a grotesquely abstruse pun on "polestar"', apparently, and who am I to deny it. I'm happy to let WS and SB have that snigger between themselves at the back of the class. If the innuendo's there, it doesn't help the poem.

The closing couplet can be read (rather unfairly, I think) as swaggering and boastful; other commentators make the rather obvious point that it's paradoxical, given he *is*, y'know, writing. I dunno. To me it reads as little more than 'if this isn't true, then the Pope's not a Catholic'.

l.10 makes brilliant use of *compass*, meaning 'mandate' or 'sphere of influence', of course – but also maintaining the consistency of that maritime-navigational metaphor.

l.11 *Love alters not with his brief hours and weeks . . .* It's important, I think, to treat the antecedent of *his* as Time, and not Love, even though it's a little ambiguous.

l.13 *error*: he may have had in mind its Latin root, *errare*, to wander, putting us in mind of that errant bark again.

117

Accuse me thus: that I have scanted all,
Wherein I should your great deserts repay,
Forgot upon your dearest love to call,
Whereto all bonds do tie me day by day;
That I have frequent been with unknown minds,
And given to time your own dear-purchased right;
That I have hoisted sail to all the winds
Which should transport me farthest from your sight.
Book both my wilfulness and errors down,
And on just proof surmise accumulate;
Bring me within the level of your frown,
But shoot not at me in your wakèn'd hate;
  Since my appeal says I did strive to prove
  The constancy and virtue of your love.

This is Sonnet 116 rewritten by Shakespeare's id, as if to provide a balanced account. Where 116 saw his mind fixed on higher things, most of this is couched in terms of filthy lucre. Rhetorically, I suppose it's an interesting tactic, though not one worth imitating. 'By all means – accuse me of failing to repay the debt I owe you, forgetting to acknowledge your dear love; yeah – say I spent too much time on other folk I should've spent with you, that I've been only too happy for the wind to carry me far from you . . . [Note how the *wandering bark* is much less passive here, and has *hoisted sail.*] Go on. Write it all down, all the

misdeeds and misdemeanours – and actually . . . that might
prompt you to consider all the *other* bad stuff I probably got up 117
to. Fix me in your frowny stare, by all means – but don't shoot me down with this newly awakened hate: in my defence (cough) all I was doing was trying to prove the constancy of your love. No really.'

There are several things wrong with this approach. It's hard to know where to start. Usually if someone says – 'Go ahead! Accuse me of this. Accuse me of that . . .' you tend to expect something like '. . . because you're *wrong*. It's only your goddamn self-obsession that makes you *see* things that way. I, on the other hand, am a paragon of constancy.' But what you tend *not* to expect is 'Well – aha! you're right! I *did* do all that. And *more*, I expect. And I did it – drumroll – so I could prove the constancy of your love! As evidenced, like, by how much you now hate me.' Genius. That's *that* point won. A more generous interpretation might be, 'I did it to prove I could get some goddamn reaction', would leave us with something more credible, but even more disingenuous. To get a reaction, you do something once, or maybe twice. You don't, unless you're pathologically sadistic, keep it up over months and months. You do *that* because you're an arsehole, but not because you're concerned with your alleged beloved in any way. WS is keen to prove – both to the YM and himself – that he *is* as concerned as ever. But he simply *isn't*.

Oh, we're adult enough to see through this, aren't we? WS's love is waning, and he refuses to recognise the symptoms for what they are. He's less interested in the YM's company than he was. The reasons he used to give for his behaviour were reasoned, if sophistical; now they're towards the flailingly, guiltily hysterical.

117 l.1 *scanted*: withheld, neglected.
l.5 *frequent*: familiar in company as in 'frequented'.
l.11 *within the level*: within the range or aim. An archery term.

❧

118

Like as, to make our appetite more keen,
With eager compounds we our palate urge;
As, to prevent our maladies unseen,
We sicken to shun sickness when we purge;
Even so, being full of your ne'er-cloying sweetness,
To bitter sauces did I frame my feeding,
And, sick of welfare, found a kind of meetness
To be diseasèd, ere that there was true needing.
Thus policy in love, t'anticipate
The ills that were not, grew to faults assur'd,
And brought to medicine a healthful state
Which, rank of goodness, would by ill be cured;
    But thence I learn and find the lesson true,
    Drugs poison him that so fell sick of you.

This is a *brilliant* sonnet, and heaven alone knows why it isn't better regarded. It should be *revered.* A quick summary's needed before we can discuss it: 'Just as we sharpen our appetites with acrid or sharp tastes [*eager* is cognate with "acrid"], just as we take purgatives to ward off sickness – so, being full of your never-sickly sweetness, I took to feeding on bitter sauces.' Of course he's talking metaphorically. The *bitter sauces*, we're surely to understand, must mean other affairs, more tart affairs (pun possibly intended) than his relationship with the YM.

The poem continues: 'And sick of being healthy anyway,

118 I found a kind of appropriateness in being *additionally* sick from what I was getting up to, before there was a real need to be. Thus my strategy in love – anticipating sickness that hadn't yet come – led to real evils.' In other words, anticipating difficulties (which is what I read into the oxymoron *sick of welfare*, as well as a rising boredom from the sheer predictability of all this sweetness) he got used to being unfaithful to the YM. 'And brought together a medicine, and a healthy state – which abounding in [*rank of*] goodness, I proposed to cure with ill. But then I learned: *Drugs poison him that so fell sick of you*.' The couplet we should read as very much within the country & western idiom, with which it intersects rather splendidly. I'd love to hear this whole sonnet sung by Merle Haggard in a codpiece.

No paraphrase can do a shred of justice to the almost inhuman cleverness of this argument, the glorious balance of the whole, its logically rigorous defence of its own irrationality, its original phrasemaking, its flawlessly pursued conceit, and the squared circle of its lyric argument. And *what* an argument. What an insight. Love is a sickness, we know that, and we've always known it. But how to treat it? And should we really treat it at *all*, when it's in that first phase, whose only symptom is a sweet delirium? The once or thrice bitten in love will see the boring second phase coming a mile off, though; and they may choose to prepare for it. (Young lovers, wherever you are: this poem isn't for you.) They may do so by weaning themselves off the beloved early; they may indulge in a bit of self-hatred-inducing infidelity, just to get used to the feeling, as they know they're going to have to; or they might prepare a soft landing or two elsewhere, so there's another mattress positioned below them when the fall inevitably comes – a practical move that nonetheless is likely to leave the lover feeling pretty sick of himself. No, this kind of behaviour isn't universal, and probably not even that typical; it's unusual. But not pathologically so.

There's also the implication in the first two lines that sexual appetite for the beloved, in the later stages of a relationship, is often sharpened elsewhere – a miserable but probably accurate observation. You can end up taking *anything* for granted, however wonderful. Paul Newman once sweetly commented on his marriage to his beloved Joanne Woodward, 'Why go out for hamburgers when I have a steak at home?' (This can probably claim to be the only non-misogynistic woman = meat comparison in the history of the species, though I still feel it's a little unfortunate.) However it can be met with two obvious objections: (a) a hamburger on Tuesday can make a steak on Wednesday taste even better; and (b) sometimes you just want a burger. A sensible defence of marital fidelity deserves a better, harder and less sensual metaphor, possibly involving the words 'money', 'bank', 'investment' and 'risk' and 'broke'.

Too many commentators read WS's defence of his away-game in this poem as contrived and sophistical – as, god knows, he often can be. Here, though, I think he's perfectly sincere, and to call this argument specious is just naive. Let's just say this isn't an area of human behaviour where academic criticism has a track record of deep insight.

l.12 SB prefers to follow the Q and keep the commas out of this line, meaning *rank of goodness* refers to the aforementioned *healthful state*, and now means something like 'this degree of goodness'; the trouble is that this proposes nothing worth curing, by ill or otherwise, and we're left with a much starker oxymoron – possibly WS's intention; however if the commas are inserted,

118 the phrase is adjectival, and can carry the senses ‘abounding in’, ‘overgrown with’, ‘lustful with’, all of which make a bunch more sense, to my mind. But it’s impossible to say which is correct, and it’s all down to taste.

❧

119

What potions have I drunk of Siren tears
Distilled from limbecks foul as hell within,
Applying fears to hopes, and hopes to fears,
Still losing when I saw myself to win?
What wretched errors hath my heart committed,
Whilst it hath thought itself so blessèd never?
How have mine eyes out of their spheres been fitted,
In the distraction of this madding fever?
O benefit of ill! Now I find true
That better is by evil still made better;
And ruined love, when it is built anew,
Grows fairer than at first, more strong, far greater:
　So I return rebuked to my content,
　And gain by ill thrice more than I have spent.

This poem continues from the last. I get the sense WS thought there was more to be mined from this conceit – understandably, since the last poem went so well. Alas, most of the good ore has gone. But it's a pretty good sonnet, at least for the first eight lines, even if it's all getting muddled in the bubbling alembic of his mad love, and WS can't tell if he's coming or going in all the chaos. The first quatrain cleverly embellishes an alchemy metaphor. A wonderful decoction is brewed up; he applies this to that, that to this. In the second quatrain, he's snatched defeat from the jaws of victory in his wanderings and mistakes,

committing errors in his heart while he thought himself blessed
119 (presumably by the love of the YM, not the temporary relief offered by his other dalliances).

l.7 is great. The performed sense of *How have mine eyes out of their spheres been fitted* runs right against the metre – you don't say *How HAVE mine EYES out OF their SPHERES been FITTed* but *HOW have mine EYES OUT of their SPHERES been FITTed* – and it's impossible to say without the words popping out of the line like a pair of bulging, bloodshot eyeballs. It's a prime example of using the metre to make your sense in a physical way – indeed making a kind of sense that *couldn't* be made unless you were writing metrically, which permits the reader to experience the expressive stress in a much more present, high-relief way.

Then the sestet tries to wheel the whole mad juggernaut round. He fails. It has way too much momentum. 'O the good of ill! I find good things can be improved by bad' – I refer you to the 'burger argument' in my notes to the last sonnet to make some possible sense of this statement – and then it all goes Sammy Cahn. '*Love's more comfortable the second time you fall / Like a friendly home the second time you call . . .*' Well, not quite like that, but perhaps you can sense my cynicism. SB cites Terence's 'The falling-out of lovers is a renewal of love' as good evidence that we've been making this observation for a long time now: no one's happier than reunited lovers. I'd like to pour cold water on that with another observation: only 10 per cent (a statistic I have just made up) of reunited lovers *stay* together, as their parting was a perfectly reliable indication that things were falling apart. The fatal tensions in the relationship will have reasserted themselves by the following weekend. In Tesco's. Unless people change, their relationships don't, and I fear the writing's on the wall here too.

119

It's not enough to say that he finds the YM more beautiful than ever, because he's been elsewhere and has gained some perspective. This is a poem of lame apology, and WS is hoping no one will see through it; including, I suspect, himself. I think his recent experiences are reduced, caricatured in this poem; and to come out with a statement like *better is by evil still made better* requires a lot of careful defence, none of which is provided. There isn't even a consistent metaphor developed in ll.11–12, where we'd expect one. Reason being, I suspect, he can't *find* one. What, exactly, *Grows fairer than at first, more strong*? Unwanted facial hair? Nah. This poem makes little real sense.

l.1 *Siren tears*: KDJ considers the possibility that WS's intention here was *serein*, a fine rain from a cloudless sky 'formerly regarded as a noxious dew or mist' (OED), but I can't see it. You'd lose the contrast between the pure, seductive distillation, and the foulness of the alchemist's alembic which produced it; a rather sharp point about the exquisite and pure sensations which are nonetheless bred from one's 'immoral' urges.

l.9 Those of you wishing to fix your telescopes on *O benefit of ill!* will find a cluster of many learned and abstruse puns, all dull.

120

That you were once unkind befriends me now,
And for that sorrow, which I then did feel,
Needs must I under my transgression bow,
Unless my nerves were brass or hammer'd steel:
For if you were by my unkindness shaken,
As I by yours, you've passed a hell of time,
And I, a tyrant, have no leisure taken
To weigh how once I suffered in your crime.
O that our night of woe might have remembered
My deepest sense, how hard true sorrow hits,
And soon to you, as you to me then, tendered
The humble salve, which wounded bosoms fits!
  But that your trespass now becomes a fee;
  Mine ransoms yours, and yours must ransom me.

Tonight on 'Seasons of Our Love' (Ep. 120): Will battles his demons – and faces up to the truth about his cheatin' and a-lyin' in the Big City. Remember two summers back, when young *Harry* was the love-rat? Will does . . . And now the boot's on the other foot, he knows Harry must be having the same *hell of* [a] *time* – but not in a good way!! – *he* had back then. Well at least it's all even Stephens. But has the thrill gone? Are our boys a perfect match – or just so bad they deserve each other? (And who *is* that dusky-skinned damsel at the bar giving *both* of them the eye??)

This *is* a sorry old soap, at times, but I'm doing this poem a disservice. A slight one. What's affecting here is WS's abandoning of *any* kind of smart argument to explain his behaviour. All the clever conceits, all the metaphysical casuistry . . . it avails him nothing, and he knows it. 'Given you put me through *exactly* the same hell – I should've been quicker to apologise for the damage I'd done. Well: I guess we're all square now.' That's pretty much it. It's just a poem of open, heartfelt and rather forlorn apology, with a bitter aftertaste in the tone, an implied resignation to the knowledge that the pair of them are as bad as each other – and maybe all the warbling about ideal love is getting a little hollow, and should stop for a while. But it's still a pretty thing. I just sang it in the bath as a Luther Vandross ballad, and it works just fine, though I'm relieved no one heard me. (HV's judgement that the poem is 'deliberately confusing' is lost on me. There's nothing difficult in this sad little unrisen soufflé.)

l.1 is a lovely double-edged affair. He's indeed comforted, 'befriended', by the thought of the YM's previous infidelities, as they offset his own; but it also allows him to access the imaginative empathy he needs to see the human pain he's caused.

ll.3–4 mean something like 'I'd have had to be made of steel not to be doubled up under the weight of my guilt.'

l.12 sends us back to the 'salve' of the YM's repentant tears in Sonnet 34: *Ah, but those tears are pearl which thy love sheds, / And they are rich, and ransom all ill deeds.*

ll.13–14 are a kind of half-hearted and belated attempt to work in a little Elizabethan symmetry, and again look back to Sonnet 34. 'My sin pays your debt, and yours serves to pay mine.'

121

'Tis better to be vile than vile esteemed,
When not to be, receives reproach of being,
And the just pleasure lost, which is so deemed
Not by our feeling, but by others' seeing.
For why should others' false adulterate eyes
Give salutation to my sportive blood?
Or on my frailties why are frailer spies,
Which in their wills count bad what I think good?
No, I am that I am, and they that level
At my abuses, reckon up their own;
I may be straight, though they themselves be bevel,
By their rank thoughts my deeds must not be shown,
  Unless this general evil they maintain:
  All men are bad, and in their badness reign.

An argument in need of précis before we can talk about it. It runs: 'You'd almost be as well just *being* vile, if everyone thinks you already *are*; because even if you're not, they think you are anyway – and ruin the pleasure of your (perfectly non-vile) acts through their criticism of you. Why should these lustful and weak-willed folk stand in judgement on *my* lust and weakness of will? I am what I am, and my accusers are just showing their own corruption. I'm the straight one. They're as bent as a nine-bob note. I can't be judged on their wicked terms – unless all they're really saying is this: *all* men are bad.'

121

'Men are bad' is a serviceable aphorism, and the famously terse Bias of Priene did pretty well out of it. Usually, though, our assessments have to be a little more nuanced. It all puts me a little in mind of my favourite Burns poem, 'Address to the Unco Guid' – another tirade against hypocritical judges, and a much better and more subtly argued poem than this, it has to be said. Though it's also hard not to read this in the context of the preceding sonnets, with their theme of the poet's trespassing and the YM's forgiveness. Here he just sounds exasperated by his own self-defence, and instead says – 'Look: I am what I am. Whatever sins I committed were no big deal'. But it's sad, I think, that we've come such a long way from the aspirational purity of the earlier sonnets, and we do start to have the sense that this whole thing is coming apart at the seams.

The most interesting part of this poem is the first quatrain, which does seem to half-imply that a sin undiscovered is no sin, unless you feel inclined to charge it against yourself; it's only a crime when you get caught. Which is an easier argument to make for consensual-if-taboo sex than recreational murder, i.e. not a great general maxim. However I wish I could have retro-emailed WS the last stanza of Burns's poem, which would have provided him with some comfort, and a better explanation for his own behaviour:

Who made the heart, 'tis He *alone*
Decidedly can try us,
He knows each chord, its various tone,
Each spring its various bias:
Then at the balance let's be mute
We never can adjust it;

121

What's done *we partly may compute,*
But know not what's resisted.

l.9 *I am that I am*, as well as just saying WYSIWYG, is of course unbelievably blasphemous, being the words spoken by the burning bush – sending us (OK, me) back to the *ever-living poet* of the dedication.

122

Thy gift, thy tables, are within my brain
Full charactered with lasting memory,
Which shall above that idle rank remain,
Beyond all date, even to eternity;
Or, at the least, so long as brain and heart
Have faculty by nature to subsist;
Till each to razed oblivion yield his part
Of thee, thy record never can be missed.
That poor retention could not so much hold,
Nor need I tallies thy dear love to score;
Therefore to give them from me was I bold,
To trust those tables that receive thee more;
    To keep an adjunct to remember thee
    Were to import forgetfulness in me.

Yes, it's not much of a poem, but let's call it tellingly symptomatic. 'That notebook you gave me – I've filled it already! Well, in my imagination, at least . . . and with words that will last a lot longer than any I could have actually *written* in that little book. And they will last for all eternity. OK, yeah – not for all *eternity*, obviously, but at least until I cark it. Yip: that poor little notebook can't hold anything like as much as my mind can, nor do I need to tally all the things I love about you. No no. I mean – it would be tantamount to admitting I'm *forgetful* of your loveliness, wouldn't it, if I kept a written record. Oh by the way I've lost it.'

122 I think there's a very good chance this is nothing more than a sonnet of apology and (wholly unconvincing) explanation for the fact that WS has either lost (implied in l.8) or inadvertently given away the YM's gift. 'Hey Will: how come I saw Mikey Drayton with that lovely book I gave you?' isn't a wholly implausible occasion for this outburst. But it's unconvincing, firstly, because by the end he's so defensive, he's on the attack: 'Are you imputing *forgetfulness* to me by suggesting I might *need* such a book?' Hmmm . . . If the beloved gives you a plastic teaspoon, you treasure it for ever. You fondle it in your pocket and sleep with it under your pillow. Secondly, it's unconvincing because throughout the Sonnets, he's been extolling the extraordinary ability of the written word to preserve both his love and the young man for future generations. But suddenly we're being told that was all an empty conceit. No, he's fooling himself. The thrill has gone, man. Face up to it. Look at the two of you: arguing over a *notebook.*

l.1 *tables*: here, a 'table-book', a pocket notebook, used as an aide-memoire or commonplace book.

l.9 *That poor retention* is a nice metonym: 'that book which poorly retains my memories'. Note how it could only work within the thematic domain of this poem, i.e. one about memory.

l.10 'nor need I a recording device [such as a tally-stick on which one would *score* a number] to keep a measurement of your love'.

123

No, Time, thou shalt not boast that I do change;
Thy pyramids built up with newer might
To me are nothing novel, nothing strange;
They are but dressings of a former sight.
Our dates are brief, and therefore we admire
What thou dost foist upon us that is old'
And rather make them born to our desire
Than think that we before have heard them told:
Thy registers and thee I both defy,
Not wond'ring at the present nor the past,
For thy records and what we see doth lie,
Made more or less by thy continual haste.
  This I do vow, and this shall ever be:
  I will be true despite thy scythe and thee.

Time hasn't boasted anything, of course; but someone *else* may have proposed WS's love is on the wane. It was most likely himself: he can sense his ardour weaken, and he doesn't like it. Unable to get angry at no one at all over love's change of state, he gets mad at Time, the engine of that change. It's all very and effective. 'Time, you can't boast that I'm changing. Your new pyramids are nothing new to *me*: they're just an old design with a new appearance.' ll.5–8 are fine and resonant, but need a bit of unpacking: 'Our lives are short, so we're fooled into admiring these old things that you palm off on us as new – and we regard

123

them as if they had been brought into being to satisfy our immediate desire, rather than for what they are: a bunch of stuff we've all seen and heard before.' The sestet says 'I defy you and your records; the past and present don't interest me – because history is a liar. In your *continual haste*, things rise and fall, come and go, wax and wane. But in defiance I vow this – and it'll stand for eternity: *I* will *be true, despite thy scythe and thee.*'

Those *pyramids* are a bit odd, but WS could well have had in mind the obelisks – 'pyramids' is just what they called them – that flanked the triumphal arches built for James I's arrival in London. (To which WS seems to have been uniquely and endearingly indifferent; everyone else was offering up tributary verses by the shedload.) This would date this poem somewhere shortly after March 1604. That being the case, we might also choose to read it symbolically, and see a political dimension here: it's not just these here-today-gone-tomorrow monuments WS is defying, it's the caprices of changing regimes, their fickle patronages and falls-from-favour.

In the end, however, the YM is *nowhere* in this poem. It's to love itself that WS pledges his eternal faith, and who's to say he was wrong. It's all we've talked about for the last few hundred pages. Larkin was right: love – love, in its pure, abstract mandala – is exactly what will survive of us.

Here's the paradox, though. There's more than just an unhealthy relationship between love and poetry, and WS's affair and this sonnet sequence are more than just roughly coterminous. They're pretty much consubstantial; I get the strong impression one would have been *unimaginable* without the other. WS knows the sequence must end soon – whether having run out of things to say, or having reached the target of 'Sidney's climacteric' of 108 poems (discounting, as I feel we should, Sonnets 1–17; I'm beginning to feel he added them just to top Sidney's final tally). The affair, too, must end; and it's either been *driven* there by the poem, or prolonged beyond its natural life, which is my reading. What poet wants to sack a good muse? (If you thought getting a plumber on a weekend was tough, try finding Maud Gonne, Laura or Beatrice in the Yellow Pages.) I'd say the chances of affair and sequence having *naturally* coincided are about zero. True: he might have knocked out the last ten poems over a weekend to engineer their simultaneous ending, but I doubt it. Easier all round that he contrive a situation where they can share the same teleology. This arrangement is ideal for the poet; alas, for the human participants, the first word that comes to mind is 'callous', closely followed by 'mercenary'.

Let's be clear. This has been an affair subservient, in the end, not to love, but to *poetry*. And it should probably serve as a health-warning to all those thinking about embarking on an affair with a poet: all those sonnets aren't really about *you*, you know. (This is setting aside the more mundane observation that the poetry is usually the *only* sensitive thing about poets. As Auden once snapped at an underwhelmed lover: 'If you want romance – fuck a journalist.')

124

If my dear love were but the child of state
It might, for fortune's bastard, be unfathered,
As subject to time's love or to time's hate,
Weeds among weeds, or flowers with flowers gathered.
No, it was builded far from accident;
It suffers not in smiling pomp, nor falls
Under the blow of thrallèd discontent,
Whereto th' inviting time our fashion calls:
It fears not policy, that heretic,
Which works on leases of short-numbered hours,
But all alone stands hugely politic,
That it nor grows with heat, nor drowns with showers.
  To this I witness call the fools of time,
  Which die for goodness, who have lived for crime.

The end is in sight. I'm convinced that we can boldly date Sonnets 123–5 around 1604, and propose that political circumstances have encouraged a bit of regime-change in the love department too. Time to be done with this gnash-fest of a sequence. The psychological manoeuvre is quite fascinating: WS will not actually *let go* of love. Instead, he severs love from the beloved, in the apparent belief that it can exist without a physical host: once more, the YM is nowhere in any of this. This is a spiritual salvage-operation of the most desperate kind. It's quite a dense little number too, so I'll annotate it line by line:

124

If my dear love were but the child of state

– If my love had been created by circumstance (*my dear love*, I'm certain, is 'that love which I love, which is dear to me' – i.e. the affection itself and not its object)

It might for Fortune's bastard be unfathered,

– it might be rejected or disowned, because it's wholly at the *mercy* of changing circumstance. (KDJ points out that Elizabethan readers would have been reminded that both Elizabeth and her sister Mary had been declared illegitimate by Henry VIII.)

As subject to time's love or to time's hate,

– it'd be subject to whatever happens to be in or out of fashion, to the mere *whim* of Time

Weeds among weeds, or flowers with flowers gathered.

– flung aside when seen as a weed, or gathered up when seen as a flower. (Here we're reminded that 'flower' and 'weed' are pretty arbitrary designations.)

No, it was builded far from accident;

– No – it was established somewhere free from the caprices of fortune (i.e. with more deliberate resolve)

It suffers not in smiling pomp, nor falls
Under the blow of thrallèd discontent,

– It's affected neither by official approval, nor is it crushed alongside those who present a challenge to authority (*thrallèd discontent* is weird, but it's some kind of attitude-for-attitude-

124 holder metonym for something like 'enslaved malcontents')

Whereto th' inviting time our fashion calls:

– (*thrallèd discontent*) being a state to which the present times tempt us' (or at least that's my best shot, though it's far from clear to what extent WS might include himself in that 'us'; probably not much)

It fears not policy, that heretic,
Which works on leases of short-numbered hours,

– It doesn't fear political scheming (OED defines *policy* as 'A device, expedient, contrivance; a crafty device, stratagem, trick'), that heretic (against truth, I suppose), which operates only over the short term

But all alone stands hugely politic,
That it nor grows with heat, nor drowns with showers.

– but stands alone, hugely wise, neither growing in the sun nor drowning in the rain (i.e. the same in fair or foul weather, times of good and bad fortune. 'These lines have a vaguely phallic cast,' writes SB, a phallic cast being exactly what one would need to maintain this kind of long-term tumescence.)

To this I witness call the fools of time,
Which die for goodness, who have lived for crime.

– As witness to all this, I call those *fools of time*, those slaves to fashion, those fickle victims of fickle time, who – after a life of sin – will repented on their deathbeds.

. . . I think. In a late 19th-century commentary George Wyndham glosses those *fools* as '. . . Who are so much the dupes of Time that they attach importance to mere order or sequence in which the events occur, and believe that a death-bed repentance can cancel a life of crime'. Which makes a fine sophisticated sense of it, for all it goes against the Christian desirability of such a conversion. The alternative is to read l.14 as 'who die as martyrs but live as criminals' – i.e. their status having been defined just as circumstantially and capriciously as that weed/flower we encountered earlier. This has the advantage of allowing us to read in the Gunpowder Plot, Catholic martyrs and all sorts of ar.–1605-type stuff (and confirms the hunch that WS was indeed expressing a more general indifference to James's pyramids in the last poem), but I prefer Wyndham's reading. However both work, and these folk are just the sort of time-bound wretches that, by way of contrastive evidence, WS would call upon to bear witness to (not to act as witness *for*, of course) the eternal, atemporal constancy of his love. I should say that HV goes for something *completely* different, and reads the line as 'those who having lived for inconstancy die to some good purpose, since they bear witness to the folly of infidelity', or something like it. But that's way too contrived, especially given that the sociopolitical frame of the conceit has been clearly established. We're free to take crime as *crime.* Sorry to repeat, but until the poem offers you a good reason to do otherwise, always take the shortest route to literal sense, otherwise there's a good chance you'll just make something up.

125

Were't ought to me I bore the canopy,
With my extern the outward honouring,
Or laid great bases for eternity,
Which proves more short than waste or ruining?
Have I not seen dwellers on form and favour
Lose all, and more, by paying too much rent,
For compound sweet forgoing simple savour,
Pitiful thrivers, in their gazing spent?
No; let me be obsequious in thy heart,
And take thou my oblation, poor but free,
Which is not mixed with seconds, knows no art,
But mutual render, only me for thee.
  Hence, thou suborned informer: a true soul
  When most impeached stands least in thy control.

Having made the psychological move to cut love free of the YM, WS has found a little closure, and is now able to move on. As you'd expect, WS feels the need to draw himself up to his full rhetorical height here, both because of the imminent end of the sequence, and the now-unavoidable need to address the YM directly – something so painful, it requires no little bravery, at this late stage. The magnificent congestion of this sonnet is reminiscent of our own Geoffrey Hill, whose own poems often resemble a logjam at the Vatican. Again, its density means we're better taking this poem a few lines at a time:

Were't ought to me I bore the canopy,
With my extern the outward honouring,

– Would it really mean much to me if I were to, say, carry the royal canopy in a royal procession (again, we can't help but be put in mind of James I's triumphal procession), dignifying such shows (of power) with my outward appearance?

Or laid great bases for eternity,
Which proves more short than waste or ruining?

– Or laid great foundations to last for all eternity (foundations for monumental buildings, we can assume; perhaps the 'pyramids' previously described) – though that eternity, as it turns out, proves to be shorter than either the forces of decay or destruction?'

Have I not seen dwellers on form and favour
Lose all, and more, by paying too much rent,

– (shifting his comparison closer to home) Haven't I seen those who are obsessed with their appearance, and on winning the favour of others, lose everything and more, by paying too high price . . .

For compound sweet, forgoing simple savour,
Pitiful thrivers, in their gazing spent?

– . . . for their fancy fare, forgoing simple tastes – those pathetic aspirants, who are destroyed by their own avaricious gazing?

No, let me be obsequious in thy heart,
And take thou my oblation, poor but free,

125

– No, let me be dutiful in your heart (*obsequious* would then have readily put you in mind of 'obsequies', so these lines have a funereal overtone, miserably appropriate under the circumstances), and accept my simple sacramental offering

Which is not mixed with seconds, knows no art,
But mutual render, only me for thee.

– which isn't cut with stuff, isn't propelled by any wily motive, but is made in the spirit of mutual surrender, myself for yourself.

In ll.10–12, it's easy to hear the Eucharist: in the simplicity of the *poor but free* sacrament; in *seconds*, which might refer (I gather) to the sort of inferior flour to be avoided in making the host; and in *mutual render*, which carries strong overtones of the kind of mutual sacrifice the Holy Communion involves (Christ's *oblation* on the cross, balanced by an offer to sacrifice a life in his service). However, to quote SB's sane conclusion: 'Though the analogy is apparent if one totes up the various Eucharistic references in the sonnet, the analogy is never applied or activated while the poem is in process.'

Fine. That's that then. Done and dusted. Oh hang on, there's another couple of lines. Sure they can't be anything important . . . Better read 'em anyway.

Hence, thou suborned informer! a true soul
When most impeached stands least in thy control.

– Get lost, you bribed informer! When an honest soul is most accused you have least control over him.

Huh? You *what*? Get lost *who*? The shock of these lines is downplayed by far too many commentators, but shock they are: essentially the YM sequence ends right here – on a riddle. *Who's*

being told to get thee *hence*? There are theories, of course, but what I don't understand is why no one seems to be terribly excited 125
by their puzzle. OK: let's analyse this. In the context of the Sonnets, (a) who might be the *suborned informer*? (b) who is the *suborned informer* working on behalf of, and what would they accuse the soul *of*? and (c) what can have *least control* over an loyal and true soul when it is most accused? SB proposes 'a straw man addressed in the character of a self-serving toady who has accused the speaker of some breach of the beloved's faith', but also notes that perhaps the final *thy* addresses the same subject as the *thy* in the third quatrain – i.e. the YM.

I don't buy this. As is often the case, I think WS hasn't intended to be so oracular, and thinks the subject has already been clearly established in our minds. (Poets always do, god bless 'em: much poetic 'obscurity' is simply down to a miscalculation, where the intensity of their feeling – which they are inclined to take as a sign of its self-evidence – has been confused with the clarity of its expression.) To my mind the poem clearly follows on from Sonnets 123 and 124 – both of which address Time, and take a bold stand against its depredations. *This I do vow, and this shall ever be: / I will be true despite thy scythe and thee.* I think *Hence!* indicates a change of address from the YM to Time. Time has been addressed *throughout* this poem, when you think about it: 'Is it a big deal if I partake in these so-called eternal projects, those great noble ceremonies – when they're as worthless before time as everything else? [In *dwellers on form* we might think of that later in*form*er – i.e. perhaps 'one who insists on form being adhered to'.] When those great investors in their own future – in their being sticklers for form, curriers of favour – all fall, consumed by their own desire? No – none of that for me: mine is a simple timeless exchange without ulterior motive, with no expectation of future reward for its present sacrifice.' Then we might read 'Get thee hence, Time, you false witness to true love! A true soul, when most accused of change and its corruptions [damage WS now observes in himself] stands least in your control, neither *subject to Time's love or to Time's hate.*' This doesn't quite solve the logical riddle of why Time has *least* influence when the true soul is *most* accused; although we might rationalise that if the accusation is false, as one might expect from a *suborned informer*, it only serves to remind the soul of its own purity.

Thus the Sonnets' major arcana plays its last card with an appropriately defiant get-thee-behind-me to Time: Time, the evil engine of the terrible change that WS has, alas, identified in his own heart.

HV takes the bizarre line that the whole poem enacts a kind of aesthetic struggle between Latinate and English diction, which is itself symbolic of a move to simplify and purify the 'corrupt Latinate court and its canopied ceremonies'. This argument is prompted (I think) by the obvious contrast between *extern* and *outward* in l.2; although my own suspicion is that *outward* is no more than a necessary 'elegant variation', to get round saying 'extern' twice. (In the first act of *Othello*, WS uses the two words in much the same way – see below – for the same reasons, and there's certainly no sign of any Anglo-Saxon vs. Latin agenda there.) Her conclusion, that 'the couplet's declaration that it is when the Latinate is being *most* Latinate that the English is least threatened . . .' is completely ridiculous. Poetry's hard enough to write as it is. There's simply no way WS would have added another dimension of difficulty to his own compositional process by simultaneously enacting his conceit through some hypertextual, interlingual struggle. There's too much damn *feeling* here.

l.14 SB hears 'in thy cunt roll' in the last line, possibly, which might tie in with a weak riff on premature ejaculation. Hence I suppose 'stands least' etc. However the shade of Kenneth Williams is but fleeting, and passes over the company leaving only a ghost of a snort.

Interestingly, many key ideas and key words (in a non-HV sense) in this poem are echoed in I. i. ll.35–66 of *Othello*, a play we usually date between 1603–1604. Iago's speech contains *outward*, *extern*, *thrive*, *second*, *forms* and *obsequious*. This certainly points to their simultaneous composition, knowing all writers' fondness for recycling (especially between literary genres, where they're less likely to be found out) and obsessing over the same ideas. Even more telling is Iago's *I am not what I am*, echoing the lines in Sonnet 121, where WS forcefully makes the opposite claim: *No, I am that I am, and they that level / At my abuses, reckon up their own.* In WS's own mind, Iago is precisely what he himself is not: Satan, the ultimate false friend. WS is as trustworthy and loyal in love as God himself (cf. our *ever-living poet*).

126

O thou, my lovely boy, who in thy power
Dost hold time's fickle glass, his sickle hour,
Who hast by waning grown, and therein showest
Thy lover's withering, as thy sweet self growest.
If nature, sovereign mistress over wrack,
As thou goest onwards still will pluck thee back,
She keeps thee to this purpose: that her skill
May time disgrace, and wretched minute kill.
Yet fear her, O thou minion of her pleasure:
She may detain, but not still keep, her treasure!
Her audit, though delayed, answered must be,
And her quietus is to render thee.
( )
( )

And so we reach the final sonnet in this remarkable gut-wrenching, tormented sequence. We'll get on to the subject of its strange formal features in a moment, but let's attend to the poem first.

Perched, as it is, on the double climacteric of 126 (i.e. 2 x 63), WS will have felt obliged to write about death and the passing of time – but of course this subject dovetails perfectly with the sequence's end anyway. He's had this end-point in mind for a long while, I feel, so plenty of time to prepare his valediction. There's the temptation (especially among the homoqueasiacs) to read *lovely boy* as 'Cupid' in l.1, but it's clear that WS is addressing the YM, and it comes as a relief after the tactical avoidance of the last three poems. Nonetheless you feel it took a certain courage. (CB points out that 'lovely boy' is also used in a homosexual context in Holland's translation of Plutarch's *Moralia*.) l.2 is interesting: *time's fickle glass* – time's changing mirror, a wonderfully scary concept – is clear, but *sickle hour* presents a few more problems, enough to have encouraged some to read it as a misprint, and change it to *fickle*. But it's *sickle*, a fine pun on *sickle*, as in 'knife', i.e. time's scythe, and sickle as in 'sickle moon' – the *waning* time that we see in l.3; in the course of which, and in contrast to which the YM has grown to maturity, while showing up his lovers as very much on the wane too. (The repetition of *grown/growest* might be a polyptoton; personally I think it might be somewhere between that and a polyp, an unfortunate little outgrowth WS didn't notice. Semi-accidental repetitions are the classic poet's goof, and arise through the intense focus on the detail at the expense of the whole. Editorial conversations often consist of things like 'You are *aware* that this is the second time you've used *adamantine* in this stanza?' I don't know one of us who doesn't make this error from time to time. You can make it sound deliberate, though, by overstressing *self*, and contrastively de-emphasising *growest*.)

ll.5–8 might be summarised 'If nature, the ultimate power over destruction, insists on holding you *back* from that destruction – she's doing it for this reason: to show, through her ability to keep you young, that she can disgrace time – and kill the wretched minute [whereby it measures out death].' I agree with KDJ that 'minute' shouldn't be corrected to the plural. To disgrace time, you have to destroy not just its 'minutes' but its very constitution, the smallest unit of time itself (the Elizabethans didn't use 'second' in the temporal sense yet). The poem concludes 'But nature's pet or not, you should fear nature; she might detain you, but she can't keep you. Her accounts will be due, and her settlement [*quietus*] will be *you*.'

Quietus (short for *quietus est*, 'he is quit', i.e. all square – something you'd write on a receipt) was already a metaphor for death. You'll recall *When he himselfe might his quietus make / With a bare bodkin* – though admittedly WS seems to have been the first writer to use it this way. Here he seems to invert the cliché of 'death as a debt paid to nature'; I hear a suggestion that nature has, through her keeping the YM back from time's decay, put *herself* into debt – and there's only one thing she can pay it off with. Yup: you. I love the admonitory and minatory tone of this poem, the way WS conceals his vulnerability, his great grief and disappointment, behind the dead baritone of this grim augur.

As HV points out, the poem is indeed rich in its lyric weaving, or what she calls 'interphonic relations'. However her claim that *audit* and *answered* are 'unpartnered phonetically and are thereby foregrounded as nonce events' is plain wrong. They sit within a veritable *garden* of proximate dentals. Toothsome consonants apart, *answered* is immediately followed by *must*, echoing both its nasal and sibilant sounds. (Apart from anything else, I hope I never get invited to a nonce event. Har.) Much worse, though, is her metrical analysis, where she finds echoed amphibrachs (– / – feet) scattered through the poem, reads them as confirmation of this, that and the next thing, and states that the poem falls into trochaic and amphibrachic pattern, not iambic. Setting aside the fact that 'amphibrachic pattern' is triple metre, this is the sort of nonsense that can arise when you proceed with a great ear but only a partial understanding of how metre actually functions. There *are* no feet in English verse, only metrical patterns; in Germanic languages the foot is a useful concept only as a limited tool of retrospective analysis, to indicate or describe a local area of *deviation* from a metrical pattern, and exists neither for the reading reader nor the composing poet; caesurae do *not* indicate divisions between feet, and words do *not* represent foot-boundaries. (In spoken language, incidentally, even the gaps between words are a purely psychological phenomenon.) The poem is in duple metre, like every other poem in the entire sequence. HV has the cart before the horse. Can everyone *please* stop marking in the feet, and imagining caesurae where there's no punctuation to indicate a pause? I know it's fun. But *they're just not there*, folks.

Sorry: it's late, and I've been drinking. Now for the fun bit, and for my money the most poignant part of the poem. You'll note that this alleged sonnet is really a 12-liner resting on an empty couplet. There's been much speculation as to the meaning of the 'missing' lines, not least because the sonnet itself is a pretty workaday affair on a well-worn theme. We can quickly dismiss the theory that Thomas Thorpe removed the lines because they were too personally revealing – a happy thought, but a hopelessly optimistic one – or that WS failed to read the proofs properly, and failed to notice there were lines missing. Because they're not missing. They're just unwritten. The poem ends, and ends firmly: it's hard to imagine a couplet of even the most redundant variety. SB thinks the brackets a printer's addition, as if he *thought* there was something missing, though he does concede that the emptiness stands as an accidental 'illustrative analogy' and seems to enact the poem's warning. Do they represent an hourglass? Well, if they'd been printed:

126 ( )
( )

. . . conceivably, yes; though they don't actually look like that, but like two spare tyres on a fat lad. Perhaps they symbolise the post-double-climacteric scene of the two dead lovers, now united in the grave? Nice, but a bit far-fetched. For all l.12's emphatic closure, there seems to me no possibility that we are *not* meant to experience a gap at ll.13–14, whether WS inserted the empty brackets or not – of the sequence has the momentum of 125 poems behind it, and ends right here. To *feel* that missing couplet is surely WS's intention. This missing pair is further emphasised by the fact that the poem is written not in quatrains, but six couplets, making twelve lines – 12/6 echoing the number of the sonnet itself.

As to the meaning of the gap: well, I hear nothing more than a simple visual pun. What are we faced with here? A missing couplet. As well as 'two rhymed lines of verse', WS would know 'couplet' as 'a pair', 'a coupling' and perhaps 'twins'. There's no couple any more. It's over. Note that this poem in some sense closes the circle of the whole YM sequence: it could easily have been one of the procreation sonnets, with the couplet proposing that it was time for the YM to act against death's approach, and make replicas of himself, perpetuating his beauty. The omission of such a couplet leaves it to stand as a cold and rather bitter warning: WS no longer has any role here, whether as lover or adviser.

With an absurd caution, SB says that 'although the sex of the beloved is unspecified in most of the sonnets, all those that are specifically and exclusively addressed to a man precede this one in the Q order, and all those specifically and exclusively addressed to a woman follow it'. Erm . . . Indeed. Pre-Raphaelite poet, painter and amateur grave-robber Dante Gabriel Rossetti suggested that 'there should be an essential reform in the printing of Shakespeare's sonnets. After sonnet CXXV should occur the words *End of Part I*. The couplet piece, numbered CXXVI, should be called *Epilogue to Part I*. Then, before CXXVII, should be printed *Part II*. After CLII should be put *End of Part II* – and the last two sonnets should be called *Epilogue to Part II*.' (I'd add a *Preface to Part I*, i.e. Sonnets 1–17.) These divisions are clear enough when you read the Sonnets straight through – but since hardly anyone does, it would certainly improve their navigability.

127

In the old age black was not counted fair,
Or if it were, it bore not beauty's name;
But now is black beauty's successive heir,
And beauty slandered with a bastard shame:
For since each hand hath put on Nature's power,
Fairing the foul with art's false borrowed face,
Sweet beauty hath no name, no holy bower,
But is profaned, if not lives in disgrace.
Therefore my mistress' eyes are raven black,
Her eyes so suited, and they mourners seem
At such who, not born fair, no beauty lack,
Sland'ring creation with a false esteem;
Yet so they mourn, becoming of their woe,
That every tongue says beauty should look so.

Well, that was that. Now we have a whole new sequence. It's doubtful, however, that the composition of these poems followed neatly on the heels of the YM sonnets, and it certainly seems that the love-affairs the two sequences describe ran concurrently, or at least that there was a large degree of overlap. It's certainly an interesting series of poems, but more from the psychological than literary perspective: the Dark Lady sonnets are remarkable testament to how little an intelligent man can know about himself. (The contrast between the intelligence of the expression and the stupidity of the content is so profound, at times, that we really have to consider this stuff from an *evolutionary* perspective.) Wordsworth *hated* them: 'These sonnets, beginning at 127, to his Mistress, are worse than a puzzle-peg. They are abominably harsh, obscure & worthless.' 'Harsh', yes; but they're certainly not without 'worth', if 'interesting, for all the wrong reasons' counts for anything.

This one's all right, I suppose; it all turns into a right old ugly misogynist affair soon enough, so enjoy this while you can. However what's interesting here is the way in which this poem – while doing its best to *praise* the DL – is already wrestling with the demons of WS's self-disgust.

This poem purports to ask the following serious questions: Where does the essential nature of beauty lie? How much is intrinsic to an unchanging *idea* of beauty, and how much to changing fashion? But the poem doesn't really give a damn about them, and like most of the DL sonnets is fuelled primarily by WS's own incomprehension at the dissonance between his desire and his aesthetic sense. Or to put it much more bluntly: he finds himself wanting to screw someone that, try as he might, he just can't find beautiful in the way he did the YM. If you read this poem as a free-standing sonnet, however, you'll likely find none of that, but the later poems in the sequence lay bare his truer feelings.

'Back in the day, dark complexions weren't thought of as beautiful – or if they were, no one called it that. But now black is the legitimate heir to that "fair" idea of beauty, and the fair that *used* to be called beautiful has a shameful reputation. Why? Because – since everyone paints their face, and imitates the fair beauty that was once in nature's gift alone – no one can *really* be called beautiful; it's too common, maybe even shameful. So my lady's eyes

127 are black, as [when you think about it] *befits* the current fashion: they seem to be lamenting those who were born ugly but now *no beauty lack*, slandering nature by faking her. But those black eyes mourn so beautifully, everyone is now saying that beauty should actually look like *this*.'

Where to start. The conceit was going passably well: 'now that *anyone* can now look fair and beautiful – *black* is the new fair'. But then he runs out of steam, and introduces the utterly extraneous idea that the DL's black eyes are like mourners. The most generous interpretation of ll.9–12 – in terms of crediting this with some coherent sense – is that the DL's black eyes look like they mourn the tragic sight of nature being slandered by the ugly folk who have painted themselves to look beautiful. However the poem doesn't really say that; the DL's eyes mourn the sight of the painted ugly *themselves*. This requires us to understand *mourners* in the sense of 'lamenters' or 'deplorers'; both possible senses of the word, certainly – but *not* if the sense has already been limited by WS's metaphor, which is 'dark eyes look like black-garbed mourners'. They don't look like deplorers. In other words it doesn't work.

This is setting aside the unprovable but nagging objection that – while the DL's dark eyes might well look *sad* – the idea that WS *really* thought of them as deploring anything at all is highly unlikely. It's just a facile and disingenuous turn in the argument, made in an attempt to work the whole into some neatly interdependent conceit. The couplet, in attempting to shore it up further, just makes matters worse. 'Her eyes look so mournfully becoming, that now everyone says beauty should look like *her*.' Thus, apparently, closing the circle of the argument, and turning the initial proposition, fair = beautiful, on its head. The point is that it's achieved via a stupid interpolated whim, not by reasoned argument. If we could translate this poem into the neat quadratic equation to which so much Elizabethan conceit aspires to, it simply wouldn't balance at all: it leaks everywhere. The DL doesn't mourn anything, and the only 'deplorer' here is WS, irrationally disgusted by his own contradictory feelings, and desperately trying to square them.

ll.9–10 the repetition of *eyes* has often been assumed to be a mistake, but I don't see why. For one thing, if you change it to another noun – *brows*, *hairs*, whatever – it muddles the antecedent of *they* in . . . *and they mourners seem.* In Sonnet 132, WS also refers to *two mourning eyes*, and it's surely *eyes* that mourn here too. If you read l.10 with a de-emphasis on *eyes* and an expressive rise on *suited*, the repetition now just reads as a rhetorically effective diacope.

128

How oft when thou, my music, music play'st,
Upon that blessed wood whose motion sounds
With thy sweet fingers when thou gently sway'st
The wiry concord that mine ear confounds,
Do I envy those jacks that nimble leap
To kiss the tender inward of thy hand,
Whilst my poor lips, which should that harvest reap,
At the wood's boldness by thee blushing stand?
To be so tickled, they would change their state
And situation with those dancing chips,
O'er whom thy fingers walk with gentle gait,
Making dead wood more blessed than living lips.
  Since saucy jacks so happy are in this,
  Give them thy fingers, me thy lips to kiss.

By the time WS wrote this, the 'O-how-I-wish-I-was-your glove/wine-glass/viol/lapdog/sandwich' shtick was very well-worn. Barnabe Barnes was already having a hard time taking it too seriously, and declared his desire to be the very wine his mistress drinks, then is intoxicated by, then pees: . . . *which down her throat doth trickle, / To kiss her lips, and lie next at her heart, / Run through her veins, and pass by Pleasure's part!* Yay . . . By the time WS came to write this poem, the conceit was subject to routine subversion and satire. With this I-wish-I-was-your-virginal number, many commentators think WS had his tongue in his cheek too, and that he's giving a knowing wink to the reader. But were that to be the case, we'd expect the poem to be either funnier or ruder than it is. It's just a bagatelle.

And it doesn't work too well, either. WS envies the virginal's keys for their kissing his lover's hand – where his lips should be; in other words we have 'keys of virginal: WS's lips' as the vehicle and tenor of our conceit, but the ground between to the two is just too thin to make it work. The DL's fingers depress the keys more than the keys rise to meet her fingers; and lips aren't anything *like* bits of wood, something the dreadful l.12, in trying to make a virtue of the difference, only hammers home. In other words, the ground is constructed from 'lips'/wood's relationship through touch', and through 'music-as-lifter-of-spirit': as l.1 says, while she *plays* music, she *is* WS's music. Alas, the latter ground is never developed, leaving us with the 'touch' alone; which thin idea gives rise to a whole bunch of increasingly creaky comparisons between ll.5 and 12. SB suggests that WS chose the virginal because of its sexual overtones (though it's etymologically unrelated to 'virgin'), appropriate here in that it's physically uncooperative. Maybe. But the most interesting thing about this poem is what follows it: the black mass of Sonnet 129. Why on earth did WS prepare the darkest sonnet in the entire 154-poem sequence with such a piece of *fluff*? To catch us off-guard?

l.5 *jack*: 'In the virginal, spinet, and harpsichord: An upright piece of wood fixed to the back of the key-lever, and fitted with a quill which plucked the string as the jack rose on the key's being pressed down. (By Shakes. and some later writers erron. applied to the key.)' – OED.

l.7 *harvest reap* marks a stylistic nadir in the sonnets; the metaphor has nothing to do with anything here at all. Dear me.

128 l.12 Everyone quotes Henry Constable's *A lute of senseless wood, by nature dumbe, / Toucht by thy hand doth speake divinely well* (c.1590), so I will too. Though I don't know why, really, as I think the similarities are superficial and probably coincidental.

l.13 *saucy jacks* can also read as 'impertinent knaves', of course, should you choose to. I have no idea if this phrase informed the author of the notorious 'Saucy Jacky' postcard, allegedly sent by Jack the Ripper to taunt the police, or indeed 'Saucy Jack', the Ripper-themed rock opera proposed by David St. Hubbins of Spinal Tap. HV is mysteriously silent on this issue.

129

Th'expense of spirit in a waste of shame
Is lust in action; and till action, lust
Is perjured, murd'rous, bloody, full of blame,
Savage, extreme, rude, cruel, not to trust;
Enjoyed no sooner but despisèd straight;
Past reason hunted, and no sooner had,
Past reason hated as a swallowed bait,
On purpose laid to make the taker mad;
Mad in pursuit, and in possession so,
Had, having, and in quest to have, extreme;
A bliss in proof, and proved, a very woe;
Before, a joy proposed; behind, a dream.
All this the world well knows, yet none knows well
To shun the heaven that leads men to this hell.

One of the most famous sonnets; a terrific display of self-directed fury, raging away in the little cage of the sonnet like a spitting wildcat. For once WS pulls back from his subjects, ditches the authorial 'I', and is moved to give us a speech on the subject of lust and shame, as if he were thundering from a pulpit. In the syntax of its disgusted litany, it sounds to me like George Herbert's 'Prayer', only read backwards in a mirror. Again, though, look at the articulacy of anger, in all its impassioned argument-for-the-prosecution exactitude and wildly original phrasemaking. HV says this is a 'judgmental, "morning after" account of the experience'. But this isn't the morning after. No one writes poems then. They drown their shame in buckets of coffee, fry-ups and black naps. This is the *night* after the morning after. The shame and disgust of the morning are reconsidered in anger, as he sees his uncontrollable id master him again, and the spectre of his lust rise to its feet, ready to go another fifteen rounds. (David West points out that this is the only use of the word *lust* in all the Sonnets.)

Omne animal post coitum triste est is invariably quoted by most commentators, and fairly. (The whole phrase, from the Roman physician Galen is much more fun, if somewhat inaccurate: *Triste est omne animal post coitum, praeter mulierem gallumque.* After sex all animals are sad, except women and the rooster.) The expended spirit means the 'vital spirit' of semen, as well as life-force. It alludes to the ancient belief that spilled seed diminishes your vitality, and perhaps even shortens your life. (And ruins your eyesight; depending on the age of their mothers, an old warning male readers might be familiar with in an auto-erotic context. WS seems to refer to this in later sonnets, where he blames his own failing eyesight for taking the DL for a beauty. This poor woman really can't win.)

The timing of this sonnet is strange, as it follows two poems of sensual praise. What lies behind this is certainly post-coital tristesse – *A bliss in proof, and proved, a very woe* sums it up rather perfectly – but one of a very particular, self-disgusted variety. Those who have experienced it will know what I mean, and its basis is surely more physical than psychological; Spinoza thought it was mere post-Santa letdown – 'But after the enjoyment of sensual pleasure is past, the greatest sadness follows'. But it's too irrational and disproportionate a response to explain by

129

anything but a bizarre reaction to a sudden flood of post-orgasmic neurotransmitters. Your anticipatory-thrill dopamine goes through the roof during arousal, but the prolactin secreted during orgasm suddenly suppresses it, so you get a mood-plummet. The cuddle-hormone oxytocin released on ejaculation to drive you into your limp 'refractory period' (this serves to stops the penis thrusting after orgasm, since that would only displace the semen it had carefully implanted) isn't always enough to offset the effect; either way, especially in younger men, we seem have the recipe for a very grim mind-bouillabaisse. The fact that this can be then misinterpreted as feelings of self-disgust, or disgust towards your sexual partner (both of which can produce generalised feelings of misogyny in the none-too-self-aware) is yet another thumb-tack in the coffin of intelligent design.

Feeding into the mix, there's also the Christian idea of sex being fundamentally sinful (great idea, guys), but I think it's a relatively small part of it. I'm trying to avoid the conclusion – perhaps I can't – that it's just a horribly misogynist poem. Now a man can say what the hell he likes about *one* woman, just as a woman can of one man: it might be true. Too many knee-jerk charges of misogyny conveniently overlook this simple point. But if it's clear that your negative assessment of one woman is informed by a *general* hatred of them, or if you generalise your bad feelings about one woman, and then extend them to the whole of womankind . . . Well, that's monstrous, and no excuses should be offered. I'll proffer one more possible explanation, if not an excuse, and it's hardly a revolutionary one: WS was so uncomfortable in his homosexuality, and so keenly aware of its 'sinfulness', that despite his contrary instincts he was often forced to try to conceive of it as a largely non-sexual and pure impulse. This

129 left only one place for his instincts to go: towards the sex that he wasn't actually attracted to.

The results were predictable. Yes, it's true to say that the pursuit of lust can turn us into savage, extreme, rude and cruel monsters, not to be trusted; we know all that. But as soon as lust is *had*, is it still *hated*? Yes, lust can wreck a life, but only under specific circumstances: when you're sexually in thrall to someone you neither love, nor like, nor respect, nor who affords you any aesthetic pleasure when you look at them. I fear that's just what's going down here. All the post mating blues apart, it's hardly a blindingly original insight to suggest that when a natural urge is forced into an unnatural expression, the attendant self-disgust is often transferred to the sexual partner. A less brilliant poem on the same subject would have been difficult to stomach.

(Thinking about this atrocious societal suppression of natural instinct and its diversion into unnatural or inappropriate sexual relations, I'm afraid it's quite impossible, at this point, not to be reminded of the current 'plight' of the Catholic church. Don't get me wrong – I'm sure many priests signed up because they were career paedophiles and saw a splendid opportunity. But there must have been many whose healthy, adult urges – through the church's deranged insistence on suppressing them – were diverted into a perverse and pathological expression, with nightmarish consequences for countless children. Why this point is even slightly controversial is a mystery, given that we accept it as more-or-less axiomatic that a high incidence of male rape in prisons is probably inevitable, for very similar reasons.)

l.1 *in a waste of shame*: a way of saying both 'shameful waste' and 'something not worth the shame it involves'.

l.2 *action*: could also simply mean 'sexual action'.

I was going to go on, but actually – the poem is such a torrent
of innuendo, with some kind of Elizabethan double-meaning in 129
every second word, you can safely assume that if you think you've
spotted something rude, you have.

130

My mistress' eyes are nothing like the sun;
Coral is far more red than her lips, red:
If snow be white, why then her breasts are dun;
If hairs be wires, black wires grow on her head,
I have seen roses damasked, red and white,
But no such roses see I in her cheeks;
And in some perfumes is there more delight
Than in the breath that from my mistress reeks.
I love to hear her speak, yet well I know
That music hath a far more pleasing sound:
I grant I never saw a goddess go;
My mistress, when she walks, treads on the ground.
  And yet by heaven, I think my love as rare,
  As any she belied with false compare.

Hmmm. Don't fancy yours much. God only knows why this wretched little poem is so popular. It's fun to teach in school, I suppose. But its mechanism – a negation of the traditional blazon, a list of the beloved's admirable attributes, often presented as elaborate similes – is a cheap trick. (The form has been mocked for ever, and some of the paraprosdokian music-hall similes are still doing the rounds: *Your teeth are like stars: they come out at night. Your lips are like petals: bicycle pedals. Your eyes are like the sea: they make me sick,* etc.) Me, I'd have been far more convinced if he'd stopped this litany of near-misogynistic, repulsed detail at the octave, and had had the decency to spend six lines trying to work out where her appeal for him might have *actually* lain. It's all very well to suggest that traditional ways of celebrating the female are tired old tropes, and that we need a new approach that conveys something of the real earthly, earthly beauty of an attractive woman – but where *is* it? At least have a *stab* at it, man.

The couplet is sort-of-clever, and summarises neatly the whole poem's real conceit – a critique of *false compare* – while belatedly remembering to pay the woman some kind of limp compliment. In l.13, note that *she* does not have the focus of WS's lust as its antecedent; it's a synonym for 'woman'. So 'I think my love just as special as any woman misrepresented by false comparisons.' But at the end of the day, does this poem *really* say more than 'Well, she's an ugly old bag, but she seems to get it up for me anyway. Go figure'? More charitably, you could say this is a poem twitting his fellow sonneteers, and attacking their lazy writing (i.e. it's really about other *guys*), and he gets so distracted that he forgets to actually address and respect the poem's declared subject. But it *could* have been a poem that said 'no: *my* mistress – unlike yours, with her ears like shells and eyes like stars and all that nonsense – is a *real* woman'. HV thinks it *does* say just that, but she's too kind. WS leaves the compliment much too late.

(While I'd defend this reading, I should point out that the poem also stands as a good example of the slightly different conclusions we can reach when we read the Sonnets individually and out of sequence. Sonnet 131 goes some little way to make up for it, and in WS's mind, at least, it probably runs on from this one.)

l.1: Actors often take great and ostentatious delight in *really* hamming up the emphasis on *My*, and every occurrence of *my*

130 and *her* thereafter; show your superior sophistication by underplaying this, and playing up the qualified similes. This way the contrast between WS's and his rival's woman, and his superior non-hysterical handling of the simile get equal billing – which is his intention.

l.8 *Than in the breath that from my mistress reeks* – isn't quite as bad as it sounds; confusingly, 'reeks' won't mean 'smell' for a hundred years yet. It's used as in the surviving Scots sense, 'smokes'.

❧

131

Thou art as tyrannous, so as thou art,
As those whose beauties proudly make them cruel;
For well thou know'st, to my dear doting heart
Thou art the fairest and most precious jewel.
Yet in good faith, some say that thee behold,
Thy face hath not the power to make love groan;
To say they err I dare not be so bold,
Although I swear it to myself alone.
And to be sure that is not false, I swear,
A thousand groans, but thinking on thy face;
One on another's neck do witness bear
Thy black is fairest in my judgment's place.
  In nothing art thou black save in thy deeds,
  And thence this slander, as I think, proceeds.

Harrumph . . . OK, but a bit late. As I say: one hazard of reading a sequence as a bunch of individual poems will sometimes lead us into making unfair criticisms (and occasionally bestowing a little unearned praise). It's clear that in some important senses this sonnet redeems the previous one, and it does pay the missing compliment. I don't doubt that was WS's reparative intention. The amazing thing is that it retracts the slur on the DL's appearance only to deliver a *far* worse insult, in the wholly unsuspected sting of the final couplet; this lashes from the poem just when you thought you were clear, like the Balrog's whip,

131

albeit disguised as a late, casual afterthought. It's as if he were channelling Edna St Vincent Millay from the future. Quite brilliant.

On a second reading, though, we can see that it was all there in the first line. That *tyrannous*, we were inclined to overlook; it's part of the stock-in-trade of the post-Petrarchan lurve sonneteer (Sidney uses the word of Stella), and within that context, it's almost a compliment. One's inamorata was *supposed* to be tyrannous. But it turns out WS *meant* it, and breathes new life into the cliché by literalising it. We don't just read it the same way on the second pass.

Still, though . . . I find ll.5–12 thoroughly stirring, viscerally suggestive of the torments of sexual obsession and infatuation. 'Yet, oh yes, some who look at you say – yours isn't the kind of face men moan over. Well; that might be true for them. Me: I can't stop groaning when I think of it. Groan after groan. In my judgement, your black is beautiful.' (I don't hear the agonies of venereal disease here, as some suggest, which I gather involve more yelping than groaning.)

And *then* . . . 'No: in nothing are you *black*. Nothing at all. Oh no . . . Apart from your deeds, of course, which is where I guess we're *really* going with all this.' (i.e. the slandering of your appearance.)

Ouch! And if it's not obvious, I should maybe say why I don't find this sonnet misogynistic where the last one was: Sonnet 130 sounded a generic disgust. That's all wrong. This one makes a specific accusation. That's all grand. Or at least would be, if we weren't reading this poem as part of a sequence.

l.5 *some say that thee behold*: some say whom thee behold.

l.11 *One on another's neck*: idiomatic, meaning 'one after another', i.e. a succession of groans.

l.12 *Thy black*: thy black complexion (and perhaps with a hint of the non-fair, i.e. the ugly), I think, since *black* in any other 131
sense is withheld until the next line.

132

Thine eyes I love, and they, as pitying me,
Knowing thy heart torments me with disdain,
Have put on black and loving mourners be,
Looking with pretty ruth upon my pain;
And truly not the morning sun of heaven
Better becomes the grey cheeks of the East,
Nor that full star that ushers in the even
Doth half that glory to the sober West
As those two mourning eyes become thy face:
O let it then as well beseem thy heart
To mourn for me, since mourning doth thee grace,
And suit thy pity like in every part:
Then will I swear beauty herself is black,
And all they foul that thy complexion lack.

Who said love had to be consistent? A much sweeter sonnet, this one, with all the hatred directed inwardly again, where it belongs. Indeed WS is deriving no little masochistic pleasure from the fact that he feels himself to be scorned and pitied; good man. He loves the way it makes the DL look. Her dark eyes are like mourners, consoling him on his grief – albeit a grief she's caused, through the torment of her disdain. (Disdainful mourning, mind you, is a hell of a complicated expression. Try it. I'm going for Stephen Rea above the nose and Alan Rickman below it, but it's coming out like Bell's palsy.)

There isn't enough information to say what provokes the pity, or what suffering invites it. Because WS is so weak, and has been sexually enslaved? Because he wants more than he's getting? Because he isn't getting any? Because *he* isn't getting any, but someone else is? Although it's made easier if we just read this poem as, essentially, an in-the-pocket Petrarchan sonnet, where a frequent theme was the cold mistress refusing to yield to the poet's ardour. I think that's the main thrust here, and as we'll see, this seems to be confirmed in the couplet.

It's far more straightforward on the subject of the DL's unconventional beauty, though. However, ll.5–9 seem an attempt to map the sky to the DL's face, and it doesn't come off so well. *Grey cheeks of the east* seems an attempt to broaden the ground of the eyes = heavenly bodies comparison, but it's very forced. (A pale pallor wasn't in any way undesirable in a woman: as SB points out, it would mark you out as a lady of leisure, or at least someone unlikely to be taken for a field-worker.) Not that WS's comparison of her dark eyes to the rising sun and a full-phase Venus is so great either; the only plausible hinge, apart from their twinkliness, lies in their vague ability to both lend *glory*. Either way, the mapping 'dark eye = bright sun' is never going to produce a great metaphor.

But it *is* a lovely argument. After the praise, WS says 'Look: since mourning becomes you, why not go the whole hog? If your heart mourns for me too, it'll then dress [*suit*, though also used in the sense of 'match'] you top-to-toe, inside-out in pity. Then I'll swear: Beauty *herself* will take a dark appearance – and all those who don't share that dark look, I'll declare unbeautiful.' This idea is proposed in ll.10–12, where HV observes that 'the plea distinguishes itself from the praise by its "logical" evenness of iambic

rationality'. Nice to agree, for once. Indeed it does. Compare the
132 stresses in this passage to what's gone before.

By *then* in l.13 I think we can hear his meaning more clearly. 'If you pity me from the heart, *really* take pity on me,[if you pity me sufficiently to sleep with me], then . . .' (The poem turns late, incidentally, on l.10.)

l.5 puns on *morning/mourning*, but you'll have spotted that.

133

Beshrew that heart that makes my heart to groan
For that deep wound it gives my friend and me;
Is't not enough to torture me alone,
But slave to slavery my sweet'st friend must be?
Me from myself thy cruel eye hath taken,
And my next self thou harder hast engrossed:
Of him, myself and thee I am forsaken,
A torment thrice threefold thus to be crossed.
Prison my heart in thy steel bosom's ward,
But then my friend's heart let my poor heart bail.
Whoe'er keeps me, let my heart be his guard;
Thou canst not then use rigour in my jail.
    And yet thou wilt, for I, being pent in thee,
    Perforce am thine, and all that is in me.

Now this is where it all gets very slightly interesting. In a way, this is another 'useless' sonnet: after the loose, quickly shifting amorous allegiances of the school playground, the chances are you'll never have to deal with this kind of situation again. The poem's interests for us are literary and prurient, but that's about it. It will shed light on nothing. (OK, that's a half-truth. There are adult subcultures which mimic the morally derelict fun-zone of the school playground, of course, but we can pursue that thought at our own reflective leisure.)

Anyway – guess what? The DL has enslaved his *sweet'st*

133 *friend*, his *next self* – and we're surely not meant to doubt who *that* is. Putting aside the observation that this is *one* socially incestuous little group (another reason – if we have a mind to – we might finger the DL as someone close to *Mr WH*'s noble circle), it's just rotten luck. You might be suffering some déjà vu at this point, and recall some identical shenanigans from Sonnets 40–2. It's a fair bet that these *are* the identical shenanigans, if for no other reason than it seems unlikely anyone would be dealt such an identically bad hand twice in their life. Again, this would make us inclined to read these sonnets as having been written contemporaneously with the YM sequence, and later divided. That scenario makes a great deal more sense than the idea he completed them *after* the YM sequence. Again – this definitely doesn't sound like *anything* recollected in tranquillity to me; WS loves writing in the heat of the moment.

'Curse that heart of yours – that heart that makes my *own* heart groan for that *deep wound* it gives my friend and me. Isn't it enough to torture me without making my friend a slave to the same slavery? [Which sounds tautological, but not if we read *slavery* as something like "sexual addiction".] Your *cruel eye* has taken me from my own nature, and my YM you've acquired even *more* completely; so I've been abandoned by him, by myself and by you – which is a triple torment, multiplied by three. Imprison my heart in your steely bosom, but at least let me use my own heart to bail out my friend. Whoever keeps me, let me at least guard my friend – and then you can't torment me in my prison [because he's compensated by the joy of looking after him, I guess]. But you *will* torment me, won't you: because if I'm imprisoned in you, of necessity I'm all yours – and everything [i.e. the YM included] is therefore yours too.'

For all its nightmarish, rack-and-screw self-excoriation – it's quite fun, really. It pursues an attractively self-defeating line: WS tries to argue for his friend's bail, but realises that his logic contains a grave flaw: if the YM is in his heart, and that heart is furthermore imprisoned within the DL's steely bosom – then she has the YM's heart too. The somewhat larger flaw is, you'll have noticed, that none of this makes an ounce of sense. If A is in your heart, and you're in B's heart, B *doesn't* have A's heart – because to say someone is 'in your heart' is a metaphor, where the preposition 'in' has a non-extensible and contextually limited meaning. WS has extended it anyway, but it's nonsense: we're not Russian dolls. The Elizabethan conceit was rarely derailed by its own speciousness.

So what *can* he mean? Oh, it's quite simple. He's just upset. I don't doubt for a second that this has led to the total erosion of his psychological centre. He now has a double jealousy to add to his own sexual enslavement; no wonder he feels it all as a ninefold torment. Talking of which . . . while it's certainly gratuitous hyperbole, it strikes me that the conceit alone can't justify the presence of these 3 x 3 torments; they must also be a deliberate echoing of the number of the sonnet. Since the number will have almost certainly prompted the line, and not vice versa (although I guess it's possible the line was flown in late), this means that WS *must* have been composing the sonnets not only in the rough sequence we find them, but numbering them as he went. But bear in mind that the YM and DL sequences were likely composed in parallel. This scenario leaves us with the interesting and not-totally-outrageous possibility that he'd had 154 in his head as a target-number from very early on in the sequence's composition – meaning that while he was composing *this* sonnet, he was

looking at the 90-sonnet gap between sonnets 40–2 and 133, and
133 already planning ahead, trying to figure out how he might fill it.
But that's *exactly* how you compose a sequence, as much as the reader would prefer to think of it as a more organic affair. This certainly explains much of WS's desperate padding in the doldrums of the 80s and 90s, and such curiosities as the juvenile Sonnet 145.

134

So now I have confessed that he is thine,
And I my self am mortgaged to thy will,
Myself I'll forfeit, so that other mine
Thou wilt restore to be my comfort still;
But thou wilt not, nor he will not be free,
For thou art covetous, and he is kind;
He learned but surety-like to write for me,
Under that bond that him as fast doth bind.
The statute of thy beauty thou wilt take,
Thou usurer, that put'st forth all to use,
And sue a friend came debtor for my sake:
So him I lose through my unkind abuse.
Him have I lost; thou hast both him and me;
He pays the whole, and yet am I not free.

This sonnet runs on from the last. What's interesting here is less the poem – which is too dry to permit us any real emotional engagement with its subject – than the wretched density of the legal and financial metaphor. The metaphorical mapping, that 'love's dealings = legal transactions', is an easy one to embroider, and has a deep truth. We *do* often feel like we're embroiled in some lengthy, agonised contractual negotiation, and WS's unusual situation is singularly nightmarish in this regard. But like all extended metaphors, this one presents itself as consistent and convincing by omitting mention of everything that *won't* fall into the

134 ground (the attributes tenor and vehicle share – I know you know that, but just to refresh). In this case, the *difference* between the tenor and vehicle – what we call the 'tension' of the metaphor – lies between love's tenderness, and the coldness of litigation. The bit of the metaphor we're consciously impressed by is its aptness, the strength of ground; but what's not often appreciated is that its real poignancy lies in the tension, and what the tenor is patently *not* – but what, through our determined comparison, *we propose that it is becoming*. In other words – what kind of love *is* it that we can think of in such legal terms? One which is losing all its tenderness and warmth and selfless sacrifice. And that's the real emotional field proposed by the comparison. Not that love *is* a legal negotiation; we know it isn't, really. But what kind of love yearns to *become* so? One too painful to deal with by any other means.

The poem is tightly knotted, so let's loosen it off a bit: 'So now I've admitted he's yours, *and* that I'm also legally contracted to your desires – I'll forfeit myself, if you'll release my friend, so that he can come and comfort me. But you won't. Nor does he want to be released, because you're greedy and he's kind: he tried to raise the bail for me – but that's just ended up enslaving him as strongly as I am. Oh, you'll insist on all your beauty entitles you to, you loan-shark, selling yourself to everyone, and then legally pursuing my friend, who was only borrowing from you for my sake. So I've lost him through *my unkind abuse* [either the injury I've received, or the injury I've visited upon my friend through allowing him to get mixed up with you in the first place]. I've lost him; you've got both him, and me; and he pays the whole debt to you [i.e. satisfies your sexual desire]; but I'm *still* not free.' And we end this dreadful little circular fugue precisely where we started: enslaved, and comfortless.

In its own way, a poem like this moves the sonnet much further
from the Petrarchan ideal than other more superficially innov- 134
atory approaches. Never had a 'love sonnet' been so arctic in
tone, nor its mise-en-scène such a cold hell.

135

Whoever hath her wish, thou hast thy Will,
And Will to boot, and Will in over-plus;
More than enough am I, that vexed thee still,
To thy sweet will making addition thus.
Wilt thou, whose will is large and spacious,
Not once vouchsafe to hide my will in thine?
Shall will in others seem right gracious,
And in my will no fair acceptance shine?
The sea, all water, yet receives rain still,
And in abundance addeth to his store;
So thou, being rich in Will, add to thy Will
One will of mine, to make thy large will more:
  Let no unkind, no fair beseechers kill;
  Think all but one, and me in that one Will.

Woman goes into a bar and asks for a double entendre. The barma . . . oh you've heard it. Look: the first thing you have to bear in mind when reading the next two poems is that there were *no movies*. You took your entertainment where you could get it. Yes, London had the most sophisticated, dedicated and demanding theatre-going population Europe has ever had, or will ever know. There was also bear-baiting and hanging at Smithfield on the weekend, while over the Channel cat-burning was shaping up as the next big thing in family entertainment. Puns were also *much* funnier than they are now. The next two poems play in multiple ways on the word *Will*, and would indeed be brilliant but for one thing: the poems. Try and paraphrase the sense *without* the puns, and you can do it in a line or two. Puns were never so thigh-slappingly hilarious, nor would be again. It was a little like the invention of stereo recording in the late sixties, when for two years everything was panned hard left and right, and producers were so besotted by the effect that they forgot to put anything in the middle. Here, there are more puns than you can shake a stick at, but the poem itself seems to have gone missing in action. (Although I do wonder if the phrase *thus I will excuse thee* in the possibly-simultaneously-composed Sonnet 42 might have lit the taper on this big stupid firework.)

The sense-paraphrase of both poems is pretty easy. It goes 'Oh go *on*. Go on go on go on go on go *on*' – like Mrs Doyle in *Father Ted*, with WS trying to foist his knob onto the indifferent DL, and win her over by sheer persistence. Oh yes. That *always* works.

Right: puns. *Will* could mean one of the following things: (a) desire, or something desired; (b) sexual lust; (c) determination, resolve; (d) the modal verb expressing the future tense; (e) William; (f) slang for the vagina; (g) slang for the penis. We have italics in the Q to perform a largely redundant Frankie Howerd service throughout. I'll follow most other editors, and pull them off. Phnaar . . . As SB points out, 'a modern reader's susceptibility to orthographical signals is so acute that Q's capitals and italics can make the poems sound even more archly precious than they were for Shakespeare's reader', and that the crude italics may oversignify some *Will*s at the expense of others. Though these two poems are so beyond help, it really makes little odds.

Let's do it in parallel translation. You be the bishop and I'll be the actress:

135

Whoever hath her wish, thou hast thy Will,

– other women have their desires, but you have your Will (desire, William, vagina)

And Will to boot, and Will in over-plus;

– and Will as well, and Will in over-abundance (either more Wills – implying that there's more than one lover called Will here, which pleases Pembrokites, who'll hear William Herbert as the third corner of the love-triangle – or just more desire, or more vagina, or more of WS than she knows what to do with; or maybe it's just cueing us up for the approaching pun-torrent)

More than enough am I, that vexed thee still,

– I'm more than enough for you, though, the sex-pest that I am (More than enough *am I* – geddit? *Will-I-am*, another brilliant pun recently rediscovered by a member of the Black Eyed Peas)

To thy sweet will making addition thus.

– would like to 'contribute' to your sweet fanny (fanny = vagina [Brit]; I find SB's relishing the use of the non-synonym 'cunt' plain creepy. This poem's creepy enough)

Wilt thou, whose will is large and spacious,

– Won't you, whose desire is large and fanny is as capacious as a wizard's sleeve

Not once vouchsafe to hide my will in thine?

– allow me to play 'hide the salami' just the once?

Shall will in others seem right gracious,

– Shall other men's knobs seem attractive to you (*gracious* rhymes with *spacious* – they'd normally be disyllabic but here they're trisyllabic – *gray-she-us*, *spay-she-us*. SB thinks they're disyllabic but he's wrong: WS never drops a syllable in a strong stress-position, and besides, it's the old Cowardian 'polysyllabism for comic effect' routine, which has clearly been around for ever)

And in my will no fair acceptance shine?

– but shine no approval upon my knob? (Am I alone in thinking *in* might not be another 'in' pun, but just a misprint for *on*? Apparently)

The sea, all water, yet receives rain still,

– The sea is full but keeps on accepting the rain (where *can* he be going with this)

And in abundance addeth to his store;

– And in abundance addeth to his store (where *can* he be going with this)

So thou, being rich in Will, add to thy Will

– Just so, you, being rich in desire/fanny/knobs/Williams add to your desire/fanny

One will of mine, to make thy large will more:

– a knob of my own, and make your already massive fanny even larger

Let no unkind, no fair beseechers kill;

– Don't be cruel and kill an eager chap (Although *Let no*

unkind . . . is highly confusing)

135

Think all but one, and me in that one Will.

– Think of all your lovers as one, and me just a part of that great consolidated desire/pile of knobs/Williams, etc.

Phew! Blimey. Don't want to have to do *that* again. Aw no . . .

❧

136

If thy soul check thee that I come so near,
Swear to thy blind soul that I was thy Will,
And will, thy soul knows, is admitted there;
Thus far for love, my love-suit sweet fulfil.
Will, will fulfil the treasure of thy love,
Ay, fill it full with wills, and my will one;
In things of great receipt with ease we prove
Among a number one is reckoned none.
Then in the number let me pass untold,
Though in thy store's account I one must be.
For nothing hold me, so it please thee hold
That nothing me, a something sweet to thee.
  Make but my name thy love, and love that still;
  And then thou lovest me, for my name is 'Will'.

. . . Right, we've got the hang of it now. This is more of the same. Actually it's slightly less of the same. First time I've glossed a poem with *Roger's Profanisaurus*, however. (When will people cotton on to the fact that *Viz*'s *Profanisaurus* provides the most remarkable documentary evidence of the continuous innovation of inter- and intra-domain trope in living speech? It's one big filthy PhD-mine.)

If thy soul check thee that I come so near,

– if the fact that I'm bothering you for a shag is preying on your

136 conscience (for this line to make any sense, we have to assume her pity here, as WS invariably does, the self-obsessed twit)

Swear to thy blind soul that I was thy Will,

– swear to your blind conscience that it's me – your Will – WS!

And will, thy soul knows, is admitted there;

– and WS/knob, your soul knows, is admitted into your bed/fanny (I know conscience is blind and all, but is he disguised as Groucho *Marx*?)

Thus far for love, my love-suit sweet fulfil.

– For pity's sake, for charity's sake – grant this much

Will, will fulfil the treasure of thy love,

– WS/desire will 'full fill' (phnaaar) the 'treasure of thy love' (phnaaar)

Ay, fill it full with wills, and my will one;

– Yep, I'll fill it full of knobs, I will – despite me being just a single knob. Oh I'm *good.* My surname's probably derived from 'one who shakes his spear', in the sense of a womaniser or exhibitionist, by the way, but I'm trying to put it behind me. At least I was

In things of great receipt with ease we prove

– In things of great capacity, say the Albert Hall – or, as our Scotch cousins would say, a tenement close

Among a number one is reckoned none.

– waving a flag or throwing a single black pudding is unlikely to register much on the Richter scale

Then in the number let me pass untold,

– Then let me pass uncounted within the large number of your lovers

Though in thy store's account I one must be.

– though I'm still *one* thing, at least, in the inventory of your possessions

For nothing hold me, so it please thee hold
That nothing me, a something sweet to thee.

– Take me for nothing, so long as the nothing you take me for is something sweet to you

Make but my name thy love, and love that still;

– Love my name, and always love it

And then thou lovest me, for my name is 'Will'.

– and then you'll love me, for my name is 'Desire'. And also 'Will'. Obviously.

Aw . . . Quite sweet, really. Started all Roy 'Chubby' Brown and ended all Barry White. I think WS was starting to realise that all the scintillating wordplay, admiring comments on the size of the DL's vagina and boasts about his own ability to impersonate many penises at once might not be the most romantic approach, and that puppy eyes are a better alternative. Although these two poems were probably for a male readership only, being too rude and too unflattering for the addressee. Which makes when you think about it – his sad sweetening towards

136 the end all the more poignant. If it's just locker-room stuff, which it is, why the loss of nerve? Y'know, maybe he *does* cuddle afterwards.

❧

137

Thou blind fool love, what dost thou to mine eyes,
That they behold, and see not what they see?
They know what beauty is, see where it lies,
Yet what the best is, take the worst to be.
If eyes, corrupt by over-partial looks,
Be anchored in the bay where all men ride,
Why of eyes' falsehood hast thou forgèd hooks,
Whereto the judgment of my heart is tied?
Why should my heart think that a several plot,
Which my heart knows the wide world's common place?
Or mine eyes, seeing this, say this is not,
To put fair truth upon so foul a face?
  In things right true my heart and eyes have erred,
  And to this false plague are they now transferred.

Oh, this is a good one. In this poem we can clearly see the terrible little equation, the twisted skeleton that WS has fleshed throughout the sonnets. I'd characterise it as a sort of psychological chiasmus, with a half-twist: with the YM he was in the grip of a pure love, but stalked by the presence of lust; with the DL he is in the grip of a pure lust, but stalked by the absence of love. Without getting all Kristeva on its ass, what tipped presence into absence was the change of genders. In terms of the sonnet tradition, WS has already moved it as far away from Petrarch's rapt descriptions of his beloved Laura as it's possible to get.

137 This poem, a riff on the dissonance between his sexual urges and 'higher' feelings, is also politically indefensible, mistaken in its self-diagnosis, and demonstrates little or nothing in the way of self-knowledge. But as an expression of an irrational sensation that at some point in their lives many men and women will simply *have*, it has, alas, an emotional truth that'll keep it relevant for many centuries to come. It's a wonderful example of the way that poetry, in its intelligent honouring of human stupidity, can be both really bad and great at the same time. It isn't paradoxical, and it doesn't even present a contradiction; if it does, you're confusing how things should ideally be with how they regrettably are. We can read poems from both perspectives, and acknowledge their emotional truth and their moral dubiety simultaneously. But if you read this *without* that ache in the solar plexus of horrible, baseless jealousy – you're probably not, as actors say, engaging your emotional memory.

Blind fool Cupid has not only shot WS with an arrow, he's also infected him with his own hairy-palmed blurred vision. WS is now wearing the penile version of beer-goggles. (I wrote 'knob-goggles', but that's an unfortunate picture. *Fool* seems to have been Elizabethan slang for 'penis', and how felicitously.) This leads him to contemplate the difference between what one knows, and what one beholds – and the worry that what one beholds might convince the better judgement of the heart that it really *is* love and beauty. (*Why of eyes' falsehood hast thou forged hooks, / Whereto the judgment of my heart is tied?* – is wonderful: 'Why, Love, have you joined my lying eyes to my heart?' It made me think of hooking the heart like a fish on a line, given the previous nautical metaphor.) Now that's a dangerous thing, and a confusion that might lead to some reckless decisions. *Be anchored in the bay where all men ride* – the innuendo here is so strong it barely deserves the name, of course. But *Why should my heart think that a several plot, / Which my heart knows the wide world's common place?* Oh man, that hurts. 'Why should my heart believe this woman is a private garden, when it still knows she's common land?' There's what you know, and there's what you want to believe.

Though who knows if she *was* sleeping with everyone, as WS plainly and offensively accuses? But even if she *was* – let's not forget to mention the obvious point that WS's response is *still* just as sexist. (Yes, of course we have to factor in the sexual mores of the age, and all that, but little has changed. Male promiscuity is often admired by other men. This situation leads the kind of men who worry about how other men regard them to understand that promiscuity might be a desirable way to behave. I know this one-rule-for-men, one-rule-for-women stuff is a trite old observation – but I pedantically mention it, because omitting to mention it can sound damn close to approval of the status quo; in the field of Shakespeare studies, it can manifest itself as a tacit approval of WS's lousy attitude. I strongly suspect that some morally backward opinions still thrive under cover of scholarly disinterest.) Either way, WS is no trustworthy commentator. He may just have been thrown by her moderate and normal sexual appetite – see the preceding sonnets – and made the familiar response of a certain type of insecure male: 'with an appetite like that, she's probably a whore'. The next thought is often something like – *stick her behind a veil, and we'll all be better off; I'll be spared the torment of my eyes, and we can save her from herself and her shameless appetites*, etc. Witness one bright imam, who at the time of writing has suggested that we might want to experiment with the

137 one-eyed burqa, since two eyes clearly present too much of a temptation.

l.14 *plague* is the woman; she's like a plague to him. But there's also a clear and more literal suggestion, a taint, of something like 'clap-riddled, because of her promiscuity'. (A fairly unusual instance of something being both a metaphor *and* a metonymy.)

❧

138

When my love swears that she is made of truth,
I do believe her, though I know she lies,
That she might think me some untutored youth
Unlearnèd in the world's false subtleties.
Thus vainly thinking that she thinks me young,
Although she knows my days are past the best,
Simply I credit her false-speaking tongue:
On both sides thus is simple truth suppressed.
But wherefore says she not she is unjust?
And wherefore say not I that I am old?
O love's best habit is in seeming trust,
And age in love, loves not to have years told:
  Therefore I lie with her, and she with me,
  And in our faults by lies we flattered be.

A rather depressing little poem. Earlier WS was in spiritual communion with the YM; but there's nothing at all like that here, just a self-flattering dishonesty in which both parties collude. Everyone's lying to everyone else, and it's all very small-spirited and tawdry by comparison. The first quatrain is wonderfully concise, though, and would have taken a less gifted poet (i.e. everyone else who ever lived) another three lines. The argument of the whole poem runs: 'My mistress swears she's honest, which I know she's not; nonetheless, I pretend to believe her so she'll be charmed by my apparent youthful naivety. In turn

138 she plays along, even though she knows my real age. *On both sides thus is simple truth suppressed.* But why do we do this? Because this way, everyone's a winner; everyone's flattered.' We have, of course, much play made on the word 'lie'.

As this poem appeared in the bootleg rag-bag of *The Passionate Pilgrim* in 1599, it allows us (well me, anyway) a fascinating opportunity to see how WS redrafts his work. I'll work through his revisions, with the earlier line first:

l.4 PP: *Unskilful in the world's false forgeries.*
Q: *Unlearned in the worlds false subtilties.*

Here, WS has made the 'education' metaphor consistent with *untutored* in the previous line. *Forgeries* to *subtilties* loses the rather noisy and pointless alliteration, but if you've already changed the first word to *unlearned, subtilties* echoes the dental music of the *d*s.

l.7 PP: *I smiling, credite her false speaking tounge,*
Q: *Simply I credit her false speaking tongue,*

Smiling to *simply* is a wonderful revision. The sound of the earlier word probably suggested its replacement, but *simply* means 'like a simpleton', as well as 'straightforwardly', and the adverb means he can make a single phrase of the line, and remove that ugly comma.

l.8 PP: *Outfacing faults in love, with love's ill rest.*
Q: *On both sides thus is simple truth supprest:*

A straight swap for a better line. WS draws it back into thetight thematic domain of the poem; the older line was more diffuse.

l.9 PP: *But wherefore sayes my loue that she is young?*
Q: *But wherefore sayes she not she is unjust?*

Interesting. In the earlier version, her lie was also one about her age; in the later, WS keeps its nature vague, preserving the distinct contrast between the lies of the two parties. More practically, of course, he was trying to get rid of the repeated *tongue/young* rhyme.

l.11 PP: *O, Loves best habit's in a soothing tongue*
Q: *O loues best habit is in seeming trust,*

Having cut out the extra *tongue*, he has to find a rhyme for *unjust*. (I'm pretty certain it occurred this way round; l.9 strikes me as the more natural of the rhymed lines, usually a sign that it occurred to the poet first.)

ll.13–14 PP: *Therefore I'le lye with Loue, and loue with me,*
Since that our faultes in louve thus smother'd be.
Q: *Therefore I lye with her, and she with me,*
And in our faults by lyes we flattered be.

In the second version Love is particularised, and becomes the DL; this works better in the context of the sequence of the Q, where the DL is constantly being addressed, and it clears up the confusion between allegorised love in l.13 and plain old 'love' love in l.14. WS also changes *smother'd* to *flattered*; what guided him here was probably just good taste. 'Smothering' is an ugly idea to import in this context this late in the day, and would've needed more figurative preparation than the poem has made.

Now you won't believe this, but 'opinion is divided' as to the relative merits of these two versions. You *what*? Well, a talent for

138 critical analysis isn't the same as one for critical discrimination, and not all commentators seem able to exercise the latter. I very much doubt WS ever revised a poem without improving it significantly. Yes, there are many duff poems in the Sonnets – but rest assured: any time they spent under WS's scrutiny will have improved them. WS's only poetic sin was a lack of patience and (occasionally) taste, which is often the flip-side of a turbocharged facility. (Certain poets – I'm thinking of someone like Hartley Coleridge – have been completely destroyed by it.) Folk would have saved time by simply starting with the more pertinent question: in what *way* is this an improvement over the original?

139

O call not me to justify the wrong
That thy unkindness lays upon my heart;
Wound me not with thine eye, but with thy tongue;
Use power with power, and slay me not by art.
Tell me thou lov'st elsewhere; but in my sight,
Dear heart, forbear to glance thine eye aside:
What need'st thou wound with cunning, when thy might
Is more than my o'erpressed defence can bide?
Let me excuse thee: ah my love well knows
Her pretty looks have been mine enemies,
And therefore from my face she turns my foes,
That they elsewhere might dart their injuries.
  Yet do not so, but since I am near slain,
  Kill me outright with looks, and rid my pain.

This is only really comprehensible if we've been following the previous sonnets pretty closely. Given that context, we'll immediately read ll.1–3 as 'Oh, don't ask me to justify those cruel betrayals with which you've hurt me; don't wound me with your wandering glances.' Then we get something similar to Sonnet 90, in its psychological strategy of self-preservation – a plea for a direct attack that one can read easily and see coming, not something more artfully tormenting. However it could easily be read as being delivered with a rising note of sarcasm, which is my own preference. 'Oh – why don't you save *time*, and just go for the straight kill?' Our man hasn't been writing consistently well recently, but *Tell me thou lov'st elsewhere; but in my sight, / Dear heart, forbear to glance thine eye aside: / What need'st thou wound with cunning, when thy might / Is more than my o'erpressed defence can bide?* are bold and robust lines. It's all very much against the grain of the Petrarchan tradition, too, with its default posture of virtue-in-wretchedness, one aspect of which is finding the beloved's cruelty wholly forgivable.

But at the sestet, the poem kowtows mightily, or appears to: *Let me excuse thee . . .* Talk about a turn. But I think it's disingenuous, and only serves to intensify the sarcasm. 'But I'll excuse you in this way: ah, my love knows well that her looks can kill – and therefore she turns them away from my face, so that they can do their damage elsewhere. But don't bother. Since I'm half-dead anyway, finish me off. Look at me, and kill me, and put me out of my misery.' Yep: it's all sarcasm, as far as I'm concerned, a snarl at his beloved, and reads much better that way – not least because we don't have to suspend our disbelief entertaining yet another largely specious conceit, and more recreational masochism. Reading this as straightforwardly ironic allows us to hear the author *believe in what he's saying*, which has to be worth something. WS might have thought of it as a twisted rewrite of a passage from *Astrophel and Stella* (48): *Yet since my death-wound is already got, / Dear killer, spare not thy sweet cruel shot: / A kind of grace it is to kill with speed.*

To summarise: it's an improvisation on the theme of the DL's killing glances, and WS's response to them. ll.1–8 go 'Please don't look at other guys! It's too much pain to bear. If you fancy them – just tell me outright, for god's sake.' ll.9–12, infected with the rising bitterness in his delivery of ll.1–8, read 'Ah – but you must be turning your eyes from me in *kindness* . . .' and the couplet, 'Actually, don't bother. The biggest favour you could do me is to fasten your fatal gaze on me, and quit prolonging the torment.' But *what* kind of looks are they? It's all rather beautifully destabilised. The looks she was turning *from* WS were looks of lust for others, hence his pain; but if the *same* look is then turned towards WS, isn't that what he really desires? Or has the DL's look altered, in its turning back, to one of utter disdain? Or – my own reading – has WS's distaste for his *own* lust simply cast the DL as Medusa, whose looks, whether baleful or lustful, always have the same fatal effect on *whoever* falls under her gaze?

l.11 *foes*. SB and others also hear WS's enemies being turned from his face by her killing glances, but it's just an elegant variation on *enemies*, and refers to her pretty looks again.

140

Be wise as thou art cruèl; do not press
My tongue-tied patience with too much disdain,
Lest sorrow lend me words, and words express
The manner of my pity-wanting pain.
If I might teach thee wit, better it were,
Though not to love, yet love to tell me so,
As testy sick men, when their deaths be near,
No news but health from their physicians know:
For, if I should despair, I should grow mad,
And in my madness might speak ill of thee;
Now this ill-wresting world is grown so bad,
Mad slanderers by mad ears believed be.
  That I may not be so, nor thou belied,
  Bear thine eyes straight, though thy proud heart go wide.

More of the same, but there's *way* too much pain and exhaustion here to sustain anything as contrived as a rhetorical façade; the sarcastic demeanour has fallen away to reveal a very desperate man. The result is a far better poem – a *great* little poem, in its way. A pathetic plea, but an utterly honest one, full of the kind of metre-wrasslin' that, in the hands of a fine poet, is often the stamp of real feeling; the i.p. manages to subjugate the expressive rhythm, but only just. It runs something like 'Look – be as smart as you're cruel. If you give me no hope, I'll go mad; and if I go mad, I'll say something we'll both regret. Tell me what

I need to hear, even though it's a lie – the same way you'd tell a dying man he was fine, just to ease his mind. Trust me, it's better for both of us if I'm silent.'

WS grows increasingly wild: 'It's even worse than that, actually – this whole world has become so twisted, they might even *believe* a nutter like me, if he started sounding off about you.' This is partly blackmail, of course; it's a threat not just to bad-mouth her, but broadcast the insult as far and wide as he can – nicely shifting the blame, and extending his own madness to the world at large, which is now so twisted that its *mad ears* are receptive to just this kind of crazy slander. In the couplet, the DL is less basilisk than Cupid again, and the arrows her eyes fire are those of love – and fired straight, however *wide* her heart might go.

There are some striking similarities between speeches in *Troilus and Cressida* and some of the DL sonnets, and you might well assume (as Harold Bloom and others have done) that WS has conflated the DL and 'false Cressida' in his mind. Compare the below, and the first two lines of this poem:

> *PANDARUS:*
> *Amen. Whereupon I will show you a chamber with a*
> *bed; which bed, because it shall not speak of your*
> *pretty encounters, press it to death: away!*
> *And Cupid grant all tongue-tied maidens here*
> *Bed, chamber, Pandar to provide this gear!*
> (III. ii.)

More telling, though, is the date. We normally place this play around 1602. Working on the generally true but totally unscientific observation that literary recycling rarely happens years before or years after the first instantiation of one's fine phrase or idea, this

140 would appear to bolster those of us who'd place the composition of the sonnets well into the 1600s; but if we assume, as I do, that the DL sonnets were written in parallel with the YM sequence – where does that leave the likes of Sonnets 40–2? Arguably *very* late; which is a big problem if we see the order of the YM sequence as roughly chronological. For that reason, I think the correspondences with *T&C* might be a red herring. Sonnet 144 appeared in largely identical form in the bootleg album *The Passionate Pilgrim*, placing it at 1598–9 at the very latest. I think the DL sequence falls in the middle of the YM sequence in its chronology, and was complete by the late nineties. The YM sequence kept on running well into the new century, and I feel – despite HV's avowals to precisely the contrary – the capstone of Sonnets 153 and 154 were very late additions indeed, something I'll discuss when we reach them.

l.12 presents us with a bad metrical glitch, and has a supernumerary syllable. This seems to trouble me alone, but WS rarely goofs so loudly. *believèd* is clearly the more natural pronunciation here, but you'd have to make it a disyllable if you wanted the line to work out. This would leave us with *mad SLANderERS by MAD ears BELieved BE*, which is plain horrible; the sense offers no excuse for it going totally against the grain of the received stress, unless it's supposed to sound 'a bit mad'. Might *slanderers* just be a misprint in the Q for *slanders*? *Now this ill-wresting world is grown so bad, / Mad slanders by mad ears believèd be* sounds like the right line to me.

❧

141

In faith I do not love thee with mine eyes,
For they in thee a thousand errors note;
But 'tis my heart that loves what they despise,
Who in despite of view is pleased to dote.
Nor are mine ears with thy tongue's tune delighted,
Nor tender feeling to base touches prone,
Nor taste, nor smell, desire to be invited
To any sensual feast with thee alone:
But my five wits, nor my five senses, can
Dissuade one foolish heart from serving thee,
Who leaves unswayed the likeness of a man,
Thy proud heart's slave and vassal wretch to be:
  Only my plague thus far I count my gain,
  That she that makes me sin awards me pain.

A wretched little number continuing where Sonnet 130 left off, and one we will do the immense service of skipping over as quickly as possible. 'Let's go through all the senses one by one and work out what it is that attracts me to you. Ummm . . . Nothing! All my eye sees is error; your tongue doesn't please my ear; nor do my nose and mouth care to be invited to any *sensual feast* in which you, m'dear, are the only entrée on the card.' He's even denying her *sexual* appeal now. Charming. . . . *Nor tender feeling, to base touches prone*? Liar. 'But for some reason – beats the hell outta me – my heart's enslaved to you. The only thing I've got out of this is the clap, frankly.'

141 The poem might owe something to George Chapman's version of Ovid's poem *The Banquet of Sense*, but I doubt Ovid will want it back. (Chapman's poem is totally forgotten, but full of good bits: *And as the air is rarefied with heat / But thick and gross with summer-killing cold, / So men in love aspire perfection's seat, / When others, slaves to base desires, are sold.*) GRL concludes 'The poet here finds himself perplexed that the woman he loves does not appeal to his five senses, as the tradition of sonneteering insists that she must, and yet he still loves and desires her.' I'd humbly suggest that it's not just the 'tradition of sonneteering' that insists on it. There are some amazingly charitable assessments of this stuff, but you can't justify a poem like this sheerly on the basis of its subversion of the tradition. I suppose it does, again, raise the question whether one's reaction to a poem can be separated from the content. I used to think you had to defend the argument that it *could*, but the truth is it's never going to come up: 'While I deeply admired your exquisite lyric in praise of the Jewish holocaust, I nonetheless remain queasy about certain aspects of your handling of the subject matter.' Nah. No one *wants* to separate their emotional and critical reactions; it's inhuman. What's the point, and where's the fun in it? Why would one defend such a level of robot-like disinterest? Who *reads* like that anyway, and would you want them round for dinner? I think good readers have a bandwidth of acceptable and tolerant disagreement, within which the literary merits of the poem are quite unaffected by whatever opinions it might express. Many poems which hold contrary views to our own can still be enjoyed – I mean, most of us rejoice in the variety of human opinion – and their worth can be more-or-less neutrally assessed. But certain

opinions can cross a line which makes such disinterested judgement impossible, and this crossed mine. All I hear in this poem is 141
his disgust of women. This guy's really screwed up, and I don't
much want to read this poem again.

142

Love is my sin, and thy dear virtue hate,
Hate of my sin, grounded on sinful loving;
O but with mine compare thou thine own state,
And thou shalt find it merits not reproving;
Or, if it do, not from those lips of thine,
That have profaned their scarlet ornaments,
And sealed false bonds of love as oft as mine,
Robbed others' beds' revenues of their rents.
Be it lawful I love thee as thou lov'st those
Whom thine eyes woo as mine importune thee,
Root pity in thy heart, that, when it grows,
Thy pity may deserve to pitied be.
  If thou dost seek to have what thou dost hide,
  By self-example mayst thou be denied.

O these Elizabethans and their boring chiasmi: 'Loving you is my sin, and your virtue is hatred: hatred of my sin, based on your own sinful loving.' Now *there's* a couple of lines to sap the heart. Always suspect a chiasmus: you can place objects in such artful symmetries, but there you're making a genuine comparison of form; however an abstract concept is just a big mess hiding behind a word. Unless we're talking in absolute binary opposites, the neatness of the construction has the effect of making the proposition seem a whole lot tidier than it is, and we're convinced by the apparent but not the *real* logic of the words. (It's this

142

flattery of our intelligence that lies behind Socrates' dismissal of rhetoric in the *Gorgias* as so much cookery and cosmetics: *I am contented with the admission that rhetoric is of two sorts; one, which is mere flattery and disgraceful declamation; the other, which is noble and aims at the training and improvement of the souls of the citizens, and strives to say what is best, whether welcome or unwelcome, to the audience; but have you ever known such a rhetoric; or if you have, and can point out any rhetorician who is of this stamp, who is he?* – Plato, *Gorgias*, Jowett's translation.)

What do these lines actually *mean*? It's a lot of nonsense. Best I can do is 'I know it's wrong for me to love you, but it's good that you hate the fact that you hate my sin, which is based on my sinful loving of you', although the following might make more sense of it: 'I know it's wrong for me to love you, but it's good that you hate the fact that my loving you is sinful, because I can see that this hatred is fuelled by the fact that, in *your* sinful loving of me, you want the best for me'; *or*, conceivably: '. . . I can see that this hatred is fuelled by your own sinful-loving-fuelled self-hatred.' Then again, I think I'm confusing me with someone who *gives* a toss. Must I go on? Oh OK: 'But compare your state with mine, and you'll find that I don't deserve to be told off – or if I do, not from your lips, *That have profaned their scarlet ornaments / And sealed false bonds of love as oft as mine . . .*' Yeah, I'm not trying. *Robbed others' beds' revenues of their rents*, I guess, means something like 'cheated on our spouses, and freely handed out elsewhere what should have been coughed up at home'. In short: 'Don't be too disapproving of me; we're as bad as each other.'

The sestet says 'If it's as permissible for me to love you in the way you love those other men you woo with your glances, as my own eyes crave you – have a little pity; then eventually you'll also

142 deserve to be pitied. If you want to keep on having those secret affairs, you might find yourself denied because of the example you're setting.' For *pity* we can reasonably read *sex*, so it's really something like 'If you want men to pity you, and sleep with you – but you don't show *me* pity and sleep with *me*, they might turn you down because of your bad example.' Aye, that makes a whole bunch of sense. That's *just* what men are like, of course. 'Well – she didn't shag Will, so *I'm* not shagging her.' What tosh. The trouble with *all* sequences is that at some point there'll be padding, poems spun out of nothing, or less; and by 'less' I mean 'lies', whether told to the reader or to oneself. I doubt he ever felt *any* of this. It's just a vapid rhetorical exercise.

l.6 those *scarlet ornaments* are interesting, though; it could be suggestive of the scarlet robes of cardinals, or, as KDJ points out, the scarlet wax seals of ecclesiastical or civic authority, which enhances the sense of *profaned.* Though there's a strong hint, too, of the scarlet woman of Revelation, the *mother of harlots*, and all that.

143

Lo, as a careful housewife runs to catch
One of her feathered creatures broke away,
Sets down her babe, and makes all swift dispatch
In pursuit of the thing she would have stay;
Whilst her neglected child holds her in chase,
Cries to catch her whose busy care is bent
To follow that which flies before her face,
Not prizing her poor infant's discontent:
So run'st thou after that which flies from thee,
Whilst I thy babe chase thee afar behind.
But if thou catch thy hope, turn back to me,
And play the mother's part, kiss me, be kind:
    So will I pray that thou mayst have thy Will,
    If thou turn back and my loud crying still.

After the last poem you're probably reading this one through your hands, but it's fairly safe to come out. It's *bizarre*, certainly, and no good, and might tell us something very worrying about WS's relationship to his mum, but mercifully it's innocuous enough. The extended simile here is that a careworn housewife (the DL) has set down her baby (WS; ugh) to chase after a chicken on the loose (its description as a 'feathered creature' implies a bit of a foppish 'peacock', so we might read in one of WS's fancy rivals). The neglected baby runs after his mother – but she's only interested in the fowl which *flies before her face*, i.e.

143 the fancyman running away from her. So far, so . . . weird; but the last four lines read: 'If you catch the one you hope for – turn back to me and act like my mother; *kiss me, be kind.* If you turn back and hush my loud crying, I'll pray that you get your *Will.*'

The proverb 'A woman will have her will' lurks here; but – as hammily indicated by the capital letter – it's not just will as *thy hope* she'll have. *Will* can just about be read as *our* Will, although since she now has the ageing bald beardy babe in her arms, the prayer is redundant. The sense more strongly implies *another* bloke called Will, namely our feathered friend. (If we conflate him with the YM in Sonnet 144, it certainly lends some credence to the Mr W. Herbert theory.) More worrying is how *pathetic* he's become. 'If you mother me, you can go sleep with that other bloke.' Oh have some *pride*, man.

l.1 *careful* can mean both 'painstaking' and 'anxious'.

l.4 *pursuit* has the stress on the first syllable.

144

Two loves I have, of comfort and despair,
Which like two spirits do suggest me still:
The better angel is a man right fair,
The worser spirit a woman coloured ill.
To win me soon to hell my female evil
Tempteth my better angel from my side,
And would corrupt my saint to be a devil,
Wooing his purity with her foul pride;
And whether that my angel be turned fiend
Suspect I may, yet not directly tell;
But being both from me both to each friend,
I guess one angel in another's hell.
  Yet this shall I ne'er know, but live in doubt,
  Till my bad angel fire my good one out.

Well, well: in the numerologically significant position of 144 (12 x 12; 12th Fibonacci number; number of the thousands saved in Revelation, etc.) we find the entire Sonnets' emotional equation explicitly declared. Coincidence? . . . Oh, probably; though there is that worrying 144-lettered dedication. Other theories include a meta-pun on 'gross', but there are other sonnets which address the subject of earthbound corporeality just as explicitly.

Here we see rehearsed all those tedious ideas of women as a corrupting influence, a destroyer of noble and pure love, the Eve

144 of the Fall, and every moronic sex-with-women-is-dirty prejudice Christians have dreamt up ever since they were fool enough to bless a virgin. We're also prompted to think of a spiritual battle in hell between the pure spirit and the rotten flesh, but the poem doesn't discharge this conceit (nor any other) in a consistent or convincing fashion. The spirit wins, -ish, but emerges with a dose of the clap.

To read this poem properly, we need to be armed with another bit of Elizabethan slang: for 'hell' we can also read 'vagina', heaven help us. However WS doesn't make play with this until later in the poem (*I guess one angel in another's hell*); *To win me soon to hell* appears to mean no more than that, since WS's agony is caused by the YM being wooed over to the DL's vagina, *her* 'hell'. Confused? Who'd blame you. It was a lousy decision to use 'hell' *both* in its punning and un-punning senses.

The most impressive thing about this poem is how good it makes everything else look: this poem is clearly misogynistic, and any alternative reading seems to me perversely wilful. Yet WS's plays abound with *every* type of woman, including the strong, noble, intelligent, pure and wise. His misogyny seems to have been a feature only of his love-life; thank heavens there's more to our lives than that. What was remarkable was WS's ability to suspend the worldview and gut feelings of William Shakespeare – or at least understand that his own opinions were just as partial and unrepresentative as those of any other character in his dramatis personae. The Sonnets disprove Borges's theory that WS's inner being was a kind of cipher, a malleable emptiness which could form itself to the shape of any and every human personality; he certainly had one of his own. However the plays show that he possessed an almost superhuman ability to suspend his *own* personality to clear the way, and permit the full engagement of his vast imaginative empathies. Love has different licences, and none of them are rational, nor do we require them to be. But what a thing to discover that the *I* of the poet – the one POV in which the writer thinks he can place trust in, his centre of gravity – is the least reliable commentator of them all. WS probably knew this, and dismissed his ego from having much of a say or hand in the rest of his creative output. But the ego cannot be dismissed in love, or the contemplation of love; it's the beating heart of the whole psychodrama.

The poem, as I've mentioned before, appeared earlier in *The Passionate Pilgrim*, and SB gives one of his stupendous, brilliant, and infuriatingly over-thorough analyses of what might have happened between the PP and the Q version, which you can read with the usual mixture of profit and despair. It's sort of interesting, but also the kind of thing that seems predicated on the reader having a very slack evening. The two versions differ only slightly, and the earlier is notable only for having a lot of parentheses – *My better Angell, is a Man (right faire) / The worser spirite a Woman (colour'd ill.)* etc. The line *Suspect I may (yet not directly tell:)* gives us one of the earliest smileys in printed English.

The last line is quite fun, and burdened with a number of different literal and metaphorical senses: *Till my bad angel fire my good one out*: until she kicks him out; until she fires him from her vagina; until she 'fires' him with venereal disease; and until she expels him from hell. The problem lies in its relation to the previous line, *Yet this shall I ne'er know, but live in doubt.* WS suspects his two loves are 'together', but can't tell if they are or not; so why on earth would the YM being 'fired' in *any* of the senses described

leave WS any wiser, unless she threw him out a fourth-storey
144 window, or the YM passed on his pox? The statement makes little sense. The poem's a dog's dinner, to be honest with you. It's a perfect example of the kind of poem that holds an understandable fascination for Shakespeare scholars, though very little interest for the contemporary general reader.

145

Those lips that Love's own hand did make,
Breathed forth the sound that said 'I hate',
To me that languished for her sake;
But when she saw my woeful state,
Straight in her heart did mercy come,
Chiding that tongue that, ever sweet,
Was used in giving gentle doom,
And taught it thus anew to greet:
'I hate' she altered with an end,
That followed it as gentle day
Doth follow night, who like a fiend
From heaven to hell is flown away.
  'I hate', from hate away she threw,
  And saved my life, saying 'not you'.

Ha – bet you didn't expect *this* . . . many critics consider this poem so awful they'd like to see it excluded from the sequence, but it's an amusing little curiosity. For one thing, it's in iambic tetrameter, and the only poem in the whole sequence not in i.p. The effect is unbearably jaunty – *yumpty tumpty yumpty tum*, not least because we've had those five stresses hammered into our brains for 144 poems now. Secondly . . . where to start. It's clichéd (*as gentle day, / Doth follow night*), incompetently rhymed (the *make/sake and hate/state* pairs are horribly close in sound; rhyme is pleasing because the ear hears it as a felicitous

145 similarity against a background of difference, and it's a golden rule that you don't have one rhyme-pair near another with which it can be confused) and tasteless: look at that couplet. All this leaves us with a poem *so* bad, there are only two real explanations. The first is that WS didn't write it. As usual, this creates more problems than it solves, and would mean he had no hand in the preparation of the Q, etc. It's a theory popular only with the hard-core conspiracy crowd. The second is that WS *did* write it, but that he wasn't quite himself at the time. The most charitable and plausible excuse for this mess is that its author was very young.

Some think we can date this poem *very* early indeed, at around 1582, when the 18-year-old WS was a-wooing the a-26-year-old Anne Hathaway. If you read it like that, the poem suddenly yields a few not-so-well-buried puns, which stand revealed as forming its entire purpose. If you ask me, there's no possible explanation for writing a poem on such a bad premise as *Those lips that Love's own hand did make, / Breathed forth the sound that said 'I hate'* – I mean who the *hell* ever says that – *unless* you're cueing yourself up for a big punchline. The poem runs: 'Those lovely lips said *I hate . . .* – and to me! I was crazy about her. But when she saw how miserable I was, she checked her tongue, and taught it something different. She altered *I hate* by putting something nice on the end of it, that followed its horrid night as the morning does blah, blah etc.'

And what could that thing be? 'She threw the hatred out of *I hate*, and saved my life, adding [I hate] *not you*.' *Hateaway*, as Andrew Gurr first argued forty years ago, is a plausible Elizabethan pronunciation of *Hathaway*. Surnames seem to have been particularly unstable in WS's time. His own name is famously spelled 83 different ways in Stratford records (my favourite being

Shagspere). By the somewhat lax orthographic standards of the day, it probably passed for a damn good pun – whether *Hathaway* and *Hate-away* were closer in pronunciation or not. *And* was almost certainly pronounced *An'*, however. So we get '*I hate*', *from HATHAWAY she threw, ANNE saved my life, saying 'not you*'. (I'd like to point out that this still isn't exactly a ringing endorsement, and it might not be too far-fetched to see the bad seeds of WS's less-than-idyllic marriage in this very poem.) When you read it this way, the poem also lends considerable support to Germaine Greer's theory that it was the young bard himself who pursued the older Anne, contrary to the shotgun wedding of popular myth. God knows she was the better prospect of the two.

(Hilda Hume's idea that it's 'hate' as in *hae't*, from *Deil hae't* ('Devil have it'), and develops the fiend conceit, is interesting, but far too convoluted, and can't possibly be right. The 'fiend' riff is down to bad taste and youthful incompetence. WS is casting about desperately for rhymes, and any old rubbish to pad the lines with. We might not have come within the foothills of WS's peaks, but lord knows we've all been *here*.)

But what on earth is this poem *doing* here? If you ask me, it's either a truly desperate bit of padding: 'Aw god – I'm still three short . . . what do I have in the drawer?' (see my note to Sonnet 133); or it's a sop to the missus. What else would an irrelevant bit of fluff he'd composed twenty years ago be doing in this sequence?

– 'I'm doing a book of those sonnets.'

– 'Are you going to stick in that lovely one you wrote for me, y'know, when you had hair? You remember – the one with me in it? About how I saved your life and that?'

– 'Oh yeah. Definitely. It's sort of a . . . y'know . . . *miscellany*
145 anyway. (Cough.) Throw me that chicken.'

You might think that the best place for such an insincere expression of WS's uxoriousness might not be sandwiched between two of the darkest efforts in the DL sequence; but *you* find a good one.

l.7 takes another wrong turn: *gentle doom* is 'merciful judgement', and this isn't the time to comment on AH's fundamentally compassionate nature – she's busy chiding her tongue. WS hasn't learnt how to structure and weight an argument yet. Nonetheless the phrase shows a certain . . . *promise*, no?

(Accidental, probably, but 145 – 14 x 5 – is the formula for a perfect sonnet. The irony.)

146

Poor soul, the centre of my sinful earth,
[ ] these rebel powers that thee array,
Why dost thou pine within and suffer dearth,
Painting thy outward walls so costly gay?
Why so large cost, having so short a lease,
Dost thou upon thy fading mansion spend?
Shall worms, inheritors of this excess,
Eat up thy charge? Is this thy body's end?
Then soul, live thou upon thy servant's loss,
And let that pine to aggravate thy store;
Buy terms divine in selling hours of dross,
Within be fed, without be rich no more:
  So shall thou feed on Death, that feeds on men,
  And Death once dead, there's no more dying then.

Where were we. Oh yes – this is a terrific poem. It has the reputation of WS's most religious sonnet, which is both a wonderful indictment of the competition, and a total misdiagnosis. This sonnet is not religious at all. It's an angry poem, a self-disgusted poem: it says that the body is a lousy home for the soul, which ends enslaved to its gaudy, pointless, sensual, self-consuming worldliness. As the only way out of all this short of death, it proposes nothing short of a renunciation of worldly things, a mortification of the flesh in exchange for the revival and revivification of the spirit. 'This way you'll consume death, that

146 feeds on living men – and once Death is dead: well, *there's no more dying then*.' Magnificent, and worthy of our deep contemplation.

Alas, alas . . . This poem contains a huge goof: in the Q, the compositor has accidentally repeated *my sinful earth* at the start of the second line. Before we get on to 'The Mystery of the Missing Foot', which inevitably tends to obsess most commentators, we should arrive at as full an understanding of the poem as we can. The poem deserves it; we shouldn't allow it to be completely ruined by a compositor thinking about his dinner. (Although the damage is so bad, and the poem so good . . . you almost have the sense of it being jealously defaced.) Like all the best poems, it resists easy paraphrase, and it's better just to read it ten times over. The poem seems to describe a conflict between the soul and the body, but the subtle and important point is that it's the *soul* who directs proceedings, here, and for some reason has elected to let itself go short while directing its energies towards bodily display and ornament. This is a far truer description, I think, of the way the psyche works than those simplistic descriptions which pitch one against the other: we *do* have self-control and choice, and the body's lower urges can be taken in hand any time we choose to. That we so often choose not to, to the great impoverishment of our inner life, is a mystery. Here WS proposes a very radical solution, something akin to an old-school early Christian or Hindu asceticism; starve the flesh to feed the soul, *Buy terms divine in selling hours of dross*, for which you might read 'exchange wasteful earthly pursuits for spiritual ones' – and in the eating up of Death itself, its awful desire-driven narrative of satiety and surfeit, adornment and adoration, decay and decline, to which we allow our bodies to gleefully subscribe – we can't fear

Death in anything like the same way again. What we fear is the body dying: so let it die now. Free it from its self-consuming desire by *consuming* that very desire, and we won't have to trouble ourselves with it again. *And Death once dead, there's no more dying then.*

Anyway, to the more mundane business of that absent foot. What *should* have gone there? C. H. Sisson called this 'the prize crux of the sonnets': 'prize', mainly because everyone has the fun of making something up. Not everyone will have any interest in or stomach for this kind of forensic detective work, so feel free to skip this bit altogether; it gets a little technical. However it might prove briefly diverting for anyone with an interest in the way poems are put together.

OK: let's see if we can work out what's missing. Metrically, it's an iamb, a *duh DAH*. However WS frequently has some fun at the start of the line, so *DAH duh* (a trochee) and DAH DAH (a spondee) are possibilities – and note that l.1 starts with just such a double stress; there are different ways of stressing this line, but this seems the most rhetorically natural. He may have echoed this spondee at the start of the second line, or may have tightened up the metre again; there's just no way of knowing. So let's keep the metre open for now. (All these terms like 'spondee' and 'trochee' are of very limited use, and useful *only* for the business of metrical diagnostics, as now. Poets don't write in feet, but in metrically patterned lines.)

Let's turn to the syntax. Here, I think, we're obliged to work out the most natural construction and build from there. To do that, we need to decide what the first two lines mean with rather more precision than we'd usually require of ourselves. In poetry, the more subtle and complex lines don't necessarily need to be exhaustively paraphrased to be understood, or anything like it. That's why we write poems in the first place – to do just that complex job, not to prompt someone else to generate a secondary text in the form of a commentary or exegesis. But here we're obliged to. The key phrase *sinful earth* is best glossed, I think, by WS himself: in *The Merchant of Venice*, Lorenzo says:

> *Such harmony is in immortal souls,*
> *But whilst this muddy vesture of decay*
> *Doth grossly close it in, we cannot hear it.*
>
> (V. i.)

SB defines *sinful earth* as, firstly, a 'substance of which my body is composed', within which the *poor soul* resides; and in the light of Lorenzo's speech, that seems very reasonable. There's great disagreement as to what the *rebel powers* are, but skipping gaily between the scholarly squabbles, the best bet is something like 'bodily passions', metaphorised here as 'rebel forces'. The body *clothes* the soul, and this idea is further developed in ll.3–4, leading us to conclude that the uppermost meaning of *array* is probably 'to dress'. (The military use of *array* as in 'marshall' has some precedent in WS's work, but it's pretty tenuous; nonetheless it's probably present here as a secondary meaning, a sense drawn forth by *rebel powers*.) So we might make the very rough paraphrase 'Poor soul, the centre of my bodily substance, [– /] these bodily passions in which you are dressed'.

Suggestions such as *Rebuke these rebel powers that thee array* won't work. Not only would this involve changing the punctuation after *array* – we just don't see WS make such inelegant lurches from the imperative to the interrogative mood, as we would do now between ll.2–3. So scratch that. However the *one* big advantage of the imperative is that it makes some sense of the emphatic demonstrative '*these* rebel powers', something most of the other solutions conspicuously fail to do. SB's preference is *pressed with these rebel powers that thee array*, which is a bit lame.

HV outrageously proposes the insertion of the ametrical *Feeding*, which conveniently offers much support to her (imaginary) 'key words' theory, echoing *fed* and *feed* later in the poem – and claiming, furthermore, that this then justifies the presence of *fading mansion,* a phrase she declares 'oddly unidiomatic (and otherwise inexplicable)'. This is a remark so patently disingenuous I could have made it myself. *Fading mansion* is perfectly natural, and just fine. Besides, the vowels are wrong. *Feeding these . . . thee* introduces an ugly, loud assonance that echoes no sense.

'Something-ed by' solutions such as *fenced by*, *starv'd by* are more plausible, and most attempts to fix the line opt for one of those. But all are ametrical (not necessarily a problem), and all carry a syntactic redundancy; if we take the subject as *poor soul*, they split the predicate awkwardly over two units. (This would only be satisfying if they were linked through being rhetorically contrastive or paradoxical, i.e. something like '[undone by, cross'd by] these [very] rebel powers that thee array'.) Furthermore, and more damningly to my mind, it makes no sense of WS's using the pronoun in preference to the article: *these* is emphatic.

Nonetheless, these solutions aren't wholly implausible. Let's concoct one for a laugh. Good default compositional practice is *not* to introduce a sound new to the line, but use one already in the lyric vicinity – here, preferably one that has not yet been fully woven in, but *might* have been by the missing sound. The lines are already beautifully musical, but the /f/ of 'sinful' (together with

146 its voiced sister /v/) is a good candidate, since its next echo is in the rather distant *suffer* in l.3. Furthermore, a vowel-sound that takes us *away* from the *ay – ee – eh* (/əɪ/ /i/ /ɛ/) sounds of the line will be perceived as more musical. So let's go for it. *Foiled by*? Maybe *Fooled by*?

(Just so's you know: the English lyric default is to pattern the consonants and vary the vowels, keep them big and open, and avoid too much short 'ih' sound, or what we call *schwa*, the indeterminate vowel. We do this to the vowels for several reasons:

(a) to lengthen the line – vowel is the main component of temporal duration in the word – and emphasise its closeness to the elongated vowels of the sung lyric;

(b) generally increasing the presence of vowel simply offers more expressive potential, vowel being the principal means of carrying the tonal variation that conveys emotional information (if you want to hear what I mean, compare all the different ways you can say 'I love you' to convey alternative senses, to the number of ways you can say the schwa-fest of 'administrative indecision' – answer: an infinite number, to about one);

(c) to keep the stress-count high, so we can draw on the strong psychological association between high stress-count and urgent speech (something metrical writing, with its higher-than-average stress-count, will partly insist on anyway);

(d) to make sure that rhyme and assonance are audible and *salient* effects – that they leap out against the default pattern of varied vowels when we *do* use them, which makes them ten times more effective. If loud sound-effects are used decoratively, though, they don't work. They always have to echo some sense. Otherwise the reader just thinks: 'why did you just make that funny noise?'.)

I think there are two further possibilities here. First, take a look 146
at that *sinful earth*: if we accept 'substance of which my body is composed' as the uppermost sense, then we need posit nothing more than a bit of connective tissue between that and 'bodily passions'; i.e. we more naturally make the subject of '[Who ——] these rebel powers' *my sinful earth* and not *poor soul*. So we might have *Poor soul, the centre of my sinful earth* / '[Who hosts, houses, breeds] *these rebel powers that thee array*', or words to that effect, and delete the final comma in l.1 (the Sonnets are over-punctuated anyway). Again, though, it makes little sense of the pronoun. However there's some mileage in the sense 'run by, controlled by'.

Another strategy is to fall in with the list of rhetorical questions asked of soul that run through the octave (the figure of *erotesis*). That would leave us with one syllable, the first being taken up by an interrogative adverb. *Who are / What are / Who owns / Who rules / Who raised these rebel powers that thee array?* strikes me as one possible solution which cuts the Gordian knot, and honours the pronoun *these*. (In a tight spot, the most lyrically inoffensive sounds are often big empty vowels.) However this assumes a second error, i.e. the punctuation after *array* now needs to be a question mark – and snags badly on Occam's razor; although we *could* run it on. True, if we accept that the meaning of *rebel powers* is readily intelligible, the question is a bit redundant.

. . . I just don't buy any of this. *All* the proposed solutions suck in one way or another. The trouble is that this exercise has been conducted in the absence of any *feeling*, never mind genius – therefore it isn't real composition. The words have gone. The words that filled the blanks were probably quite surprising, and our chances of finding them via the 'good compositional defaults'

146 method – even though to try and fill them in by any other means would be crazy – are probably nil. With the compositor's error, the poem has been spoiled beyond repair. Short of holding a séance, all we can do is interpolate the solution that causes the least racket. And that, I'm afraid, is silence.

147

My love is as a fever, longing still
For that which longer nurseth the disease,
Feeding on that which doth preserve the ill,
Th'uncertain sickly appetite to please:
My reason, the physician to my love,
Angry that his prescriptions are not kept,
Hath left me, and I desperate now approve
Desire is death, which physic did except.
Past cure I am, now reason is past care,
And frantic-mad with evermore unrest;
My thoughts and my discourse as madmen's are,
At random from the truth vainly expressed;
  For I have sworn thee fair, and thought thee bright,
  Who art as black as hell, as dark as night.

The first of four sonnets on love's derangements. This poem seems to have been inspired by a passage in Sidney's *The Old Arcadia* which ends 'Sicke to the death, still loving my disease' – though the emotional context there was rather different, and concerned unfulfilled desire. Lack of fulfilment is not the problem here: addiction is. Addiction is a habit of fulfilment, or a fulfilment of habit, that leaves you feeling less fulfilled and more habituated than ever. The first two lines capture the whole hideous febrile vortex quite brilliantly – *nurseth the disease* is a wonderful irony.

147 Ted Hughes thought highly of this sonnet, and you can see the appeal for a man of his temperament. Either you recognise this kind of destructive, going-nowhere, don't-actually-like-you-but-can't-stop-sleeping-with-you crazed lust or you don't. We can travel far in our imaginations, and identify with just about anything the poem throws at us – because we already *have*, in our own lives. We can identify with a poem about a murder; most of us haven't killed anyone, but most of us will have fantasised about it, however fleetingly. We can identify with the sick and the dying and the bereaved, as they represent our worst and therefore most irresistible fears. But no one *would* daydream about this absurd situation; it doesn't even hold the attraction of a morbid fantasy. It doesn't make any sense. Like insanity, it's not going to come up. Until, of course, it comes up.

Look how WS extends the conceit. *Reason* is his physician in love, the thing that offers him a way of easing its mad fever; but *reason* – angered by WS's failure to take his advice – has abandoned him, both in the sense that he offers himself no sensible counsel, and that he is now insane. This would have occurred to most of us as two separate ideas, but here they're seamlessly run together.

I hear three shades of sense in the couplet: (1) I'm mad and here's the evidence: I swore black was white; (2) I'm mad and here's the evidence (i.e. the crazy outburst of the poem itself); and (3) the 'all Cretans are liars' paradox, i.e. as we cannot believe or not believe the words of those who declare themselves mad so 'I'm raving, and who *knows* what's up or down or day or night any more.' But he's mad, alright.

148

O me! what eyes hath Love put in my head,
Which have no correspondence with true sight?
Or, if they have, where is my judgment fled,
That censures falsely what they see aright?
If that be fair whereon my false eyes dote,
What means the world to say it is not so?
If it be not, then love doth well denote,
Love's eye is not so true as all men's: no,
How can it? O how can love's eye be true,
That is so vexed with watching and with tears?
No marvel then, though I mistake my view:
The sun itself sees not, till heaven clears.
  O cunning love with tears thou keep'st me blind,
  Lest eyes well seeing thy foul faults should find.

It's clear WS is a man for whom appearance means a very great deal, but who has so little faith in his own judgement he can't trust it. Most likely he was one of those guys who can't value a woman until or unless he sees others do so too – i.e. he has *other men* uppermost in his mind, which let's just say is rather revealing. His primary concern seems to be less the object of his desire than his assessment of its worth, and to what extent that value has been set by the consensual judgement of his circle.

The surface meaning of this poem is very plain. He blames love for having deranged him, and either warping his sight or

148 judgement; he can't square their conflicting opinions. He *sees* his lover as attractive, but *knows* she isn't. (Again, the more interesting question is why you'd insist on the dissonance in the first place.) Or is it the *world's* judgement at fault, a judgement with which WS is reflexively siding? *then love doth well denote, / Love's eye is not so true as all men's* is just a periphrastic way of saying a person in love can't see straight. (He's just making the rhymes here.) How can love's tear-blinded, insomniac eye be *trusted* to make a clear judgement anyway? The sun's judgement, too, gets clouded in much the same way, so no wonder the human eye does. 'O you're a cunning one, my dear; you keep me blind with tears so I can't see your faults.'

Love is very ambiguous, though, and can refer both to the woman and to love itself. If we read it as the latter, it's love's own *faults* being indicted here; perhaps Love keeps the lover blind to the fact that Love just isn't such a great thing. If you bear in mind that Cupid himself has a dog and a stick, the accusation is perhaps more broadly one of infection with Love's own blindness.

At a more mundane level, SB points out that ll.7–9 have at least five buried slang references (*well*, *no*, etc.) to something he calls, I note with relief, the 'vulva'. This makes *all men's: no* look like another accusation of sexual infidelity, and probably leaves us winking back at *Love's eye* too. Fair enough. But you have to know when to stop. HV finds them everywhere in the scattered O sounds, but that forms only part of a kabbalistic tour de force that uncovers many buried correspondences, DEFECTIVE KEY WORDS, chiastic and structural patterns – absolutely none of which, I suspect, WS was either aware of or had intended. By now, you may be getting the impression that I don't think Vendler's is the way to do criticism. Yes and no: HV is often

brilliantly illuminating, but her commentary on the Sonnets suf- 148
fers from a double-whammy of misperceptions.

Firstly, too much stuff is described as deliberately planned effect that I'm *certain* arose from nothing more than human feeling and instinctive decision-making, driven through the local compositional exigencies of the sonnet form. Secondly, and more sinisterly, HV seems to assume that the poem actually *has* a deep essence, pattern or structure which we can usefully abstract and codify in this way. It doesn't; the game of poetry is to keep these things in play, and to fix and codify them is to misrepresent their protean nature, and their total dependency on the dynamic process of subjective reading; otherwise you're conferring a reality they don't possess. This is the theistic fallacy in another guise. I think many of the deep patterns and symbolic underpinnings that HV diagnoses are not integral to the poem itself, but only back-formed from her somtimes too-careful reading; which is to say they're hers, and not Shakespeare's. If they do *really* exist, they must be in the hands of some remote third party, who at some point will confirm the accuracy of the brilliant exegesis. But there's just you, me, and this wee poem. That's an open game. However HV too often plays a closed one, poring over the Sonnets as if they were a holy book – as if it actually *possessed* rather than generated some meaning, and finds nothing more or less than the richness of her own mind. A relief that it's so rich, since one invariably learns so much from its company. But the Sonnets were the work of a brilliant and fallible human, and they shouldn't be interrogated like the Book of Thoth.

Everyone composes in a roughly similar way. Frost's notebooks are pretty much like mine and like those of my friends, the difference lying only in the genius of the results. There are both a

148 thousand ways to write a poem, and precisely one: messy procedure. The poem may take on a crystalline and even algebraic appearance in the end, but for all its ferocious technique, that final poem was reached through a dynamic process with feeling and instinct at its heart – and was not guided by the kind of structural blueprint and organisational intelligence that critics like HV divine at every turn. You see the problem: it looks like a subtle distinction, but there's actually a massive difference between suggesting that the structure is somehow anterior to the poem, as opposed to merely an emergent feature of its final form, with which its pattern of feeling and lyric is not properly separable.

Poets want us to lose ourselves in the surface of their language, not its hidden machinery – not least because that machinery is often hidden from the poets themselves. Not that we should always honour that desire: as you'll have noticed, I'm all for putting the poem into dry dock, so we can see what's going on beneath the surface, find what keeps it afloat, and marvel at its construction. But to talk as if that's where the deeper or *larger* truth of the poem might reside is wrong. To find that, we need to set it back in the water. The truth of a poem is in the cut of its jib, the breath in its sails, the clever route it charts to its new port, and the skill and speed and grace with which it moves.

149

Canst thou, O cruel, say I love thee not,
When I against myself with thee partake?
Do I not think on thee, when I forgot
Am of my self – all, tyrant, for thy sake?
Who hateth thee that I do call my friend?
On whom frown'st thou that I do fawn upon?
Nay, if thou lour'st on me, do I not spend
Revenge upon myself with present moan?
What merit do I in my self respect,
That is so proud thy service to despise,
When all my best doth worship thy defect,
Commanded by the motion of thine eyes?
    But, love, hate on; for now I know thy mind:
    Those that can see thou lov'st, and I am blind.

He's losing it again. Nothing conveys desperation like a series of pointless rhetorical questions:

(a) How can you say I don't love you when I take sides with you against myself?

(b) Do I ever think of myself instead of you?

(c) Do I ever call an enemy of yours my friend?

(d) If you glower at me, don't I moan in pain?

(e) What virtue do I see in myself, exactly, that would make me too proud to serve you, when the best in me worships the worst in you, and your merest glance is my command?

149 There's really no such thing as a *true* rhetorical question; we know what we'd *like* to hear, and the question itself is often a form of admission that you're not going to hear it. The answers he desires, of course, are:

(a) I can't, my love
(b) no, my treasure
(c) no, my darling
(d) yes, my sweet
(e) none, my shining prince.

The tension of the poem comes from the dissonance between the answer he wants, and the reality that likely prompted this nervous barrage of questions in the first place. Were the lady permitted to answer, chances are they'd be more along the lines of:

(a) that proves nothing – it's a hobby of yours.

(b) and I suppose this bloody sonnet is all about *me*, is it? Spare me.

(c) yes, actually.

(d) you moan at everything, so it's hard to distinguish one moan from another.

(e) oh leave it out.

The couplet is interesting, as it not only suggests that WS's blind enslavement has left her unimpressed, but that what she really wants, what she finds attractive, is someone *less* thrall to her dark charms. If it's fun trying to make yourself irresistible, what kind of game can you play with one who has no resistance? Answer: a very short one. But there's a little life-lesson here for any men under twenty, which is that most women *hate* desperation. They can smell it under your aftershave. Oh, it might indeed be your truest and most intense feeling, and therefore the one for which you feel you should be rewarded – but most women *do not find this sexy.* You may have noticed that the alpha male gorilla does not advertise his appeal via a proud display of neediness. Stop blubbering. Stop worshipping the ground on which she treads. She treads on your *dreams*, dude. Stand up and have a little respect for yourself. *You* play a little hard to get, for once.

WS is casting about within the somewhat threadbare sonnet conventions of tyranny and blind enslavement for some kind of relief, but he won't find it. WS's analgesic is logical containment, and he needs a far more ingenious turn than these knackered tropes can provide him; the little flounce of the couplet isn't enough. Such poetry as we might find here is all in the intensity of the flailing, not in the argument itself.

l.4 is murder to punctuate; KDJ accepts Malone's *Am of myself, all, tyrant, for thy sake?* But if we're going to make *tyrant* parenthetical in this way you might as well have a dash before *all*, i.e. *Am of myself – all, tyrant, for thy sake?*

ll.13–14 really upset SB, who calls them 'inappropriate', and hears a kind of witless variation on the couplet of Sonnet 148, thinking them insufficiently prepared for. I dunno; there's been, as he points out, little in the way of eye- and seeing-related stuff until l.12, but *lour'st* and *respect* both nod towards the idea, at least. And heaven knows he's written worse couplets.

150

O from what power hast thou this powerful might,
With insufficiency my heart to sway?
To make me give the lie to my true sight,
And swear that brightness doth not grace the day?
Whence hast thou this becoming of things ill,
That in the very refuse of thy deeds
There is such strength and warrantise of skill
That in my mind thy worst all best exceeds?
Who taught thee how to make me love thee more,
The more I hear and see just cause of hate?
O, though I love what others do abhor,
With others thou shouldst not abhor my state:
    If thy unworthiness raised love in me,
    More worthy I to be beloved of thee.

OK, that last poem didn't work out so well – but WS obviously thought it was worth persisting with the interrogation. This new round of questions are certainly far *more* rhetorical than the last lot, and are a thinly disguised excuse to wail. Although we might just say that they're too crazy to warrant an answer: '*Where* did you find this great power to make me love you, despite your clear moral shortcomings?' *Where* did you learn to make bad things look so good on you, that even your least worthy actions make me think that your worst is better than anyone else's best?' 'Harlesden' is not the kind of reply he's looking for. Such answers as are implied are positively satanic, of course.

The couplet does finally make some sense of it all, at least in terms of WS's own perverted logic, and we can only hope that this gives him the closure he needs. It's utterly double-edged: a first reading might yield 'my selflessness in loving one so unworthy has been appropriately rewarded by your love'; but read it again, and it's clear WS also intends 'if it was your unworthiness that made me love you – I suppose your love is exactly what a wretch like me deserves'. This is 'I wouldn't want to belong to any club that would haev me as a member' taken one step further, that of *resigning* yourself to the fact that this, let's face it, is right where you belong. Like Sonnet 116, this poem nods to the marriage vows, but more darkly: *if any man can show any just cause, why they may not lawfully be joined together, let him now speak, or else hereafter for ever hold his peace.* In l.10 WS is yelling, inwardly and against himself, the *just cause* that *should* prevent this hellish marriage; but he's powerless to stop the ceremony going through. The groom can't raise an objection: these two were meant for each other, and he knows it.

I hear odd parallels between this poem and Sonnet 43 – *All days are nights to see till I see thee, / And nights bright days when dreams do show thee me,* and do wonder if they were composed at around the same time. Who says you can't be nuts for two people at once.

ll.11–12 'whore' pun alert.

151

Love is too young to know what conscience is:
Yet who knows not conscience is born of love?
Then, gentle cheater, urge not my amiss,
Lest guilty of my faults thy sweet self prove;
For, thou betraying me, I do betray
My nobler part to my gross body's treason;
My soul doth tell my body that he may
Triumph in love; flesh stays no farther reason,
But rising at thy name doth point out thee
As his triumphant prize, proud of this pride:
He is contented thy poor drudge to be,
To stand in thy affairs, fall by thy side.
  No want of conscience hold it that I call
  Her *love*, for whose dear love I rise and fall.

A very rare sonnet which openly addresses sex; but what it gains in the bold apprehension of its subject it loses in its sheer obscurity. OK, sleeves up . . . The first thing we need to know is that the *con-* in *conscience* also alludes to the female sex organ (the French word was common); so *con-science*: knowledge of the *con*. 'Conscience' is also a sort-of pun (a pun on an abbreviated form, to be nitpicking), and is supposed to put us in mind of 'the prick of conscience', as well as the male prick, which has none: *penis erectus non habet conscientum.* (If I may be forgiven for quoting my own aphorism on the limitations of the 'hanging brain': *The male genitals are worn externally as evolution is in the process of expelling them from the body. Another million years and they'll be stored in a drawer.*)

So let's attempt a paraphrase. 'Cupid's too young to know what right and wrong are; but who doesn't know that it's love that teaches you all that?' (For which also read 'Cupid's too young to know about sex; but we all know sexual desire comes from love.' Actually I'm already disagreeing. While we know a lot of sex goes *on* in early love, I've always found that most of the *thoughts* of the beloved aren't sexual in nature at all. But that's maybe just me.)

The next lines are very murky indeed: 'Gentle deceiver, do not bring up my fault: if you do that you might be guilty of the same faults; and [playing on its double sense] if you *urge* my amiss – if you drive me into making the same mistake again – I betray the nobler part of myself to the grosser part. My soul tells my body that he might win in love; my penis doesn't wait for another reason, but as soon as your name's mentioned, rises to point you out, his prize. Proud of his own swelling [OED: 'proud: of organic structures: overgrown, exuberant, too luxuriant; swelling or swollen, tumid'], he's happy to be always at your cervix; he's a stand-up guy, there whenever you need him; he'll flop down beside you when you lie down. I don't feel bad about calling her "love", when I'm so ready to rise and fall for her *lurve*.'

Nice he doesn't feel bad. This is what passes as an Elizabethan psychological innovation: the idea that love and sex might conceivably overlap. Dear god. Mind you, I think WS speaks for himself alone, here. My larger problem, however, is this: I didn't get into poetry to do this much *work* – at least not to just figure out the plain sense. If my mind's going to be blown (no innuendo intended; SB is making me paranoid), fair enough. But

151 as evidenced by the scholastic fury of the commentaries, the kind of hyper-sophisticated reader who will *casually* be able to follow WS's line of thought here does not exist. For me, the problem with the most elaborate Elizabethan poetry is that it's predicated on a non-existent type of reader, and I'll stop there, before I say something career-destroyingly unfashionable about John Donne. (I suspect a lot of folk of pretending they enjoy him rather more than they do, or at least enjoying the wonderful music while conveniently ignoring the dullness of some of Donne's algebra.) As I've said, the poem's still of some interest, inasmuch as it's one of the very few to address sex directly, along with Sonnet 76 of Barnabe Barnes's *Parthenophil and Parthenophe,* and its talk of 'upright parts of pleasure'. But it does it so *annoyingly*, I do wish he hadn't.

It's interesting, I suppose, in that it's a pretty bold alternative to WS's standard Neoplatonic wordview, where – for all the derangements of the flesh – the soul's aspirations are the only ones we should really trouble ourselves with. To which you can only hope he'll make a swift return. But the argument doesn't cohere at all, and reminds me of an armchair which, while it *looks* perfectly comfortable, turns out to be all loose springs and lumps of horsehair and falls to bits as soon as you sit on it. As well as noting a blasphemous reference to the Resurrection, KDJ also suggests that the last line might direct us to the two final sonnets: 'the reader may discover an implication that the speaker has "fallen" sexually through infection'. Y'know I'm so brassed off with this poem, I almost hope he *did*.

152

In loving thee thou know'st I am forsworn;
But thou art twice forsworn to me love swearing,
In act thy bed-vow broke and new faith torn,
In vowing new hate after new love bearing.
But why of two oaths' breach do I accuse thee,
When I break twenty? I am perjured most,
For all my vows are oaths but to misuse thee,
And all my honest faith in thee is lost:
For I have sworn deep oaths of thy deep kindness,
Oaths of thy love, thy truth, thy constancy,
And to enlighten thee gave eyes to blindness,
Or made them swear against the thing they see:
  For I have sworn thee fair: more perjured eye,
  To swear against the truth so foul a lie.

And here we reach the end of our odyssey, with WS boldly demonstrating that he has learned nothing of any worth whatsoever, either about himself or anyone else. (The two poems that follow represent, as we'll see, a bizarre coda.) All the more reason to take the 'true' end of the sequence as Sonnet 126, where real wisdom has been won.

And what a mess, what a mess: 'I know I'm breaking my promise [to the YM, or his wife; I appreciate the latter seems unlikely] by loving you, but by swearing that you love me you break *two* promises: firstly your own marriage vow by shagging

152 me, and secondly – by making a new declaration of love for me – your promise to hate your new lover. [This could be either her husband, if she was recently married, or the YM. Or some other bloke. Or woman. Who knows.] But why do I accuse you of breaking two oaths when I break twenty of them? I've out-lied you, because my vows were made only to use and abuse you; and I've given up on the truth, as far as you're concerned. For I have sworn great oaths about your great kindness; oaths about your love, your fidelity, your constancy. And to illuminate you [also *enlighten* as in 'to make lighter', her being so dark] I blinded myself, or made my eyes swear to the opposite of what they actually beheld. For I've sworn that you're beautiful; my very *eye* has perjured itself, telling such a disgusting lie against the truth!'

We can strip away the rhetoric even more, however. To make a linguistic point, this poem may be written in the acrolect, but it's a subject that would be more clearly revealed for what it is in the basilect. I'd do it in Dundonian, but I'd lose you pretty quickly, so let's stick it in *EastEnders*-speak. Which is all this tawdry little soap is worth: *Daant get me wong – I knaa it snot roit that I'm wiv you an' all – but when you said you woz intah me, it was twoice as bad – first, coz this is be'ind your old man's back, and second coz when you said you was intah me you said you 'ated Harry now and all – but yew only said you was intah him just last week. Moin you, I've a bladdy nerve moanin bat you bein dodgy – at's nuffink: all that time I woz saying ow laavely and sweet you woz and that, it woz porkies all the way. Just so's you know. Slaaag.*

What and indeed whose sympathies are supposed to be engaged by this Neanderthal bullshit? Oh he speaks fancy, and all. But make no mistake: this is literary skill of the highest order used to express human sentiments of the very lowest. This, from

GRL's otherwise excellent and informative website, is typical of the sort of bending-over-backwards claptrap still offered up in the way of critical fig-leafing (it's interesting that so much energy has been expended not only in denying WS's homosexuality, but ennobling his misogyny too): 'He cannot find the words or reasons that will sanction this love, yet he will not abandon it, and if it is a lie against the truth, then so be it, for love must sometimes break the mould of the predictable world around us and enrich our lives with the tawdry and imperfect, rather than provide us with the ideal and cold beauty which is the subject of our endless and futile searching.' *Our* lives? Not mine, friend.

I'm not saying that WS's feelings are not sincere; I am saying I don't believe they needed sharing. Writers choose what they write and publish, and they chose as carefully in 1609 as they do today. Would that this sequence had ended better, but in a sense it's beautifully symmetrical, having started so poorly.

153

Cupid laid by his brand, and fell asleep;
A maid of Dian's this advantage found,
And his love-kindling fire did quickly steep
In a cold valley-fountain of that ground,
Which borrowed from this holy fire of love
A dateless lively heat, still to endure,
And grew a seething bath, which yet men prove
Against strange maladies a sovereign cure:
But at my mistress' eye love's brand new fired,
The boy for trial needs would touch my breast;
I, sick withal, the help of bath desired,
And thither hied, a sad distempered guest,
  But found no cure; the bath for my help lies
  Where Cupid got new fire: my mistress' eyes.

Well, here we are. Almost there . . . The last two sonnets form a pair, a bizarre closing couplet of sonnets to tie up the entire sequence. Most often treated as a rather lame and jocular coda, they're far better poems than they're given credit for. (They're often rather lazily referred to as 'Anacreontics', though that usually implies the presence not just of love, but also booze, of which Anacreon was equally fond.) They form two variations on a very old conceit, first recorded in the Greek Anthology, and attributed to Marianus Scholasticus, a sixth-century Byzantine poet. It's proved impossible, however, to say what source WS drew upon. For a number of reasons, it's unlikely to have been the original text – not least that his *lesse Greek* would have left him ill-equipped to read it – and it's more likely that he came across it second- or third-hand. The trouble is that these two Sonnets play *very* closely to their original, and imply something like a first-hand acquaintance. One ingenious and perfectly plausible explanation forwarded by KDJ is that WS came by the epigram via Ben Jonson, who owned a copy of the first Latin translation of the Greek Anthology – and who might have adapted it for his projected second book of epigrams. Of this, alas, there is no trace, so idle speculation it will remain.

However, if it *were* true . . . this would place the composition of these sonnets after 1603, when Labinus's Latin edition was printed in Heidelberg. Which would suit me fine – I'm sure WS was still writing them after that date – but doesn't fit with many more widely accepted chronologies. Not least HV's, who dates these poems far earlier, perhaps contemporary with the clearly juvenile Sonnet 145. There are indeed some superficial similarities in the syntax, but I think they're accidental. Sonnet 145 was simply rugged and amateurish. The sentences in these two poems, on the other hand, derive their shape more directly from the original text, and from the conventions of the epigrammatic-fabular form more generally, which is far more didactic and deliberately laboured in its style than the kind of fluent, hypotactic lines WS employs elsewhere. Moreover, the two sonnets slyly echo the Greek practice of writing epigrams in pairs, as two variations on the same theme (Marianus himself wrote another epigram which accompanies this one), which frankly seems a sophistication beyond the means of the author of *'I hate', from hate away she threw . . .*

153

Following the note to Sonnet 140 on the Sonnets' chronology, where I argued that the DL sequence is wholly detached from these two poems, I'd like to add this: if we assume WS was still working on the finalised version of the Sonnets close to their publication, and look at the play that coincides most closely with that schedule – it's *Pericles, Prince of Tyre*, which we place around 1608–9. WS is very much taken up with Diana throughout this play, where she also has a role as defender of Marina's virginity:

MARINA:
If fires be hot, knives sharp, or waters deep,
Untied I still my virgin knot will keep.
Diana, aid my purpose!

(IV. ii.)

Just saying. Incidentally, the unfamiliarity of the syntax, as well as the mystery of WS's source, have led some to simply deny WS's authorship of these poems – but this really isn't worth wasting our time with. (l.6, to pluck one out, has the mature WS's signature, surely.) I'd point to strong syntactic similarities with *A Lover's Complaint*, which follows these two poems in the Q. (I'm totally unconvinced by recent attempts to attribute *ALC* to John Davies. Cut into the poem anywhere, and it screams Shakespeare.)

Anyway, let's have a look at the poem, and start with J.W. Mackail's translation of Marianus' epigram:

Here beneath the plane-trees, overborne by soft sleep, Love slumbered, giving his torch to the Nymphs' keeping; and the Nymphs said one to another, 'Why do we delay? and would that with this we might have quenched the fire in the heart of mortals.' But now, the torch having kindled even the waters, the amorous Nymphs pour hot water thence into the bathing pool.

Hmmm. Already quite a complex proposition. These are wood-nymphs, and so indeed the *maids of Dian* WS describes; in other words, virgin handmaidens of a chaste goddess, and thus Eros' natural enemy. The burning torch is an older attribute of Eros' than his bow and arrow. (It belonged to Hymen, the god of marriage, with whom Eros gets a bit blurred.) The nymphs decide that this is a grand opportunity, and that they will stop the torment of the human race, and extinguish the fire of desire. But oh dear . . . the torch is so powerful that all they do is set the very waters alight. So these virgins have done nothing but make things worse; the bathing pool, supposed to cool and calm the bather, now just heats and inflames. (A tissue-paper's thickness behind this conceit lies the provocation the virgins *themselves* represent, of course.)

All this is more-or-less replicated in WS's octave. The sestet we'll get to in a minute, but as we'd expect, WS has put a lot of what US pool-players call 'English' on his retelling of the original, and has both problematised the situation and compounded the already paradoxical sense. First is the suggestion that the waters themselves have some sexual valency; it's not just a cool pool, but a metaphoric extension of 'the virginal' itself. And maybe something even more specific: KDJ glosses *cold valley-fountain* as suggestive of both the cool springs associated with Diana, and 'the female genitals in which the hot male member seeks to be cooled or quenched'. I'm pretty dubious about that; the female genitals are often described as at least as hot as blokes' bits – but as a *virginal* vulva, cool-for-now but ready-to-be-ignited,

153 the metaphor just about holds, I think. Once torched into life, it's, y'know, hot for ever.

So that's the topspin. The sidespin is the suggestion of disease, which is a bit unfortunate, as it lowers the tone considerably, and the final poem *really* isn't the place to do it, but there we go: WS often had dodgy taste. We find this sounded especially keenly in ll.7–8. l.7 is just a line about the general healing properties of hot baths, but *strange maladies* seems to suggest venereal disease. Syphilis, especially, was something you'd contract from abroad – and came with negative associations of the foreign, the strange and exotic. Now if we factor *that* in, the metaphor is folding into itself in a dizzying fashion. We have a paradoxical bath, which both assuages love's maladies, in both the physical and spiritual senses – but further raises the temperature of and *infects* the bather, proposing an hideous feedback loop, a *mise en abyme* of endlessly reawakened desire; in other words, a *hell.* However I think that while the STDs are present, their presence has been seriously overstated by nearly all commentators, who talk as if these are 'poems about venereal disease'. They're not, really. They're about how love *feed'st* its *light's flame with self-substantial fuel*, if you'll cast your mind back to Sonnet 1 (And I do feel WS might have deliberately echoed his first subject in his last). What's changed over the course of the whole sequence is this: WS has realised that the accusation thrown at the YM is more properly hurled at love itself. It's *Love* that loves herself, Love that will not leave the stage, Love that will not let herself die: she'll see you die first. This, in short, is what our man has learned.

With the sestet, WS develops the story of the epigram and adds his own code. Within the context of the original, however, it's is easily interpretable. 'But with one look from my mistress,

Cupid's torch was fired up again [i.e. my love was reawakened]; and he decided to test if it was working, by touching it to my breast. I was then sick with desire, and wanted a healing bath to ease my pain; I went to the healing springs – a sad, crazy guest – *but found no cure.* The only *real* healing spring that could help me was the very thing that sparked Cupid's brand in the first place: my mistress' eyes.' Bringing us horribly back to the *mistress' eye* in l.9, and beginning the whole vertiginous cycle again – of desire and assuagement and desire, of infection and cure and reinfection.

HV reads these poems as placing a comic distance between the speaker and the 'realm of Eros'. I admit, I seem to be disagreeing with HV on principle these days, but it doesn't sound too funny so far. The lightness of tone disguises a very dark subject. The paradox of the bath as a place of both cleansing and debauchery is very old; certainly the men-only version dates back to the 15th century, even if we tend to think immediately of West Coast bathhouse culture in the late 20th century, mainly through its being the tragic site of so many early outbreaks of the HIV virus. SB directs us also to James Revel Smith, author of *Springs and Wells in Greek and Roman Literature* (NY, 1922), which I dug up and will quote from more fully:

> *The Springs of Baiae appear to have been first known to the ailing, and those who in search of health found, among its numerous fountains with their diverse ingredients and temperatures, reliefs or remedies for many bodily troubles. Rising within sight of each other were Springs of various natures, some containing sulphur, some alum, and others of an acid character.*

153 *The neighborhood abounded in beautiful locations for outing residences, and, in the course of time, wealthy idlers and luxurious pleasure seekers built villas on those charming locations, along the coast an hour's ride west of Naples; and then, for centuries, life about the Springs of Baiae moved in that eccentric round of opposite purposes that seems to become its natural orbit in most of the world's gay watering places, where a part of the visitors are feverishly seeking a respite from sickness in draughts and baths, while others, without maladies, are plunging into every variety of dissipation and depravity that conduce to the destruction of health and sow the seeds of disease.*

l.14 is often left as the Q has it, *mistress' eye*; however the case for not fixing it is weak. It's surely a misprint, and must be *eyes*. The difference between *eye* and *eyes* might be morphologically small but it's phonologically huge, and WS is a poet ruled by his ear as much as his brain. It's therefore very unlikely he intended *eye*, though KDJ gives four reasons he might have, the most intriguing of which is an allusion to what Chaucer calls the *nether ye*.

154

The little love-god lying once asleep,
Laid by his side his heart-inflaming brand,
Whilst many nymphs, that vowed chaste life to keep,
Came tripping by; but in her maiden hand
The fairest votary took up that fire
Which many legions of true hearts had warmed;
And so the general of hot desire
Was, sleeping, by a virgin hand disarmed.
This brand she quenchèd in a cool well by,
Which from love's fire took heat perpetual,
Growing a bath and healthful remedy,
For men diseased; but I, my mistress' thrall,
  Came there for cure, and this by that I prove:
  Love's fire heats water, water cools not love.

Last poem. Group hug! This is the second half of our double epigram. ll.1–12 offer a fairly straight retelling of exactly the same tale, with a few deviations. Little Cupid has *Laid by his side his heart-inflaming brand*, which you might think a difficult move while he's actually asleep; but I think we're just about within our rights to read the brand as 'erect penis' here, which makes a little more sense of the image. As we know, it's capable of *all* sorts of tricks while the rest of the body slumbers on. The fairest nymphs steal the brand, try to quench it in the well, and merely give the spring *heat perpetual.* And yes – as several commentators

154 point out – that last couplet may well allude to a certain burning sensation that requires a swift course of penicillin. Song of Solomon 8: 7 is a better bet: *Many waters cannot quench love, neither can floods drown it.* God knows I hope so, otherwise we're faced with the prospect of the Sonnets ending with a bang *and* a whimper.

So why 154 sonnets? There are many reasons, I think. Firstly, my money's on the huge climacteric of 21 x 7. (21 is a Fibonacci as well as a climacteric number, incidentally; the identification of the Fibonacci series, you will be fascinated to hear, had its origins in Sanskrit prosody.) 3 x 7 x 7 also has its appeal. Then again, the fourteens that have driven this entire enterprise are loud in this number too: 14 x 11; 140 + 14. None of this need run counter to KDJ's theory of our 154 also being composed of 108 (YM sequence) + 28 (DL sequence) + 17 (procreation sequence) + 1 (Sonnet 126).

KDJ points to the last word in the poem, *FINIS*, perhaps also alluding to the 153 fishes in John 21: 11 – *Simon Peter went up, and drew the net to land full of great fishes, and hundred and fifty and three: and for all there were so many, yet was not the net broken.* We get 153 through the slightly dodgy accounting of omitting the non-sonnet 126. (More plausible is counting 153 and 154 as one poem.) So 153 is as much as the net can hold without breaking; time to head for the shore. Seems a stretch, frankly, though it'd certainly tie in with my own half-baked 'John 3: 16 dedication theory', giving us a Johannine frame for the whole sequence. (By the way, have a look at Sonnet 1: *only herald*, forerunner of the undying rose, keeper of the light . . . remind you of anyone in John, chapter 1? Just mentioning it.)

Numeromania might then lead you to John 15: 3–4; I don't

doubt that this is total coincidence, but it's a weirdly poignant and eerily familiar note to end on: *Now ye are clean through the word which I have spoken unto you. Abide in me, and I in you. As the branch cannot bear fruit of itself, except it abide in the vine; no more can ye, except ye abide in me.* And so our everlasting maker has delivered his final word. But whatever he claims, he no longer abides in his love, nor his love in him, the branches are now empty of fruit, and no birds sing in them.

Although I'm sworn to make as little mention of *A Lover's Complaint* as possible, go read it, if you still have the energy; it's a fine thing. I mentioned before my rejection of the theory that it was the work of John Davies. Many things stand against this, not least my deep conviction that WS oversaw the publication of the Q – and the simple fact that the story of the *Complaint* provides a too-exquisite coda to the Sonnets. A woman stands sobbing by a river, into which she throws love-tokens, letters, rings, all the evidence of her former lover. An older man sits down beside her and asks her why she sobs and wails, and she tells him the story of the man who pursued, seduced, and finally abandoned her. The lover himself, though, might sound more than a little familiar:

'But quickly on this side the verdict went:
His real habitude gave life and grace
To appertainings and to ornament,
Accomplished in himself, not in his case;
All aids, themselves made fairer by their place,
Came for additions; yet their purposed trim
Pieced not his grace, but were all graced by him.'

(ll.113–19)

154

Isn't that lovely? (And *clearly* Shakespeare?) Away and look at Sonnet 67, and tell me that he doesn't have his own YM in mind. The maid finishes her tale by admitting that she'd fall for the young man's false charms all over again. And after what we've just been through – it's hard not to see her face turn into WS, smiling wryly under his maid's bonnet, whispering: 'Yes, yes . . . I know. But damn it! I'd do it all over again . . .'

'O, that infected moisture of his eye!
O, that false fire which in his cheek so glowed!
O, that forced thunder from his heart did fly!
O, that sad breath his spongy lungs bestowed!
O, all that borrowed motion, seemingly owed,
Would yet again betray the fore-betrayed,
And new pervert a reconciled maid.'

(ll.323–9)

Appendix

A Note on the Sonnet Form

I promise I won't actually thump the next person who mentions my 'love of the sonnet form' – I'm not that sort of guy – but I will attempt some kind of big flounce. Interest doesn't imply love. I love what fills some sonnets of Shakespeare's, Milton's, Frost's and Rilke's, and I find the form useful to write in sometimes (I guess I'm especially queasy about being fingered as a 'sonnet-lover' in this context, as it might imply that I 'love writing poetry', which is definitely an oversimplification), but I don't love the sonnet, because there's nothing to love. The sonnet isn't anything, other than a bunch of vaguely agreed rules to which some poems subscribe. I do, however, think it's a remarkably versatile and useful form, and one that answers some basic human requirements, appeals to some basic human desires, and reflects some basic human turns of mind.

Poems are still generally written to be both spoken and printed. Why we *speak* poems the way we do is beyond the scope of this little sketch, but I'll say why we print them this way. Poems are still generally read on a ligneous and lamellate substance called paper, by warm-blooded mammals of an average height of about 5'6", held at a distance from their light-receiving organs of about a foot and a half, and usually printed black on white. If you leave more white than black, it looks like you're saying something really important, because we synaesthetically confuse white with silence. Poems have a visual as well as an acoustic life, and it's natural that they would seek out a form that reflects and advertises their project of unified, important and beautiful statement.

Prime amongst those formal aspects is symmetry. A sonnet is, first and foremost, just a square of text on a white ground. Wipe every sonnet from human literature and from the human memory, and it will reappear in pretty much the same form by tomorrow afternoon. The square might be slightly different in size, but would be formed by the same pressures and forces that shaped it first time round – optimum page-size, typeface and line-length, all of which are themselves formed by physical considerations: the size of books that are easy to carry in the hand, and the font-sizes capable of being read at arm's length.

Line-length is determined by human neurology. All cultures have a default line-length instinctually fitted to the human auditory present, a time-slot of around three seconds or so, which corresponds to what we can hold in our minds as an indivisible instant. This makes it easier to commit these instants to memory. (There's a data-consideration too; our short-term RAM holds about five to seven bits-worth of information, which is why eight-digit phone numbers are much harder to memorise than seven.)

In any art form which is interested in being memorable, the ease with which it can be memorised is going to be a major consideration. In an art-form like poetry whose project is additionally *memorial*, it's going to be a *fundamental* consideration.

For this reason, poets converge on line-lengths and line-speeds which correspond to our most convenient neurological units. Those line-units are not discontinuous, of course – one moment bleeds into the next – but they do establish our deep poetic measure. The line is the carrier-wave of our poetic sense-making, with three seconds its rough frequency.

The line that currently goes least against the grain of the natural rhythm, syntactic structure and delivery of the elegiac, lyric modern English that is the default speech of most poems these days, and comes out at about three seconds long, is something like an iambic pentameter. (Not medieval, conversational, journalistic or certain dialectal Englishes, I should add; the idea that i.p. is 'the natural rhythm of English speech' is a fantasy.) Hence that line tends to operate as our mean, against which others are measured: when we say 'short lines' or 'long lines' we really mean 'long or short, compared to a line of around ten syllables long' – and what's more, we'll unconsciously read the short or long lines more slowly or more quickly, in an attempt to bring them closer to the baby bear's bed of the three-second median. (This isn't an argument for the superiority of i.p., just an explanation of its popularity.) Make a nice square out of these lines in 10–12-point type, and you'll get a thirteen- or fourteen-line poem. Thirteen has been very bad news for some time, and was never likely to be a serious contender; this left the way free for the even-numbered form.

That's one explanation for the sonnet existing; but the most robust forms owe their longevity to their answering more than one need. As well as the physical stuff, there are also the forces of tradition, cultural necessity and private innovation. I'll give a very truncated history of the form here (cribbing freely from a longer essay I wrote ten years ago, in an anthology called *101 Sonnets*). Poets have been writing sonnets for about 750 years, and in English for around 450. The Italians gave the form its first kick away from shore, but the most useful forms emerge, and are rarely 'invented'. It looks like the sonnet grew out of a popular Sicilian song-form already in circulation. Giacomo da Lentini, a Sicilian poet of the early thirteenth century, produced the earliest sonnets as we would recognise them now; the form was further developed by Guittone d'Arezzo (1230–94) who introduced the bold thematic *volta* or 'turn' between octave and sestet, giving us the classical Italian form – a fourteen-line poem divided into two stanzas of eight and six lines, and usually rhymed ABBA ABBA CDCDCD. Then we get to Dante (1265–1321) and Petrarch (1304–74), who brought the sonnet to an early perfection in the sonnet-cycles *Vita Nuova* and *Canzoniere* respectively, and established an early tradition for its subject matter: love.

The sonnet has almost become synonymous with the love poem in the popular imagination, but things were never quite that straightforward. The object of Petrarch's lyric affections was called *Laura*; this puns on *laurel* – laurel wreaths were presented to poets in classical times in formal recognition of their gift (hence 'poet laureate'). Petrarch thus conflated the idea of winning his love with that of seducing the muse through his poetic prowess. The love-sonnet has long been a way of proving your lyric skill in the deft handling of the form, as much as winning the heart of the beloved.

The Italian sonnet was steadily exported throughout the sixteenth and seventeenth centuries, until it was embraced by almost the whole of Europe. But nowhere did they go quite as crazy over it as in the English court. It swept through its strange little microculture like a designer drug. (The truth is that it was regarded as a *technological* advance, as useful new forms in poetry often are. Music's evolution has always been closely tied to technological innovation – from the pianoforte and valve trumpet to sequencing software – but other than the revolution of the printing-press, literature has generally advanced through *formal* experiment. My own theory is that this is down to literature – and poetry especially – being a meta-art. Unlike music and the visual arts, which have the physical media of air, light and silence to work in, poetry rides on language; which is to say its transmissionary medium is of a secondary nature. Poetry stands in the same relation to the structure of language as music does to the structure of physical law.)

Thomas Wyatt was among the first and best sonneteers, through his virtuosic imitations of Petrarch. Henry Howard, the Earl of Surrey, innovated the so-called English form of the sonnet – three quatrains (a verse of four lines) and a closing couplet, usually rhymed ABAB CDCD EFEF GG. The strict form of the Italian sonnet rhymes, as we've said, ABBAABBA in the octave, then something like CDCDCD in the sestet. The English sonnet (alternatively known as the 'Elizabethan' or 'Shakespearian') was primarily a solution to the problem of trying to write a fourteen-line poem using only four rhymes in a rhyme-poor language, and so came about more through compositional exigency than anything else. Claims that the English sonnet developed out of the need to find a form more fitting to the 'English' turn of mind are chauvinistic rubbish (even if, I admit, the couplet often seems tailor-made for the pompous ass).

Convention dictates that the closing couplet should summarise the argument of the poem in a pithy and epigrammatic way, or should abstract a 'moral' from the poem. But the best sonnets do nothing of the sort. Those couplets that do no more than summarise the proceedings, WS's included, often sound tedious and otiose. Since poetry is largely the art of saying things once and only once, a pithy summary of the poem *within* the poem is thoroughly redundant – because poetry *is* the art of pithy summary. It's interesting to look at how the most satisfying of Elizabethan English sonnets often begin their final couplet with 'But' or 'And' or 'Yet', where the poem is still singing the song of itself to the end – and the least satisfying with 'So' or 'Then' or 'Therefore', where the author has tacked on two lines of pointless annotation. The truth is, though, that despite their appearance, the best English sonnets are most often just thinly disguised Italians, and 'turn' exactly where you'd expect them, between lines 8 and 9.

Ah yes . . . that turn. About a week after the abolition and reappearance of the sonnet, we'd see the emergence of the *volta*. This is a sudden shift or twist in the development of the sonnet between octave and sestet, and manifests itself as a break between exposition and development, or the proposition and counter-proposition of an argument, or a point of narrative dénouement, or twist in the plot. It might be a no more than a quiet shift in tone or rhetorical pitch. But why does it occur just *there*? There are theories, but for me the most obvious one is that it just feels right. The point is far from universally accepted, but I've always been struck by how this break corresponds roughly to the golden ratio. The golden ratio is that natural division of roughly 8:13 that we find forming patterns everywhere – from the shell of the nautilus and the seedhead of the sunflower, to the spiral arms of the galaxies (as well as many breeding and branching patterns, in the form of the Fibonacci number series). This invariably turns out to be to do with the optimisation of volume, generative power, and so on, and is a weird corollary of our physical law. Musicians and artists have long employed the golden section, either consciously or unconsciously. Whether the 8:5 division of the octave into tonic and dominant (the natural relationship that defines the way the ear works in nearly all western music) can be counted as a golden section division is still controversial, but many composers have also used the ratio to order tonal and temporal information in far more deliberate ways. Similarly, artists have looked to it as a basic principle of harmonious organisation, using it to calculate the placing of significant detail on the vertical or horizontal axis of a painting, as well as far more complex systems of spatial arrangement. Literature, too, seems to be fatally attracted to forms which reflect the golden ratio. The sonnet strikes me as the most obvious example of the way the ratio can be used to optimise the economy of human thought.

In the Italian form, the turn is often signalled explicitly in a stanza break between lines 8 and 9, implicitly by a change in the rhyme scheme, and syntactically, with a clear 'signpost' at the start of line 9. In the English form, we only see the latter, and some will even turn without indicating – but just where you'd expect them to. Despite frequent claims to the contrary, it's pretty rare to see an English sonnets where each successive quatrain introduces new material, or breaks the argument down into thesis, antithesis and synthesis, or the premises and conclusion of a syllogism. The turn seems a far more potent and attractive way of organising the poem's material, and reflects a highly characteristic shape of human thought. Shakespeare's sonnets are as heavily watermarked with the volta as Petrarch's.

The Elizabethans began to steer the sonnet away from the Petrarchan model, subverting their readers' love-lyric expectations, and experimenting with riskier and more varied subject matter. Increasingly, Drayton and Davies and Donne began to use the sonnet as a means of ordering their minds, of developing original argument; often the pill would be sugared by presenting this in the form of an extended metaphor or 'conceit'. No one, however, took the sonnet further from its Italian roots than Shakespeare, in whose hands it became a truly modern form. He did this by the most astonishing subterfuge: he didn't change it at all. He didn't increase the thematic possibilities of the form by abandoning the love sonnet: he simply realised that 'love' was the one theme capacious enough to encompass every other, and that he needn't stray from its centre. Secondly, unlike his contemporaries, he did this with a minimum of formal experiment, writing the form into transparency, until it became as effortless as breath; he converted the rules of the sonnet to motor skills. The form, liberated from itself, was then free to engage with any thought or theme where it might identify the motif of its golden square.

A Note on Metre

I've discussed WS's use of metaphor, metonymy, rhetoric and sound-patterning in the commentary, but in the context of the Sonnets, the subject of metre requires a little separate discussion. My own theory of metre is not entirely conventional (it's a kind of train-wreck between something called generative metrics, and the linguistic subject of pragmatics), but don't tense up; I'll only give an informal, bare-bones outline of it here.

At its heart is a very simple and uncontroversial idea. A 'prosody' describes a pattern of agreement or disagreement between a metre, which doesn't exist, and a speech-rhythm, which does. Metre is just an idealised pattern of weak and strong stresses that the poet had in their mind when they composed the poem, and which they allowed the spoken rhythm of their lines to follow, to a greater or lesser degree. The second, the speech-rhythm, is just what it says. This rhythm I tend to hear as bring composed of three different kinds of stress. Firstly, there's 'received stress'. These are the rhythms of the words and syntactic structures of the language itself: the fact that, firstly you know to say *baNAna*, not *banaNA*, and 'What's the *TIME*?' not 'What's THE time?' To give one of a thousand possible examples, it's a bit unnatural in English to de-stress a monosyllabic adjective before a monosyllabic noun. Thus 'blue door' is usually spoken with an equal stress on both words, not 'blue *door*' or '*blue* door'; we perform it as a hyphenated compound, because that's the way we think of it. Secondly, there's 'sense stress': this describes the pattern of emphasis and de-emphasis you naturally put into your speech to convey and dramatise its meaning. Thirdly, we have 'expressive stress', the pattern of emphasis and de-emphasis you naturally put into your speech to convey and dramatise its emotion. (No *way*, alas, are these three clean and distinct categories, but let's pretend they are for now. However the last two really represent a continuum, as our conscious minds often don't distinguish between arguments made from logic and arguments made from feeling, and most human speech sees them freely mixed together.)

Stress has three main components: volume, pitch and rhythmic displacement. (The last is performed by either lengthened or shortened vowels, or by lengthened or shortened gaps between the syllables.) They are intermixed. In the case of 'received stress', the stress that gives our Germanic tongue its natural rhythmic shape, there's a very gentle and simultaneous increase in pitch, volume and vowel-length when we perform a stressed syllable, and a gentle drop for an unstressed one. With 'sense stress', we see a more emphatic rise in volume and pitch; in the case of 'expressive stress', there's often a far greater rise in pitch and volume, frequently together with an elongation or shortening of the vowel sounds. 'Expressive stress' is the one you can hear most clearly when speech is acted, and where varying speeds of delivery and greatly lengthened vowels feature most prominently.

(With both sense stress and expressive stress, there are also corresponding drops in both pitch and volume for reasons of de-emphasis, but we're ignoring those for now. An accurate blueprint for a poem-performance – one which reflected *real* speech – would register wave-like gradations in both pitch rise and fall, volume and vowel-length. In other words it would look something like a musical score, though there are many reasons why musical notation is badly suited for the task. For now, though, I just want to point out the main deviations from the i.p. metre.)

All the Sonnets (with the exception of one poem) are written in iambic pentameter, which I'll abbreviate as i.p. This is the same metre that WS uses for the great bulk of his dramatic writing; it was introduced into English by Chaucer, at a time we were casting about looking for a good 3-second-long replacement for the four-stress Anglo-Saxon alliterative line, which no longer suited the grain of the language. I.p. is still a popular default for many poets today. It goes *duh DAH duh DAH duh DAH duh DAH duh DAH*. In fact if you say '*duh DAH duh DAH duh DAH duh DAH duh DAH*' over to yourself ten times, you've learned all you need to know about the metre of the Sonnets. You'll then be fully equipped to hear how WS composes his language around that pattern, allowing his speech to fall naturally towards it – and register where he pulls away from it for expressive effect. (I always think of the metre 'magnetising' speech to its pattern.) Good poets always have a lot of fun with the metre, and one of the first myths you have to scotch with all students is that 'a line of iambic pentameter has five stresses'. It doesn't. Iambic pentameter *metre* has five strong stresses. The stresses in the real, living, spoken line can vary between ten stresses and none at all. It all depends on the sense the lines make in the context in which they're spoken, and the emotion they convey.

The good thing about WS's i.p. is that it's *so* strongly sounded and so seamlessly woven through the Sonnets, you'll hardly need to think about it at all. This, incidentally, is not the case elsewhere in WS's work. His dramatic writing also runs on the engine of i.p., but the late plays are object lessons in how far you can bend it without breaking it. Compare any random snatch of *The Comedy of Errors*, say, with *The Tempest*. The difference between the two is the difference between listening to Miles Davis play the same tune in 1949 and 1969: his time. Miles no longer felt the need to play every quaver in order to convey the time-signature, and understood that, within the context of a longer composition (the crucial point), a well-phrased line carried the metronomic information within it, even if it only consisted of two notes and a long silence. The listener will feel its presence anyway. Just so, later Shakespeare operates on the principle that while no single line need enact the i.p., a whole series of them which *converge* upon it, which dance with it, will communicate its rhythm just as strongly. The Sonnets have a more straightforward relationship with the i.p. All you have to do is remember that the rhythm is *already in the language*, and that you don't need to dig for it. Just read the line, with a steady delivery, and with an understanding of its sense – and let the club do the work. The i.p. will be immediately apparent.

These poems are certainly dramatic; all poetry is. It's just not the way we normally speak. However they are *not* primarily dramatic constructions, and should *not* be 'acted'. Acting differs from normal speech-performance in two regards. Firstly, as I've already mentioned, greater emphasis is put on 'expressive stress', which is the most subjective kind. This leads to highly individual and subjective readings, which can often actively deny the listener their right to their *own* reading. Secondly, their emphasis on the use of expressive stress means actors also vary the pace of the syllables, slowing some and racing through others. Now you can do what you like, of course; but I'd propose that if you put in too *much* expression, you will lose the layers of ambiguity and multiple sense the poet has built in, through your overcommitment to one way of reading the poem. Here's the paradox: a more neutral performance, in poetry, can be far more expressive, as it *expresses* the fact that the meaning is nicely ambiguous. And if you go speeding up and slowing down as you enact the drama of the speech – you'll ruin the music by not giving the stressed vowels their full value. WS has put a lot of work into the shape and placement of these vowels – more so than he did in the bulk of his dramatic verse, where the musical aspect of the verse, while complex, was nowhere *near* as sophisticated as it is in the Sonnets. Respect it, because half the meaning is in the sound. Actors who race through lines of poetry just because they hear some dramatic urgency in them are really just wrecking them.

I'll give an example of how all those kinds of stress work within one individual poem, Sonnet 18. The important thing to remember is it's *your* sense that you'll perform in your stressing of the poem, not mine, so this is a subjective exercise. I've marked the way *I* stress it according to the sense I make of it. The underlying metrical stress of the i.p., the *duh DAH* stuff, we can take absolutely for granted in the Sonnets, and should. There's no need to mark it in. Just allow your speech to reflect the fact that WS wrote the lines that way. All we need to mark in are the places where the stresses *deviate* from our *–/–/–/–/–/* pattern. (This holds, incidentally, for any regularly metred poem. You don't have to mark in the regularity; just the deviation.)

The first kind of mark just registers that the received stress of normal English word-rhythm and syntax somtimes runs counter to the metre, producing out-of-position or consecutive strong stresses. These I've marked with a dot over the vowel. Mostly WS has made the received stress fit the metre closely, but here and there it doesn't. Sometimes it will run deliberately counter to the metre, and you'll want to *perform* that to show that, metred or not, what you're speaking is still English. Read those words with just a nice, even force on their vowels. This will have the effect of naturalising the speech of the Sonnets.

The second mark collapses 'sense stress' and 'expressive stress', and indicates the dramatic performance of your interpretation of the poem. I've marked those with an acute accent over the vowel. Read these with more force, and a gentle-but-moderately-emphatic rise in pitch. (These stresses go against the metre less frequently, because they represent much bolder deviations. Sometimes they do, though.) This is where you convey and perform the sense of the phrase *within the context of its larger argument.* It's how you broadcast the fact that you really understand what you're reading – or how you'd stress the poem if you'd written it yourself, or had just improvised it brilliantly in mid-conversation. Often WS will make elaborate comparisons and contrasts, and this is a way of making them clearly audible. (If you want to hear how this works, try this: take the phrase 'If you want to hear how this works, try *this*', and read it aloud several times, each time moving the italics to another word. Listen to how each shifted accent implies a very different sense, emphasis, intention, or feeling. '*If* you want to hear how this works . . .'; 'If *you* want to

Shall I compare thee to a summer's day?
Thou art more lovely and more temperate:
Rough winds do shake the darling buds of May,
And summer's lease hath all too short a date;
Sometime too hot the eye of heaven shines,
And often is his gold complexion dimmed,
And every fair from fair sometime declines,
By chance, or nature's changing course untrimmed:
But thy eternal summer shall not fade,
Nor lose possession of that fair thou ow'st,
Nor shall death brag thou wander'st in his shade,
When in eternal lines to time thou grow'st.
   So long as men can breathe or eyes can see,
   So long lives this, and this gives life to thee.

hear how this works . . .'; If you *want* to hear how this works . . .', and so on.) My point is simply that it's the *deviation* from the metre that make the poem expressive. Metre not only brings our speech back to the song and the dance: it also serves to make our speech *more* dramatic, because it provides a method of emphatic contrast.

Prosody is a highly subjective business, and that's the joy of it. You're *asked* by the poem to make your own interpretation of it – and you're entitled to perform that sense, to yourself and to others. This is one reason why prosody must remain an inexact science. If anyone ever says to you 'this is, definitively, how you scan this line' tell them to get lost, because the statement is founded on an imperfect understanding of what prosody actually is. You're always entitled to say 'that's just not the way I understand it'. So that's how I understand Sonnet 18, and how I stress it when I read it. (I use a little subscript to mark de-emphasis too, but if I'd marked those here it'd start to look like an ant-farm.) When I read Shakespeare, I often find these little pencil-marks a useful way of remembering the sense I made of his lines; when I come back to the poem again, I can hear my own voice perform my original interpretation, and I'm up to speed in no time. Pencil-marks are advised, though, because poems change as you do.

One last word of advice: don't ham it up. That's the poet's job.